MAKING
ANIMATED
WHIRLIGIGS

Anders S. Lunde

DOVER PUBLICATIONS, INC.
Mineola, New York

Copyright

Copyright © 1984 by Anders S. Lunde
All rights reserved.

Bibliographical Note

This Dover edition, first published in 1998, is an unabridged and unaltered republication of *More Whirligigs: Large-Scale & Animated Figures* originally published by The Chilton Book Company, Radnor, Pennsylvania, in 1984.

Library of Congress Cataloging-in-Publication Data

Lunde, Anders S.
   [More whirligigs]
   Making animated whirligigs / Anders S. Lunde.
     p. cm.
   Originally published: More whirligigs. Radnor, Pa. : Chilton Book Co., 1987.
   ISBN-13: 978-0-486-40049-5 (pbk.)
   ISBN-10: 0-486-40049-2 (pbk.)
    1. Wooden toy making. 2. Whirligigs. I. Title.

TT174.5. W6L8635 1998
745.592—dc21

98–4576
CIP

Manufactured in the United States by Courier Corporation
40049208
www.doverpublications.com

TO ELEANOR
and
THE CRAFTSPERSONS OF NORTH CAROLINA

With appreciation to Barbara and Jim Grizzle,
Kerry Nelson, and Ted Elkins for sharing their old whirligigs,
and with gratitude to Tucker Respess for her research assistance

CHAPTER 1

THE WONDERFUL WORLD OF WHIRLIGIGS

Whirligigs have been around for hundreds of years. In the past in the United States, they were very popular, particularly in the nineteenth century, and they are returning to popularity today. Artisans have always found designing and building them intriguing. They require few materials, and the wind that moves them is free; hence, they are inexpensive. Observers have always enjoyed viewing them; they are fun to watch. Because of the integrity of their design and their handcrafted beauty, some have been looked upon as works of art. Even the crude old whirligigs tell us something about the social life of the people, what they did, and how they looked upon their world. Perhaps more than anything else, the whirligigs tell us that however hard the people's lives, they had a sense of humor and expressed joy in creating a thing of whimsy.

In modern American usage, the term whirligig refers to a decorative object or a model of a person with moving arms or parts operated by the wind, a wind toy, or a small wind machine. Museum and private collections have helped formalize this definition because their whirligigs include figures with moving arms, various types of human or animal activity motivated by wind propellers, and various objects set in motion by the wind. To some, the principal mechanical characteristic of the whirligig is that it should turn and twist in the wind, and therefore they consider that the types like the sailor waving flags while at the same time spinning as the wind shifts are true whirligigs. To others, any object which swings with the wind and has a propeller attached to it somewhere is a whirligig. The term has been extended to include huge contraptions using several propellers to produce many independent movements of figures and objects. Whatever the type, a whirligig is expected to be whimsical, humorous, fascinating, and fun to observe as it goes through its motions.

The word itself appears to be a combination derived from two Old Norse words which give us whirl, a rotating movement, and gig, to turn. This seems to imply that a whirligig is something that does two things at once, and this appears to be true; most whirligigs turn on both a horizontal plane and a vertical plane at the same time. In the English language, the spelling has varied through the centuries: whyrlegyge, whirlegigg, whirlygigge, worlegyg, whirlie-gig, and whirlagig, among others. According to the Oxford English Dictionary, it appears as far back as about 1440 as a term for spinning tops. The term was also used for activities and objects that could best be described as whirling or turning. It was the name given to a revolving punishment cage for criminals (1617) and to the first merry-go-rounds at English fairs. It was the name given to a winter sport first played in the Netherlands, then in England, and reported as being played by Washington's soldiers during the Revolution. This was a kind of "crack-the-whip" played with sleds on ice. Thomas Jefferson (1743-1826) invented a rotating chair he called a whirligig chair; the term swivel chair was not used until years later. It is also interesting that Whirligig beetle is the common name for about 700 species of water bug of the order Coleoptera, family Gyrinidae. These insects are usually seen spinning and whirling about on the surface of quiet ponds.

Aside from early references to whirligigs as toy tops and miniature windmills, there appears to be little said in the literature from the sixteenth century to the nineteenth century about whirligigs as specific objects, and apparently no detailed description of very early whirligigs exists. The term has had frequent figurative use, however. Shakespeare referred to "the whirligig [circling course] of time" (Twelfth Night, act V, scene 1, line 388). Samuel Johnson spoke of one woman's wicked tongue as a whirligig (1781). In recent American literature, Joseph C. Lincoln wrote about a whirligig maker on Cape Cod in his book, Shavings (New York: D. Appleton & Company, 1918). However, don't look for whirligigs in O. Henry's work by that name; Whirligigs (New York: Doubleday, Page & Company, 1910) is a collection of short stories with plots that twist and turn with surprise endings!

Whatever the background, the American whirligig is a distinctive creation. Immigrant crafts people may have brought many designs with them, but as with many other items of culture, in the course of time the figures they built became distinctly American. A Pennsylvania farmer whirligig made in the last century doesn't look like any other farmer anywhere in the world. A North Carolina woman churning butter seems to belong there. The cheerful and colorful animal whirligigs of a black artisan from Louisiana could have been made nowhere else. And as for George Washington on his horse, waving his swords . . . especially American!

This book deals with whirligigs that have been popular in the United States and introduces some new designs. My first book, Easy-to-Make Whirligigs (New York, NY: Dover Publications, Inc., 1996. ISBN: 0-486-28965-6), served as an introduction mainly to the smaller whirligigs. Presented in this volume are the larger whirligigs and those which include activated figures and objects. A portion of the book touches on the principles of design and the parts that make up a whirligig. The major part of the book deals with the actual construction of typical whirligigs. By following the step-by-step directions, a person should be able to re-create these whirligigs. They have all been built and tested, and they work.

Do Your Own Thing: In addition to serving as a guide to constructing the whirligigs illustrated throughout these pages, this book has still another purpose: to encourage people to make their own individual whirligigs. While the models in this book can be copied and constructed, readers are urged to try, sooner or later, designing and manufacturing their own whirligigs. The sections of the book that treat design and mechanisms provide the basic information and instruction for proceeding on one's own. At first there may be some problems with making a whirligig work, but once the job is completed, most people will say, "It was easier than I thought!" and go on to think about the next one.

From observing people approach the construction of whirligigs, it seems that the principal problem facing beginners, or people who are making large whirligigs for the first time, lies within the people themselves. There is an uncertainty about approaching the task, a certain lack of confidence in oneself, and a fear that perhaps the work cannot be accomplished or won't end in success. This may sound silly when applied to a person making wind toys or experimenting with wind machines, but it is a common phenomenon. These are the same feelings that any creative person experiences, especially when beginning something new and untried. There is only one cure for this anxiety, and that is to go ahead and start the job.

Ideas for Whirligigs: As soon as you get into the construction of whirligigs and your friends and neighbors learn of it, you will get more whirligig ideas than you can possibly keep up with. Just recently, two people living in different towns talked to me about whirligigs they would like. One was a computer programmer, and she wanted a lady sitting down typing at a computer keyboard. The other was a man who had just moved to the country, and he wanted something distinctive over his rural mailbox. He wondered if he could have an airplane whirligig with "Air Mail" printed on it. Both these ideas can be turned into interesting whirligigs, and the mechanics of doing so are illustrated in this book. My grandchildren have suggested swimmers, dogs, and goats with waving ears; I have made them all. Neighbors suggested the fisherman, and the suggestion for the concert whirligig with the violinist and the pianist came indirectly from a man I never actually met. A book of old drawings of the Jules Verne era suggested the Moon Ship, and while making that, I thought of a modern submarine with a group of sailors inside working hard to make it go. The sub would be an outline frame, and the propeller would be at the back instead of at the front. I don't yet know if it will work, but that is how the ideas come—and the ideas for whirligigs are endless.

Women and Whirligigs: In the correspondence that followed the publication of my first book on whirligigs, there were a number of letters from women. While some explained that they wanted the book for their retired husbands, who apparently were hanging around the house with nothing to do, others said they wanted to get into woodcraft themselves. A few of these women indicated that they might get their menfolk to help them with the cutting and sawing, but most said they intended to learn to do all the woodworking themselves. There is no reason why women cannot learn to use the tools used in woodcraft and make whirligigs. Manufacturers employ thousands of women who seem to be more dexterous than men and more nimble with their hands, particularly as regards smaller objects and more delicate tasks. Woodworking is not sex oriented, and it is time that more women engaged in this most enjoyable hobby.

Principal Tools and Materials: The whirligig maker does not need many tools. Some households may have a basic set of tools that may be sufficient for whirligig construction, and others may not. The following list includes most of the tools that were used to make the whirligigs described in this book. A careful reading of the instructions for the whirligig you wish to make will indicate which of the tools you will need for any particular job. As in most craftwork, a guiding principle regarding tools and materials is "make do with what you have," but it is also true that the right tools will make the job easier.

Tools and Materials

Hammer

Screwdrivers:	Small and large
Saws:	Crosscut saw, compass saw,
	Hacksaw, and coping saw
Brace Drill:	With 3/16", 5/16", 1/2", 3/4" bits
Hand Drill:	With 1/16", 1/8", 3/16", 7/32", 1/4" bits
Files:	Wood file or hobby rasp
Pliers:	Regular and long-nosed pliers
Square:	Try square or combination square
Rules:	Any ruler, yardstick, or tape measure
Carving Tools:	Chisels or carving knives, as needed
Tin Snips:	For cutting metal sheeting

Wood Vise and Clamp

Sandpaper:	Coarse to fine grades

Some woodworking shops will be supplied with power tools. The most useful for our purposes would include a scroll saw with sander attachment, a drill press, and a table saw. Such tools are essential for anyone intending to make a large number of whirligigs and especially for a person planning to build them in commercial quantities. However, they are not essential for the individual making whirligigs as a small hobby.

One reason power tools are not necessary is that whirligigs do not require much in the way of materials. They usually involve a large rounded or flat piece of wood with other smaller wooden parts attached. If you do not have the equipment to saw out thin pieces of wood for wings, the service center in your lumberyard may do it for you at little cost. As for the wood used for the whirligigs in this book, most of it was inexpensive pine; the pine available for shelving is very good if you can work around the knots by taking extra care in laying out the patterns.

As for adhesives, there is a variety on the market today, many of which are both water-resistant and strong. Carpenter's glue and epoxy are very good; urethane glues are excellent for attaching wood to metal because of their sticky nature. Holding wood together on whirligigs often requires that they also be secured with nails or screws. Many households have a collection of screws and nails that may fit the immediate construction needs. Do not be afraid to substitute if it works. The main thing is to attach one piece to another firmly and permanently.

As whirligigs are designed to remain outdoors in all sorts of weather, it is suggested that they be painted with at least two coats of a good oil paint. If they are to remain as natural wood, they may be sealed with a water-resistant finish or a stain and further protected with a tough coating such as polyurethane varnish. Whirligigs designed for indoor display only may be painted with oil paints, water colors, or water-soluble paints. Frequently these are antiqued or wiped with a stain after painting to make them appear old; directions for antiquing objects may be found in a hardware or hobby store, or in a craft book in the public library.

Organization of the Text: The material in the book is divided into three sections. The first section introduces you to the world of whirligigs and deals (chapters 2 through 4) with the basics of whirligig design. Chapter 2 describes the various types of whirligigs and their principal parts, going into detail on the materials used. Chapter 3 discusses the various mechanical parts that make whirligigs move. Chapter 4 covers the design and construction of propellers used to power the larger whirligigs and to serve as decorative elements on others. This section was planned to serve as a reference to return to when you want a reminder of the basics of design and construction.

The next section (chapters 5 through 12) deals with making the various types of whirligigs identified by their distinctive characteristics or their power mechanisms. Each chapter contains step-by-step instructions and illustrations that show how to make each whirligig. Many of the models are based on traditional patterns that have been around for over a century. Others are models of my own design. In every case, their design and construction details were developed in my shop. When completed, the whirligigs were tested, and they all work. Chapter 5 deals with the large birds, chapter 6 with direct drive models, chapter 7 with camshaft designs, chapter 8 with the traditional silhouette models and bent-driveshaft mechanisms, chapter 9 with whirligigs with exceptionally large arms, chapter 10 with whirligigs designed principally as weather vanes, chapter 11 with designs that fall into no particular classification, although some are called "windmills," and chapter 12 with complicated mechanical whirligigs which have a great deal of action to them.

The last section contains information for those who wish to exhibit and market their whirligigs. Whirligigs are becoming more popular, and there seems to be an increasing demand for handcrafted ones.

You Are One of a Few: During the past 200 years in our country, thousands of people have made hundreds of thousands of whirligigs, many of them unique and all at least slightly different. The best of them were much more than a cut-out or a copy; they had individuality. Somehow they tell us across all the years that the crafts people who made them appreciated the wood and lovingly formed it to give the models character. The wonderful antique whirligigs that we see in collections attract us not because they are old but because the personalities of the artisans come through, and the whirligigs tell us that life had its moments of fun and creativity.

Today there are only a few older whirligig makers left in the country. By these, I mean people who have developed traditional or original whirligigs from materials in their own backyards. At a crafts fair in the mountains, I met a skilled woodcarver who told me that his grandfather had built complicated whirligigs, spending weeks making all-wood devices that even featured gear transmissions. The woodcarver said these models were too difficult for him to construct and would take too much time. Now and then one reads of a person who makes original whirligigs, but these people are distinguished by their rarity. This is not to say that a lot of people are not making whirligigs. They are, but they are frequently making them from kits, and some of the kits are not worth the cost. So there is a lot of room for crafts people in the field of making original whirligigs or even making handcrafted copies of traditional and antique models.

Considering the history of whirligigs in our country and the significant role they have played in the recreational and creative lives of the people, those who design and construct whirligigs today are participating in a great American tradition.

CHAPTER 2

DESIGN OF THE LARGER WHIRLIGIGS

GENERAL

Design in the arts and crafts field means more than laying out a pattern or plan for a piece of work. It involves the nature of the materials used, the methods employed to fashion them, the interrelationships among all the parts to produce a coherent whole, and the effect on those who see it. Whirligig design principles relate to the facts that these objects are essentially wind machines, that they must pivot and turn easily in response to the wind, and that they must perform in a way that is interesting and amusing to the observer.

To understand whirligigs, it is necessary to know their main types, the principal elements of their design, and something of the mechanical and constructional details. Knowing these things will make the directions given in the later chapters on construction more comprehensible and, perhaps more important, will provide the information needed to design original whirligigs. An overview of these points will be followed by more specific references pertaining to designing large birds and mechanical whirligigs.

TYPES OF WHIRLIGIGS

Winged Types: These are usually of birds, of which the most popular in the United States seems to be the mallard duck. Readily available in kit form, it is found in many yards and on farms. Any bird from a tiny hummingbird to a California condor can be made into a whirligig. The next section will go into birds in some detail. The accompanying illustration shows the basic structure of a cardinal, the state bird of Illinois, Indiana, Kentucky, North Carolina, Ohio, Virginia, and West Virginia. The major parts, from the point of view of design, are indicated. Note that the wings are propellers. Winged whirligigs are so balanced that they turn aside from the wind and do not face it; this position enables the breeze to spin the wings, giving the bird the appearance of flying.

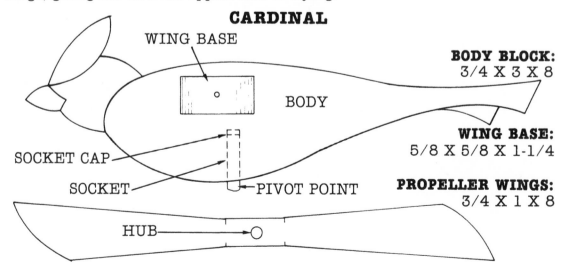

CARDINAL

WING BASE

BODY

SOCKET CAP

SOCKET

PIVOT POINT

HUB

BODY BLOCK:
3/4 X 3 X 8

WING BASE:
5/8 X 5/8 X 1-1/4

PROPELLER WINGS:
3/4 X 1 X 8

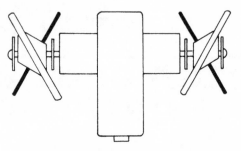

WINGS MUST BE ANGLED IN
OPPOSITE DIRECTIONS.

The winged types are not restricted to birds. They include Mercury's winged foot, the waving ears of a Nubian goat, and the wings of Pegasus, the winged horse.

Arm-Waving Types: Whirligigs with waving arms and hand-held objects are among America's oldest. The sailor waving signal flags, the soldier waving swords, the lady with kerchiefs, and the farmer with scythes are examples of this type. The arms and items that the models hold are propellers. Like the birds, they do not face the wind, but neither do they remain steadily in an off-the-wind position. The upright body is so balanced that it actually twists while the arms twirl. An example of an arm-waving type is shown below.

Traditionally, vertical whirligigs are not usually very large, because for their height they require relatively long arms and solid support systems. There are also

FLOWER GIRL

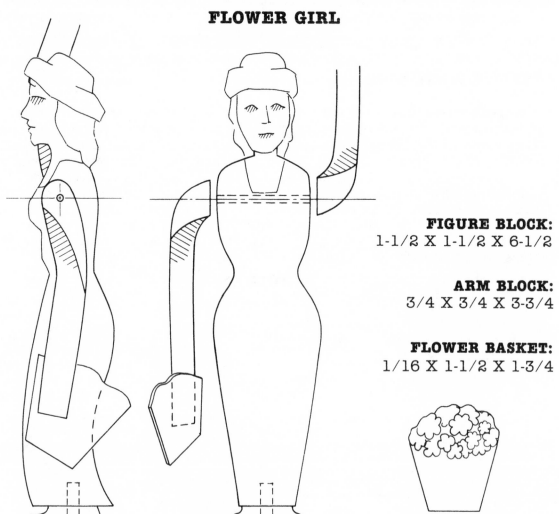

FIGURE BLOCK:
1-1/2 X 1-1/2 X 6-1/2

ARM BLOCK:
3/4 X 3/4 X 3-3/4

FLOWER BASKET:
1/16 X 1-1/2 X 1-3/4

balancing problems to consider. This does not mean that very large arm-waving whirligigs cannot be made if the design principles are followed.

Weather Vane Whirligigs: The weather vane whirligig is principally a wind-direction finder that becomes a whirligig when a propeller is attached to it. Some traditional American weather vane models that have been ''converted'' into whirligigs are whales, fish, farm animals, ships, and aircraft, but just about anything can be made into a weather vane whirligig. A modern rocket model, but of a traditional type, is shown here. Note that like a true vane, the whirligig must be balanced so that it always faces the wind.

Weather vane whirligigs can be made as large as is practical; the only restrictions to size are the support system required and the purpose for which the model is intended.

ROCKET

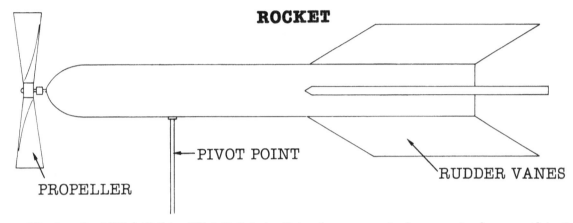

PROPELLER

PIVOT POINT

RUDDER VANES

Mechanical Whirligigs: Whirligigs in this class use wind power to do something besides turning a propeller. The propeller moves a drive shaft, which then moves something else. Because the propeller must face into the wind, a special rudder is frequently necessary, and this becomes a major part of the design, as indicated below.

Mechanical whirligigs are relatively large to begin with, and they can be quite big and heavy depending upon the amount of mechanical activity that goes on.

Other Types: There are, of course, many other types of whirligigs, but they usually are related in basic design to the ones already mentioned. They differ in operation, as in the case of the horizontal propeller types; in function, as in the mole-deterring types; and in objectivity, as in the purely decorative types. A few representatives of these will be presented in chapter 11.

WOMAN WITH BALKY HORSE

WHEN THE CAM GOES DOWN,
THE HORSE'S HEAD GOES DOWN, AND
THE LEGS AND TAIL FLY UP.

KEY ELEMENTS IN WHIRLIGIG DESIGN

The parts of a whirligig that have to be taken into account during the design phase are discussed here. These will be made more specific with respect to the large birds and the mechanical whirligigs in the second and third parts of this section.

The Base: Every whirligig has a base. In some types, like winged types and weather vane models, the body includes the base. In mechanical whirligigs, the base is a platform which supports all the mechanical contrivances and houses the mounting and rudder elements.

The Pivot Point: The point at which a whirligig is suspended differs from one type to another. Birds must sit sideways to the wind, as must the arm wavers. Weather vane and mechanical whirligigs must point into the wind. In all whirligigs there is a relationship between the balance point of the model and the pivot point (where it's supported). In birds and vertical types, there is, in addition, a relationship between the pivot point and the location of the hub, the point where the spindle for the wings or arms will be.

Mounting: A whirligig is supported by a spindle at the pivot point. In design, consideration must be given to the support elements, such as the socket, spindle size, and recommended exhibition stands, poles, and posts for displaying the whirligig.

SOCKETS AND SPINDLES

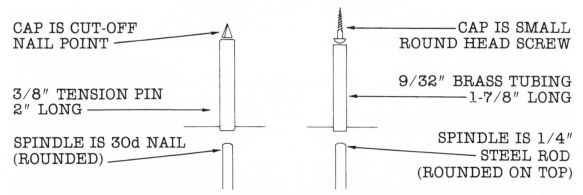

CAP IS CUT-OFF NAIL POINT

CAP IS SMALL ROUND HEAD SCREW

9/32" BRASS TUBING 1-7/8" LONG

3/8" TENSION PIN 2" LONG

SPINDLE IS 30d NAIL (ROUNDED)

SPINDLE IS 1/4" STEEL ROD (ROUNDED ON TOP)

The Propeller: All whirligigs use wind propellers either as the principal moving parts or as decorative elements. In mechanical whirligigs, they operate drive mechanisms. The design and construction of propellers is covered more fully in chapter 4. Propellers used as wings are discussed in the next section.

Propellers may be designed to move in either a clockwise or counterclockwise direction, depending on the slant of the blades. This factor is of primary importance in the winged types, because the wings must be made so they turn in opposite directions, even though the outside edge of one and the inside edge of the other face the wind. It is not so important in most mechanical whirligigs because the driving mechanism should move in either direction. The design of the propeller for any particular project will depend on several factors: the purpose of its function, the type of drive shaft, the type of mechanism, the size of the moving objects, and the appearance of the propeller. The principle of propeller design is not to make it larger than needed to do the job under average wind conditions, yet the whole whirligig should be strong enough to withstand heavy weather. As for the style of the propeller, this is a matter both of practicality and of aesthetics. The propellers on antique and classic whirligigs were made entirely of wood, and a well-designed and well-constructed wood propeller is a sign of true craftsmanship, as well as being a pleasure to behold both at repose or in action.

In some whirligigs, especially mechanical whirligigs, special attention must be given to propeller mountings, which will be discussed throughout the book.

The Driving Mechanism: The moving parts of some whirligigs are essentially propellers, and no other mechanisms are involved. With mechanical whirligigs, the propellers are attached to a drive shaft, which in turn moves wheels, cogs, and connecting rods. This mechanism may be relatively simple or quite complex. A number are illustrated in the book, and they should be taken only as examples of what may be done. An inventive mind can think of many other ways to use wind power to make things move.

Moving Objects or Figures: The mechanism is attached to objects, or persons, or animals, and causes them to move. The figures, whatever they are, make defined and repeated movements. They are often composed of jointed parts connected at points where the movement is most free and unimpaired. The figure may be attached to other objects and may cause them to move. There should be an ease of movement overall; all parts should move with the least friction possible. It is important to emphasize this point, because any restraint will only result in a stuck whirligig or in bent drive shafts or connecting rods.

The Tail or Rudder: Many whirligigs do not require tails if, as in the case of the silhouette whirligig, the figures or objects themselves serve the same purpose. The rudder or tail functions to point the propeller into the wind and works in combination with the pivot point and balance point of the base. The tail may be made of metal or wood and may have a functional shape. It may be square, round, oblong, or irregular; or it may show a design suitable to the subject of the whirligig's activity.

MAKING A PLAN

Putting together all these elements into a meaningful whole is the essence of design. The first step in making any whirligig is to develop a plan in as much detail as possible. This means a full-scale drawing with accurate measurements indicating the sizes of parts and the location of key points. Using a smaller scale drawing is also feasible as long as the measurements are accurate and the drawing lends itself to expansion to full size. The point of making a master drawing is that you can always go back to it and alter it as you work out any bugs in the design. Also, if you wish to reduce the whirligig or make it larger, you can go back to the drawing to do it. Some crafts people, particularly when working with new or one-of-a-kind designs, prefer to proceed by making judgments as they go along. This method has its limitations, particularly for beginners. A lot of time will be wasted in trying to figure out where to go next. Also, no record will exist to show how the design began and then proceeded through to the final product.

There are, of course, times when exceptions must be made to this procedure. There are times when a drawing simply will not suffice, and there is nothing like the hands-on process, seeing if one thing or another will actually work. Nevertheless, it is important to record what you do. When parts are made and tested, take time to draw them exactly as you finally made them.

A sketch or series of sketches showing the general layout will usually precede the final plan. These rough drawings simply show the main parts of the whirligig, particularly the driving action or moving parts. Other rough sketches may show details of how the moving parts or figure are related, and provide the first indication of where the various sections will be joined together or the objects connected to the drivetrain. These rough sketches can be translated into a working drawing that gives exact sizes and measurements for the entire structure. This drawing will become the construction plan for the whirligig.

MATERIALS IN DESIGN

While each section on construction will list the specific materials needed to complete the specific models in this book, a review of the basic materials will indicate the relatively few items needed for constructing whirligigs.

Wood: While there is no limitation on the type and quality of wood that can go into making a whirligig, soft woods such as white pine, western pine, sugar pine, and basswood (if you can handily find it) are recommended for the carved bodies or figures. Platform bases can be made of the same wood or of southern pine or fir. Pine shelving is excellent for most purposes. The length and width of the wood you'll need will vary, but the thicknesses available are standard; for ordinary use, get one-inch boards, which are actually 3/4" milled or finished lumber. Measurements sometimes call for 2 X 4 lumber; this comes finished at 1-1/2" X 3-1/2". Other standard sizes needed occasionally are the 2 X 6 (milled 1-1/2" X 5-1/2") and the 4 X 4 (milled 3-1/2" X 3-1/2").

Waterproof plywood is recommended for whirligig use. Plywood comes in various thicknesses (1/4", 1/2", and 3/4"); the 1/4" size is used most frequently. If 1/8"-thick wood is indicated, as in wings or vanes, it can be sawn from thicker stock.

Dowels are sometimes used; those mentioned in this book are 1/8", 1/4", 1/2", 5/8", or 3/4" in diameter, and there are other sizes available, too.

All these materials can be found in lumberyards, and in most places, yard personnel will assist you in selecting the appropriate wood. Many yards have a surplus wood section or bin where small pieces can be bought at bargain prices.

Hardware: Some of the hardware mentioned in the book is not essential for the operation of the whirligigs, but it's better if it is used. For example, a metal socket liner is not absolutely necessary, but it prevents the wood from wearing and also keeps the whirligig turning efficiently. Many items may be found around the house: Cafe curtain rods of 3/8" diameter make excellent sleeves for 1/4" bolts, and larger round curtain rods can be used as socket liners for 1/2" rods. Frequently mentioned hardware is listed below. For bigger and heavier whirligigs, an individual assessment of support requirements in terms of bolts, rods, pipes, or whatever, will have to be made.

Socket Liners and Spindles: The simplest socket liner for most whirligigs in this book is a rigid 2" tension pin of 3/8" diameter. This will accept a spindle made of a 30d nail with the head cut off and the top rounded. A tension pin 5/16" in diameter will suffice for a narrower platform and lighter whirligigs, and will ride on a smaller nail (16d or 20d). Every socket should have a metal cap placed in the top after the lining is in position. A piece of nail or a screw turned in will do the job. A ball bearing or steel BB inserted between the cap and the spindle will reduce friction and help allow the whirligig to spin easily. Some other liner and spindle measurements are given below. In every case, it is advisable to test the materials to make sure the pieces fit together properly before finally fitting them to a whirligig. The word <u>tubing</u> refers to brass tubing; adjustments may have to be made for the relative thicknesses of other tubing.

Type	Socket Liners	Spindles
Small whirligigs	7/32" tubing	12d nail
	1-1/2" tension pin (1/4")	10d nail
Silhouette whirligigs	7/32" metal tubing	12d nail
	2" tension pin (5/16")	16d nail or 3/16" rod
Large whirligigs	1/4" metal tubing	3/16" or 7/32" rod,
	2" tension pin (3/8")	or 20d and 30d nails

(**Note:** 3/8" tubing for a 1/4" rod, and 5/8" tubing for a 1/2" rod)

Sleeve Liners: Metal tubing is also used wherever there will be considerable wear on moving parts, and the size used will depend mainly on the size of the rod or bolt being used as an axle. For example, if a 1/16" brass rod is used, the tubing could be 1/8" diameter (3/32" rod might be a tight fit). If the size is not specified in the pattern, it is advisable to go to a hobby shop or lumberyard and match the items to see that they fit. For example, if clothes hanger wire is being used as an axle, take a piece of it to the store to find the tubing that it fits into best. Some standard sizes of tubing and compatible rods and machine screws are:

	Tubing	Rod or Screw
Arm hole lining, etc.,	3/16″	1/8″ brass rod,
Wing sockets, small		No. 4 screw
Other lining,	7/32″	16d nail,
Base sockets, birds		No. 6, 8 screw
1/4″ dowels, or	5/16″	1/4″ steel rod
bolts, etc.		

Bolts: Two kinds of 1/4″ bolts are mentioned: machine bolts and carriage bolts. The hexagonal machine bolt head has no stock ridge and is excellent for large wing axles, since their hubs can revolve to the end of the bolt. The carriage bolt will hold well in a block or wheel if the stock is countersunk. Standard bolts are made of soft metal and can be cut, bent, filed, and drilled fairly easily. There are also other sizes, small and large, which are used in whirligig construction; a visit with notebook in hand to a hardware store is sometimes in order. A very important "bolt" used to join moving whirligig parts (like arms to torso) belongs to a class called machine screws. Some frequently used ones are No. 4 X 1-1/4″ and 1-1/2″ in length.

BOLTS AND SCREWS

1/4″ SQUARE

STRUCTURE OF A 6″ CARRIAGE BOLT

5/8″

5-1/8″ — 3/4″

1/8″

STRUCTURE OF A 6″ MACHINE BOLT

7/16″

5-1/4″ — 3/4″

1/8″

MACHINE SCREW

1-1/2″

2″ TENSION PIN

3/8″

Screws: While standard screws are mentioned for each pattern, any screw that will do the job can be used. Those most frequently used here are:
No. 4 X 1/2″ or 3/4″ round head brass screws for attaching arms, etc.;
No. 6 and No. 8 X 1-1/4″ or 1-1/2″ flat head steel or brass screws for securing figures or objects to baseboards;
No. 5, No. 6, and No. 7 X 1/2″ or 3/4″ flat head screws for securing hardware, like angle irons;
No. 6, No. 8, and No. 10 X 1-1/4″ and longer round head brass screws for various hubs (No. 6 for small birds to No. 10 X 3″ to 3-1/2″ for windmill hubs).
Besides drilling holes through wood for the shanks of screws to pass through, smaller guide holes should be drilled into the pieces of wood to prevent splitting them when the screw is seated.

Nails: Very few nails are required and most are quite small. Nail sizes are given by a number followed by the letter d̲ (the designation for the British penny). Common nails have heads and finishing nails do not. The most frequently used sizes are: 4d (1-1/2"), 6d (2"), and 8d (2-1/2"). For spindles, 16d (3-1/2"), 20d (4"), 30d (5"), and 60d (6"), can be used. The 60d nail is about 1/4" thick. Brads (1/2", 3/4", and 1") are sometimes called for as are the small-headed nails called wire nails. For attaching the parts of the larger mechanical whirligigs, the individual will have to decide what nails or screws to use.

It should be emphasized that some of the details about hardware provided above and throughout the book are for initial guidance only. Sooner or later, each craftsperson will find his or her own way through the hardware field. There are some practical things to remember at this point. A rough propeller will spin on an old rusty nail; if you don't wish to bother with liners or sleeves and the fancy stuff, you don't have to. The whirligig makers of a century or two ago did not have access to all the items we have today. The old whirligig-building rule was: "Use what you have on hand!"

FIGURES IN DESIGN

The Human Figure: Another point in design is to develop a consistent pattern in figure proportions. These may be altered for humorous effects, but it is helpful to understand the basic structure of the figures used. Artists use a traditional scale for drawing human figures based on head size. Body length is between seven and eight head lengths, for example, and points on the body can be determined by this measurement, as indicated in the body charts.

The use of proportional figures will make it easier to make parts in sections of the human body, and the points where parts of the figure will be attached to make the model function realistically will be more easily discerned. While using proportions is helpful in designing all whirligig figures, it is especially useful if one plans to sculpt figures in the round to make them more lifelike. In these cases, it will be necessary to draw the figures in as much detail as possible, taking into account the proportional measurements.

The human characters in the illustrations are meant to be that, just human. They

THE HUMAN FIGURE

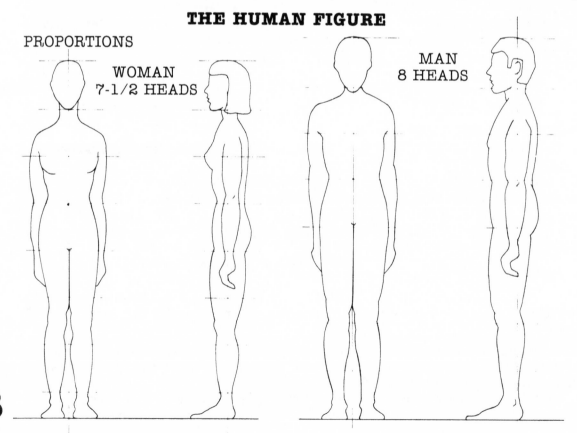

PROPORTIONS

WOMAN
7-1/2 HEADS

MAN
8 HEADS

may be black, white, native American, or have any other features. Whirligigs with human figures and features have been made by crafts people of all ethnic groups, nationalities, and genders. Whirligigs have a universal character and appeal. They can be enjoyed and appreciated by all members of the human family.

Other Figures: Animal figures, traditionally farm animals or pets, are frequently used on mechanical whirligigs. They are, more often than are the human forms, made out of proportion to look funny. So even if you can't draw well, your animal is bound to look right. The only exception seems to be the winged birds; they are usually created life-size and are made to look like the real thing.

DESIGN OF THE LARGE BIRDS

Designing large birds is not much different from designing small birds nor is their construction more difficult. The principal difference is that their size requires the handling of larger pieces of wood and heavier hardware. The main problems have to do with weight, which must be reduced as much as possible, and with the bearing points at the hub and at the pivot point, where the friction must be kept at a minimum. These problems are not severe, and most new bird whirligig designs, when constructed properly, work very well to the astonishment of many craftspersons.

Bird design focuses on the body of the bird, the pivot point, the wing base or support pieces, and the wings.

The Bird Body: First, decide which bird you intend to construct as a whirligig, then draw it life-size in outline, marking in the major features and color patterns. Birds can be made larger than life, or smaller, but as whirligigs, they look best the same size as they are in real life. Any good bird book will provide the basic facts of structure, outline, principal features, and color you need. Most birds are quite compact in appearance with the head, the torso, and the tail almost inseparable, as can be seen in the gull model. Some large birds, such as the loon in flight, are characterized by a long neck. Each has individual characteristics that should be emphasized to make the outline distinctive: a large beak, a specially shaped beak, a long neck, a plump body, a long, narrow tail, a spread tail, and so on. The final drawing should concentrate on these main features; upon completion, it can be transferred to the wood with as many details as you wish to show.

The Pivot Point: With birds, the pivot point is extremely important. Its location determines how the bird will fly and where the wing hubs will be. First, locate the balance point of the bird body. Place the pivot point a short distance forward, toward the head (1″ in smaller birds and 2″ to 3″ in larger birds). At this point, drill the socket for the spindle. Locate the hub point on the upper side of the body 1″ to 3″ in front of the pivot point.

The Wing Base: The wing support or base is attached to the body to keep the wings from striking the body. It is positioned by means of the hub point. A typical wing base might measure 3/4″ X 1-1/2″ X 6″ on a large bird. It should be curved or angled back from the outside to permit the wings to move freely. If the pivot point is in a different location and in a different relationship to the hub point, the bird may still fly, but it may not respond so well to the wind, facing slightly into it and failing to adjust readily to wind shifts.

Wings: All birds' wings are propellers, and those most preferred are the two-winged whirligigs with twin-bladed props, because the wings' movements seem real. They are also less likely to have maintenance problems than are the single-armed, split-propeller types.

Essentially, each of the two wings is a simple double-bladed propeller, fitted at the hub on each side of the body on a wing base. Each wing, however, must turn opposite from the other; this is absolutely essential to the operation of the bird whirligig. Hold the ends of the wing blades in front of you and mark them with different pitches or angles. Then mark the other ends at opposite angles. When the propellers are finished, mount them in the same way.

19

POSITION OF THE WINGS FROM FRONT

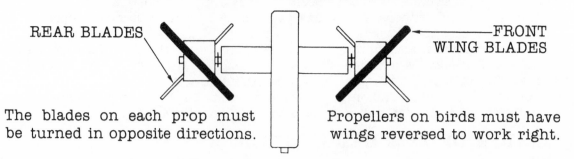

REAR BLADES

FRONT WING BLADES

The blades on each prop must be turned in opposite directions.

Propellers on birds must have wings reversed to work right.

For some very large wings, because large sizes of wood are not available or cutting out the wood would prove too difficult, the wing blades are made separate from the hubs. A typical construction of a wing may include a hub measuring 1-1/2" X 1-1/2" X 3" with a hole drilled in the center, and two separate wing blades 1/4" X 3" X 10", though the dimensions of the blades should correspond to the type and size of the bird being made. Slots are cut into the hub at the same opposite angles as indicated in the preceding paragraph, and the blades are glued in place. The straight or flat sides of blades should be on the inside, and any wide curving feature should be on the outside so the wings won't strike the body.

Mounting the Wings: Bird wing hubs get a lot of wear and should be lined with metal tubing. The size of this tubing will depend on the size of the screw or bolt used to secure the wing. This matter will be discussed more fully under model construction in chapter 5. Large screws (No. 10 X 3-1/2" round head brass screws), for example, can be used to fasten large wings to birds, but in some models the force of the wind and the constant twirling can bend or loosen them. For such large wings, it is recommended that a 1/4" carriage bolt through the body at the hub carry the weight. To determine the length of the bolt, construct a crude cross-sectional diagram with the measurements of the parts you propose using.

A single divided propeller constitutes some birds' wings. The construction involves making two wing blades and joining them at the hub to a single axle through the body. The principles of design and construction are the same; the blades are slanted in opposite directions. The hub hole in the body should be lined with metal tubing to facilitate turning and permit greasing. Early whirligigs featured axles of wood, and these can be made of 1/4" or 3/8" dowels to which the wings can easily be glued and nailed. Metal rods or bolts are recommended only because they wear longer. There are several ways hubs can be attached to metal axles. Thick wire can be fastened with epoxy glue, or the wire can be bent and stapled to the hubs. Thin wire axles should not be used with large birds. Bolts may be used as axles, and bolt heads and nuts can be countersunk at the wing hubs However, bolts are relatively heavy and should be used only with very large wings.

Remarks: Aside from real-life birds, fanciful birds may be designed. They may be of any form or color and will always be interesting. Also, common bird forms may be exaggerated; a rooster, for example, may be made with a huge crest or a big open beak saluting the dawn. Fanciful birds are fun and make people laugh.

Some large birds can be made to fill a special role. The author made one for a church retreat; it is a large white dove of peace carrying in its beak a branch of green leaves. The dove, about 24" long, was designed as indicated, constructed, and painted white with black eyes and yellow beak. Small leaf shapes were cut out of aluminum sheeting (tin cans would have done) and twisted onto a length of coat hanger wire. A small hole was drilled through the beak, the wire stem inserted, and the olive branch painted green.

DESIGN OF MECHANICAL WHIRLIGIGS

A mechanical whirligig, more than any other type, requires detailed planning from the start. Designs should be drawn to scale, showing side, top, and end views of the whirligig. If the detail is satisfactory and the plan seems to indicate that the whirligig will work, construction of the whirligig can begin. This is how it would be if all things in life were perfect and operated as expected, but most whirligig makers design and construct at the same time. That is, they have a plan and make a working sketch, but before settling on a final design, they make part of the whirligig to see if that part will work. Then they make another part to see if that fits. They go along by testing and by trial and error until all the parts work together.

In constructing Too Many Chickens, I made several separate sketches—front and side views—of the main structure, the chickens, and the farmer. Then I constructed the platform and the support piece. I found I had to change the shape of the ends of the chicken house to accommodate the chicken bodies. The chickens were going to be held in place by wooden legs, but it suddenly struck me that it would be simpler to have them move on a common axle, in this case a 1/4″ dowel. The first farmer was too small; when I made him larger, his arms turned out to be too heavy for his originally planned shape, and I had to provide more weight to his rear. The drawing did not show the farmer in action, and I had to widen his shoulders to make room for swinging arms, and so on. . . . Therefore, with respect to new ideas, it's best to begin with a plan drawn to scale and to move directly into constructing some of the moving parts, keeping in mind that changes will undoubtedly have to be made as you go along.

The design will usually include a base, an activity or movement of some kind involving figures or things in motion, various mechanisms by which the whirligig is powered and objects moved, the means by which the whirligig is turned toward or off the wind, and the support or mounting of the finished whirligig. This section deals in general with what must be considered in developing an original design, the component parts of a mechanical whirligig, and how they relate to one another.

The Base: The base is vital to the structure of the mechanical whirligig. The propeller and drive mechanisms are mounted on it; the action takes place on it; the tail (if there is one) is attached to it; and the support is built into it or added to it.

The base may be of a large platform type, such as a piece of wood 1″ X 6″ X 24″, or a narrow silhouette type about 1″ X 2″ X 16″, or any other size board that will serve as a mount. Oddly shaped bases may be designed; some have crosspieces which serve as special mountings for action. The shape of the base will depend upon the overall design of the whirligig and the activity that is expected to take place on it.

The first sketch or drawing should tell how much space is required on the base to mount the action. Allowance must be made for the mechanisms that make the whirligig work, as well as free space so the figures or objects can stand clear. The tail arrangement and any special trimming of the wood in the front and back ends must be planned for. The support at the pivot point must also be indicated.

When the drawing is completed, cut out the baseboard, leaving some surplus length. Mark off known measurements on it in pencil. It is sometimes advisable to draw a centerline and then mark it off in inches. This will save time when you are measuring, estimating distances, and making adjustments. You may wish to shape the front of a platform base in some way, like cutting a curve into it, so that you will have a feeling that the whirligig is already taking shape.

Activity, Movement, and Figures: The type, size, and details of the moving elements are the most important part of a mechanical whirligig, because this is not only "where the action is," but where the story is told and where the fun is. Traditionally, mechanical whirligigs have two elements: First, they consist of people, animals, and objects; and second, these things move and do something. Some complicated whirligigs have several people or animals or objects doing many things at the same time.

When the moving parts are first drawn, it may appear that they will work well together as planned. This is rarely the case. A figure may not bend over far enough, arms may get stuck, or hands may not reach their objective. One moving part may not connect properly with another moving part or may somehow get hung up. I once had problems with opposing parts that froze up; they were on dead center, which once created problems for early locomotive drive shafts. After planning the action, make the moving parts (they can be rough cut at this stage) and see if they will move together as planned. Also, think of the extent of the movement and if the camshaft or wheel, together with the connecting rods or wires, is allowing for too little or too much movement. There may be a number of adjustments to make: Maybe the position of the arms must be changed or the legs made longer, or perhaps the bodies need to be moved forward or back on the base. Much patience is required in making whirligigs work, and the more complicated they are, the greater the patience required! Many designs are never carried to completion, because they cannot be made to work as originally planned. After three years, I am still trying to simplify my design of the Blacksmith at the Forge. At first, I had too many joints in the body and arms, and the smithy got all twisted up. In the case of a dancer, when the action was powered from the bottom, the whirligig never worked; when I moved it to a cam that pulled from the top, the model worked just fine. Sometimes a little carving is necessary to make things right; sometimes major surgery is necessary. The point is that everyone making whirligigs must expect to make a number of adjustments before everything works smoothly.

One main problem with objects and figures is their size. The figures and objects must move with the least possible friction and not be so large or out of balance that weight becomes a problem. Sometimes a figure can be weighted at one end to counterbalance a heavier weight at the other. The man with the wheelbarrow has an external counterbalance; the farmer in Too Many Chickens has a long-tailed coat, and a handkerchief in his back pocket balances him. Propellers may not be large enough to power hard-to-move figures, camshafts may get stuck, and connecting rods and wires may break and bend. Test the movement of the figures and other parts to get the easiest motion possible. Mark the places on these parts where the connecting rods will work best. This will determine the appropriate location of camshafts or drive wheels, and lay the basis for cutting the necessary openings in the base if the operating mechanisms are located beneath the platform.

Mechanisms: All mechanical whirligigs have parts that transfer wind power to some form of mechanical or machine action. This starts with the propeller (discussed in detail in chapter 4) and its supporting parts and continues with various mechanical attachments (chapter 3).

The Propeller: In designing the whirligig, it is necessary to take into account the amount of wind power that will be necessary to move the parts. Although I have never seen one, or even heard of one, it would be possible to construct a whirligig with life-size human figures doing various tasks. This would require a substantial support frame and a huge propeller with blades perhaps five or ten feet in length. The point is that the size of the propeller depends on the work expected of it. Of course, wind conditions must also be taken into account; in a hurricane, a small propeller could move just about anything, provided it was sturdy enough to hold together. The propellers described in this book are adequate for powering the mechanical whirligigs included here. Larger propellers may have to be designed where larger figures or heavier moving parts are involved or where there are a large number of mechanical elements. It is also possible to have several propellers on one whirligig with each propeller moving a separate section. Often extra propellers are placed on the whirligig solely for decorative and entertainment purposes.

It is important to test propellers. If a propeller proves too big or powerful, it can be exchanged for a smaller one and vice versa. Sometimes it is necessary to improvise. I securely fastened a small propeller I thought would work to a whirligig but soon found that it was not sufficiently powerful. Since I could not remove the propeller without destroying the camshaft, and perhaps part of the whirligig, I added large vanes of light metal to the small wooden blades, and it worked.

The Drive Shaft: The propeller may be attached to the drive shaft, which may be one of several designs. A direct drive shaft is usually short and is commonly made from 1/4"- or 3/8"-diameter bolts. The bolt may be bent to allow for the transfer of power from a circular to a vertical or horizontal motion, or a wheel or other pieces may be attached to the bolt to perform the same operation

A camshaft mechanism will allow the same shaft to activate several figures or objects. The first consideration is the wire for the shaft, and it may be hard to locate the right kind of wire. This may be made of a 1/8" metal rod, threaded at the front end so machine nuts can hold the propeller in place. Such rods are found in welding supply houses or in hardware stores. Drapery hanger wire may serve the purpose. The wire should be soft enough to be bent easily in a vise.

Connecting Wire or Rods: Another consideration is how to attach connecting wire or rods to the shaft. If wooden rods are used, they may be widened at the base (or where they tie in to the drive shaft) to hold them in place. If wire is used in a cam, it is sometimes best to make a riding sleeve or spool on which the wire can be attached. This will prevent the wire from sliding off or getting hung up.

These are the main mechanisms commonly used. More complex whirligigs employ gears, pulleys, wheels, levers, and other mechanical means to transfer power. Most of this type of work requires a lot of time, and some old-time whirligig makers had plenty of that. A few of these mechanisms will be discussed in chapter 12. People who are mechanically minded and have an engineering bent can have lots of fun inventing new mechanisms.

Support of the Moving Parts: Planning for the mounting and installing of the mechanical parts begins with the basic design. Wood posts, metal tubing, angle iron, and metal or wooden brackets of all kinds are used. The mounting must be solid and secure. Whirligigs will not last long with wobbling propellers or loose shafts. In planning the mechanism mounting, the exact location of the drive shaft must be determined. Will it be below the platform or above it? Where will the shaft be located in relation to the figures or objects? The position of the mechanical parts and their mounting accessories will have to be located on the base. Cuts may have to be made to accommodate the action; screw holes may have to be drilled. This planning and layout on the base should be done before any other work is begun.

Socket or Pivot Support: The whirligig must be supported in such a way that it will be kept turned to the wind; the spinning movement this entails is made possible by having the whirligig suspended on a spindle placed in a socket in the whirligig. Some silhouette-type mechanical whirligigs do not require much in the way of support except for a hole drilled at an appropriate point. That hole should be fitted with a metal cap and a metal lining. Platform-type whirligigs will usually need a strong wood block support also drilled to receive a socket, lining, and cap. In some whirligigs, a main front post serves as the propeller support and the pivot support at the same time.

The location of the support socket or block depends on the overall design and weight distribution on the whirligig. Customarily, the socket on larger whirligigs is located behind the propeller, either directly behind it or back about one-quarter the length of the base. This helps make it a weather vane of sorts and keeps the propeller facing the wind.

Tail: A special tail or rudder assembly may not be necessary on a large mechanical whirligig. If the figures and moving or standing parts serve as a vane that will hold the whirligig facing into the wind, then no special rudder assembly is required. Silhouette-type whirligigs, however, usually have a tail, such as a tree or barn, built into their design. When a tail is needed, it may be constructed out of wood or metal. Aluminum flashing pieces are very useful. The metal or wood may be fashioned to fit into the story of the whirligig or may be painted with a related picture. The key to whether a tail is needed is simply how the whirligig responds to the wind. A mechanical whirligig must face into the wind at all times.

CHAPTER 3
WHIRLIGIG MECHANISMS

This chapter deals with the mechanisms that are involved in the operation of the whirligigs. Once the simple mechanical principles are understood, a person can go beyond the whirligigs described in this book, plan his or her own designs, and make new and unique ones. It also deals with the hardware frequently used in whirligig mechanisms and provides measurement details that are important if one is laying out a design with measured parts. The text also discusses how the parts are used and the role they share in making the whirligig work. This eliminates having to provide detailed explanations for every illustration in the chapters on constructing specific whirligigs.

SUPPORTING DEVICES: BRACKETS

Several types of brackets are used; their principal function is to serve as bearings for the drive shaft which moves through them. They support the shaft and keep it in line. We start with the consideration of brackets because such supports are decided upon and attached to the base before any moving part of the drive mechanism is added.

Angled Iron Brackets, or Inside Corner Braces: One of the standard brackets most useful for whirligig construction is the inside corner brace.

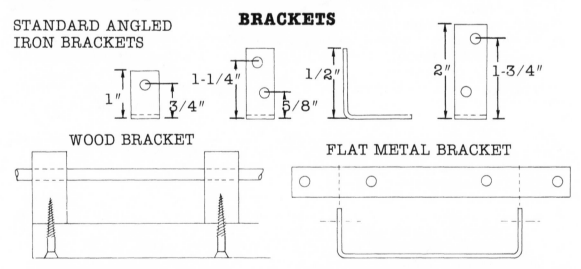

STANDARD ANGLED
IRON BRACKETS

BRACKETS

1"   1-1/4"   3/4"   1/2"   5/8"   2"   1-3/4"

WOOD BRACKET

FLAT METAL BRACKET

A commonly used size is the 1-1/2" bracket, which has four countersunk holes 1/4" in diameter. The centers of these holes are 5/8" and 1-1/4" from the corner, though sometimes the holes are slightly off these measurements. One side of a bracket I measured had holes 11/16" and 1-5/16" from the corner, so if slight variations are important to your design, you should take accurate measurements of the brackets you purchase. For most whirligigs, such small variations are not important. Standard brackets come in several sizes, as shown.

Special Metal Brackets: Special brackets, such as double brackets, for direct drive mechanisms can also be made of flat metal of a thickness sufficient to support a turning rod or shaft. Construction of the bracket is relatively simple. The really difficult part is lining up the drive shaft holes. Determine the exact size of the bracket needed in terms of its length: 2″, 3″, 4″, etc. Cut the flat metal to size and locate the positions of the holes to be drilled and the lines along which the metal will be bent.

Drill the holes first, making them large enough to accommodate the shaft and allow it to turn freely. A 1/4″ bit can be moved about in the hole to enlarge it so a 1/4″ shaft will turn freely in it. If the hole is too large, there may be too much play, and the mechanism may not work efficiently; it may not even work at all. The bending process is next. Any bending should be concerned with having the holes in line and having them the exact distance required from the base line. It is best to make the bend in a vise. If the metal is thin or soft enough, an error may be corrected by testing and rebending. The final test is to place the shaft in the holes to see if it turns properly.

Wooden Brackets: Most early mechanical whirligigs had all wooden parts, though some used an odd piece of metal here or there. Wooden brackets can be used today; they are simple enough to make. If the builder is concerned about wear and tear, sleeves or bushings can be made of metal tubing. In the illustration on the opposite page, the wood supports are 3/4″ thick, which points to a problem with wood brackets. Usually they must be thicker than metal supports, and unless the aperture is large enough, they may have a tendency to bind the drive shaft. It often is necessary to make the holes larger than usual and to use sleeves.

Additional Hardware for Braces: There are several other kinds of brackets or braces that are useful in whirligig construction.

Outside Corner Braces: These are usually used for back reinforcement of right-angle joints, such as in window frames and screen doors. They may be used as drive shaft supports in special places or to hold camshafts in position. The most useful sizes are 2″, 2-1/2″, and 3″, and there are larger sizes. The holes in the smaller braces are adequate for narrow wire, but they will probably have to be filed or drilled larger for 1/4″ or larger shafts. The example shown below is of a 2-1/2″ corner brace.

ADDITIONAL HARDWARE FOR BRACES AND SUPPORTS

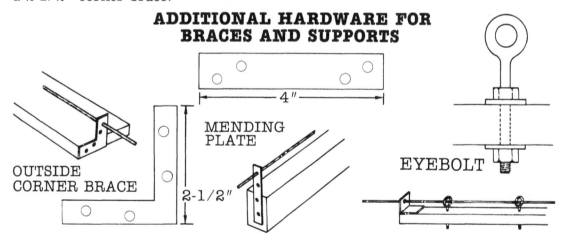

OUTSIDE CORNER BRACE

MENDING PLATE

EYEBOLT

Mending Plates: These are straight, flat pieces of heavy metal customarily used to reinforce wooden joints or repaired breaks. They are useful as shaft supports. Under some circumstances they may be bent, but special care will be necessary because the metal is relatively thick and, once bent, will resist straightening out or bending in another place. Such a plate is particularly useful where strength or rigidity is essential.

Shelf Braces: These are fairly large and would be used with very large whirligigs. Their great advantage is that they are self-braced and very strong and rigid. They will permit the operation of a deep cam in the shaft. The distance from the curve to the aperture on the smaller end ranges from about 4″ upward.

Other Supports: Two other articles are very useful in the construction of the larger whirligigs: eyebolts and screw eyes. Eyebolts come in various sizes given in terms of length and inside diameter of the eye. Smaller standard lengths are 1-1/2″, 2″, 2-1/2″, and 3″. The diameter of the stock in these sizes is 5/32″, and the opening of the eye ranges from 3/16″ to 1/4″. If an eyebolt is to be used for holding a drive shaft or other moving part in position, it must be carefully measured to ascertain that it is suitable in all dimensions. Screw eyes of the most useful size range from tiny, 5/8″ long with an aperture of about 1/8″, to ones with eyes about 7/8″ in diameter. The larger ones may be used to support drive shafts in some cases, and the smaller ones are used extensively for securing connecting rods to the moving parts of the whirligig.

DRIVE SHAFTS: THE USE OF BOLTS

Most of the bolts used in whirligig drive shafts are 1/4″ in diameter, although 5/8″ bolts are also used. They are available in all lengths, and those most frequently used are 6″, 6-1/2″, 7″, or 8″ long. Carriage bolts are distinguished from machine bolts by their heads, as indicated on page 17. For some whirligigs, the square end of a carriage bolt holds a wheel firmly. However, the square end would interfere with the movement of large winged whirligigs, so a hexagonal-headed machine bolt is used for those models.

Standard bolts are made of relatively soft metal, so they can be sawed, cut, bent, flattened, and drilled, although not without some effort.

The Direct Drive Mechanism: A true direct drive mechanism is one in which the drive shaft is attached to the main whirligig object or figure and makes it move. It would be like the main shaft of a sawmill if this were directly attached to the saw blade instead of going though a series of wheels and pulleys. Very few whirligigs operate in this way, although some old designs, such as the Acrobat, are direct drive whirligigs. In our definition we have included those which have a minimum of attachments. In the illustration below, a 1/4″ carriage bolt 6″ long serves as a drive shaft. At one end is the propeller and at the other a drive wheel. The wheel's circular motion is transferred to the object by means of a connecting wire or rod.

The drive wheel need not be circular. It may be of any shape; the motion imparted by the rotating shaft will, of course, remain circular. In one of the whirligigs in the book, the wheel is replaced by a rotor arm, which serves the same purpose.

When a bolt serves as the drive shaft, it must be securely supported. The various iron brackets are excellent for this purpose. In many whirligigs, the shaft goes through part of the main frame. In such cases, a piece of metal tubing will serve as a sleeve and also hold the propeller and drive wheel in place.

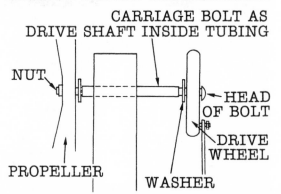

DIRECT DRIVE MECHANISM

CARRIAGE BOLT AS DRIVE SHAFT INSIDE TUBING

NUT

HEAD OF BOLT

DRIVE WHEEL

PROPELLER

WASHER

The Bent Bolt Mechanism: One of the most popular drive shafts, which has been used for generations, is illustrated on the opposite page. Its popularity stems from the fact that is it easy to make, is strong and rigid, and therefore long-lasting, and can be applied to a number of mechanical whirligigs. The mechanism in the illustration makes use of the following materials:

(1)   1/4″ carriage bolt, 6″ long
(2)   1/4″ nuts
(2)   1/4″ washers
(2)   1-1/2″ corner brackets
(1)   1/8″ bolt, 1″ long, and nut

BENT BOLT MECHANISM
POWER FROM BENEATH BASE
OR PLATFORM

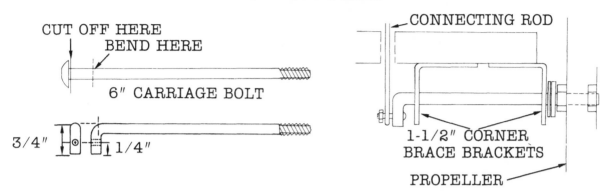

To make the mechanism, the head of the bolt is cut off, and the bolt is put in a vise and bent at right angles about 1/2" from the unthreaded end. This end is then hammered or filed flat, and a 1/8" hole is drilled through the center of the flat end. This may seem like a difficult task, but standard bolts are relatively soft and can be bent and drilled without heating. If you have the equipment and are familiar with blacksmithing and the use of torches, you may wish to apply heat. Note that you can use a longer bolt, and your plans may call for a longer bent arm to obtain a more extensive motion.

For the supports, one corner bracket is usually screwed in position at the end of the baseboard, either on top or beneath it. The position will depend on the action desired and the room you have for it. The second bracket is screwed in a position that allows for the free play of the drive shaft and gives room for the washers and propeller parts. A washer or washers are placed against the front corner bracket. Sometimes, depending on the propeller design and the size of the vanes or blades, it is necessary to move the propeller out from the end of the baseboard. In such a case, metal tubing may be inserted between two washers. Wooden washers made from beads are also excellent for this purpose. One 1/4" nut is turned hard into the bolt. The propeller (which has a 1/4" hole drilled through the center of the hub) is placed next to this and another 1/4" nut is turned fast against the propeller. For additional security it is recommended that the nut be partially countersunk, at least 1/8", into the propeller hub. This can be done by drilling with a 1/2" bit before drilling the 1/4" hole through the hub. When the 1/8" bolt, or any other metal attachment, is put through the hole in the drive shaft, it is ready to serve as the rotating arm of the mechanism. A connecting wire or rod can be attached to it for testing purposes.

CAMSHAFTS

In mechanics a cam is an irregular form of a moving part which alters the motion of another part. In whirligig mechanisms the cams ordinarily are those built into the drive shaft, which makes it a camshaft. Camshafts may be made of any bendable metal which, even when bent, maintains rigidity throughout its length. Coat hangers have been used where weight or pressure was not a problem. Drapery hangers are superior in that they are made of heavier wire. Highly tensile wire, such as the very hard piano-type wire, would be excellent if it were not for the fact that it is so difficult to bend without heat. Wire that can be bent by hand with the use of pliers and a vise is best. For the whirligigs in this book, most of the activity, such as that involved in moving human figures, does not require a cam deeper than 3/4" to 1". Deeper cams can be made, but their effectiveness is usually limited in that the larger they are, the less power they will deliver, at least in the same size whirligig. The cam can be bent into the wire at the point where it is needed to move the figure, and presumably this point has been indicated in your plan or is drawn on the baseboard. Make the cam so that the center is located where you will expect to secure the connecting rod. Several cams can be made along the length of the camshaft, and this provides an opportunity for a whole series of moving figures and objects.

CAM TYPES FOR CAMSHAFTS

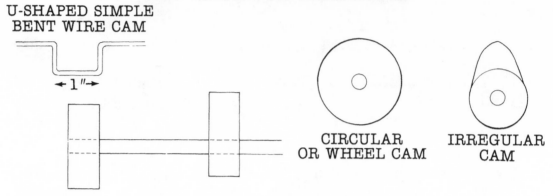

U-SHAPED SIMPLE
BENT WIRE CAM

← 1″ →

CIRCULAR
OR WHEEL CAM

IRREGULAR
CAM

Attachments to the Cam: Many whirligig makers find it difficult to attach connecting wires or rods to the camshaft, mainly because they slide off to the side or get stuck on the main shaft. The problem can be solved by making a ''rider'' to keep the wire in place. A typical rider is shown below. Slip the rider onto the cam before turning the third bend, or slip the tubing liner on first, then later cut the wooden rider in half and glue it in place over the tubing. The rider will hold the connecting wire firmly and permit free movement of the cam. A word should be said about the wire for the connection between the drive wheels and cams. If a rigid wire can be used, thin clothes hanger wire works well. However, the best wire is semirigid; it is stiff enough to do the job and hold up under some pressure, but it is bendable and somewhat flexible. I like a wire that will give a little. Besides, if a very high wind should strike the whirligig, a semirigid wire will bend rather than break all the attachments. Another type of attachment is a wooden rod. If it is thick at the cam end, this prevents slippage and binding. A hole for the camshaft should be drilled, then a small slot can be cut from the end of the rod to that hole. The camshaft can be forced into it. The large flagpole in the Waving the Flag whirligig is an example. Under ordinary circumstances the camshaft will be held in place, but if it's not, the end slot can be closed with a wooden wedge glued in place. If a metal liner is desired, then the liner should be put in position first, and the slot made big enough for it. At the other end of the rod, where it connects with another moving part, the connecting socket should be lined with tubing to reduce wear.

ATTACHMENTS TO THE CAMSHAFT

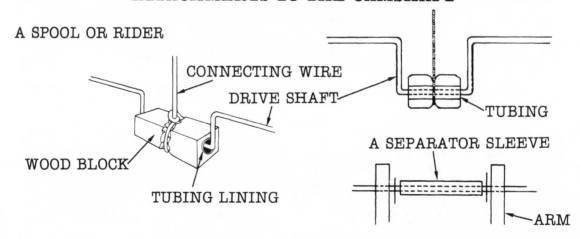

A SPOOL OR RIDER

CONNECTING WIRE

DRIVE SHAFT

TUBING

A SEPARATOR SLEEVE

WOOD BLOCK

TUBING LINING

ARM

Support for the Camshaft: The camshaft is supported by brackets and braces in the same way as is the direct drive mechanism. Special problems may arise because of the number of cams in the shaft and the length of the camshaft, both of which may contribute to the shaft's bending. This may be overcome by the use of the eyebolts placed between the cams and by the use of additional brackets.

Attachment to the Propeller: The front end of the camshaft can be threaded for the propeller. If the shaft is 1/8″ in diameter, for example, thread the shaft with a 6/32 die back to where it can hold the propeller secured between two machine screws. Drill the propeller hub with a 7/64″ bit; it can then be turned on the shaft, with a bit of glue to hold it firm. If the shaft is not threaded, allowance must be made for enough wire to pass through the propeller and be made secure. A hole of small diameter is drilled at the propeller hub. The wire may be bent at the hub and stapled. It may also be bent entirely around the front of the hub and then around the side. If the wire is not secured at the propeller, the propeller will turn, but the camshaft won't.

METHODS OF ATTACHING WIRE
SHAFT TO PROPELLER AT HUB

BENT OVER
AND SECURED
WITH STAPLE

BENT AROUND
CORNER OF HUB

BENT TWICE
AND INTO HUB

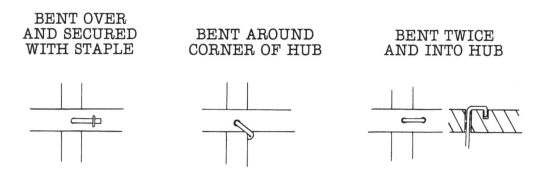

In most of the whirligigs in this book that use a wire shaft, it is secured at the front of the propeller. An additional method is shown in the Too Many Chickens whirligig. There two hub braces are glued to the propeller and, together with the propeller, are glued to the wire. This thickening of the hub area and the use of epoxy or urethane glue will prevent the propeller from spinning off.

The Loose End: The tail end of the camshaft is often simply bent over to prevent the shaft from slipping from the supports and causing trouble with the connections. However, this end can serve a purpose, and many old whirligigs demonstrate inventive use of the loose end. If it extends beyond the base and is not in the way of the whirligig tail, it can provide an additional cam to make something work, or it can spin a decorative piece of wood.

CHAPTER 4

PROPELLERS: PRINCIPLES AND DESIGN

The power of a mechanical whirligig is obtained through the use of a propeller. Technically, a propeller is a device with a central hub and radiating blades so placed that each blade forms part of a spiral surface, or a screw. When powered, as in a ship or aircraft, it produces thrust and forward motion. When put in a position to be moved by air currents, as in a whirligig, it acts in reverse, producing power that can be used to move objects. Propellers used on wind-driven electric plants can be huge, with blades over 100 feet long as on the one constructed for an experimental power station in the western North Carolina mountains. The vanes of large windmills in the Netherlands and Great Britain were over 25 feet long. Smaller propellers harnessing wind power for pumping water graced windmills on farms all over the United States a century ago, and these devices are still in use in some areas. Whirligigs, of course, use very small propellers, but they act on the same prinicple as the huge ones. When properly made and balanced, they are very efficient. During every first test of a whirligig, I am always surprised and pleased when I see how well the whirligigs, particularly the big ones, work in the wind. I always worry about the propeller. Is it big enough? Is it too big? Does it look right? And I am always astonished at the power of a small propeller. Under the right wind conditions it can move anything, almost. I mention these thoughts and questions because they are common to all whirligig makers. The propeller is, after all, the most important moving part of the whirligig mechanism; without it you have only a piece of woodwork.

While some old basic and newer models are discussed in this chapter, the craftsperson should bear in mind that there is no end to propeller design. Once the main principles are grasped, a person can invent new propeller designs that haven't been tried before. Designing propellers can be fun in itself, particularly if each design is radically different. Propellers don't cost much to make and the wind is free.

THE SIMPLE PROPELLER

The Single Two-Bladed Propeller: The basic propeller consists of a hub and two balanced blades, which in turning cut through the air in the same direction, or angle. This means that when formed from one piece of wood, as these props generally are, the cuts must be made at opposite directions on either side of the hub. Otherwise the piece will not turn.

Construction of a typical propeller, such as used for a wing on a Cardinal whirligig, is shown here. It is made of a wood block 3/4" X 1" X 6". The location of the hub is marked, then the ends are marked at the wingtips: Note the opposite angling. The hole at the center of the hub is drilled large enough to allow later insertion of brass tubing which serves as a sleeve or bearing. The wings are then whittled out; they may be finished by filing and sandpapering.

CONSTRUCTION OF A SIMPLE PROPELLER

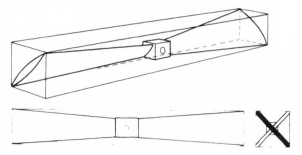

Propellers must balance. Spin the wing at the hub; if one end is heavier than the other it must be filed or sanded down until the weight on each end is the same. This size propeller is used for making smaller birds' wings, aircraft propellers, and extra decorative pieces.

The Three-Piece Propeller: If a larger two-bladed propeller is required and it cannot be made from one piece of wood, it can be made in three sections, a hub and two blades. The hub shown in this illustration is made of a wood block 1-1/2" X 1-1/2" X 2-1/2". It is carefully measured, and the center of the hub and the ends where the blades will be fitted are marked. The blades shown are made of wood pieces 1/4" X 3" X 10". After they have been cut out, they are glued in the slots in the hub. When the glue dries, the hub can be trimmed down and the entire piece sanded lightly and finished. The hub can then be fitted with a metal lining. This is recommended to prevent wear on the wood at this point. Such larger double-bladed propellers are used principally for the wings of big birds. They are rarely used for the larger mechanical whirligigs because of the size that would be required. Multiple-bladed propellers are more efficient for such purposes.

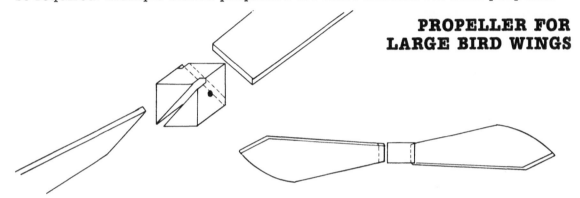

PROPELLER FOR LARGE BIRD WINGS

The Split Propeller: The split double-bladed propeller has had wide and varied use. It forms the flailing paddles of the canoeist, the flashing oars of the fisherman, the waving ears of a Nubian goat, and is found on numerous other whirligig subjects. The propeller consists of two blades separated at the hub and joined by an axle that passes through an object or body.

SPLIT DOUBLE-BLADED PROPELLER

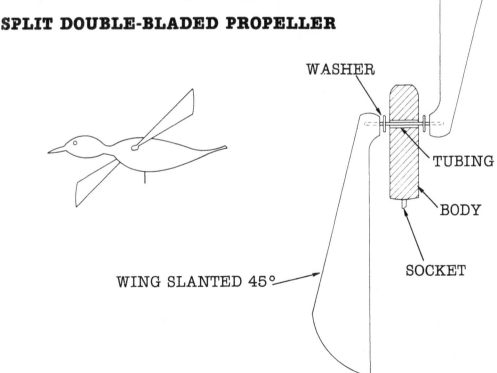

WASHER

TUBING

BODY

SOCKET

WING SLANTED 45°

The Winged Foot of Mercury, pictured here, was made for a friend who presented it to her professor of podiatry. The wings were cut from pieces of pine 3/4" X 3" X 7" and shaped carefully until they were quite thin and showed feather outlines. The hub was kept about 3/4" square. The foot was cut out and rounded off, and a hole was drilled over the heel, as shown. The hole was lined with brass tubing. The two opposite wings were joined by a thick wire axle, which was secured with epoxy glue in small holes drilled in the wings. When mounted, the wings performed perfectly.

WINGED FOOT OF MERCURY

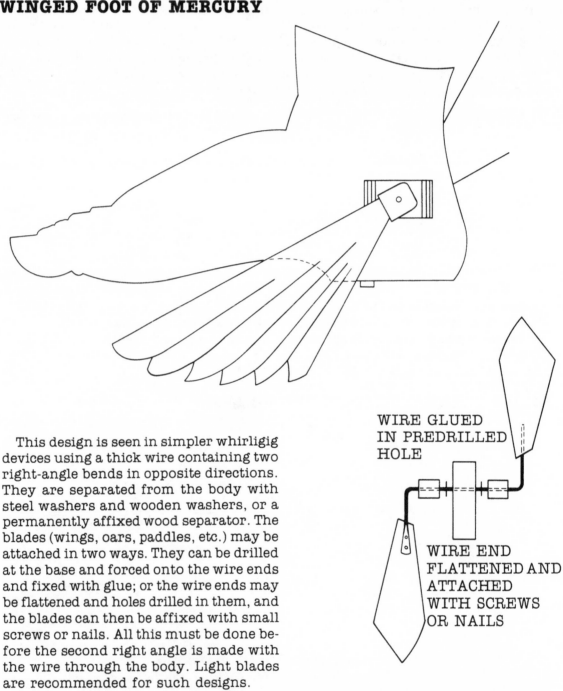

WIRE GLUED
IN PREDRILLED
HOLE

This design is seen in simpler whirligig devices using a thick wire containing two right-angle bends in opposite directions. They are separated from the body with steel washers and wooden washers, or a permanently affixed wood separator. The blades (wings, oars, paddles, etc.) may be attached in two ways. They can be drilled at the base and forced onto the wire ends and fixed with glue; or the wire ends may be flattened and holes drilled in them, and the blades can then be affixed with small screws or nails. All this must be done before the second right angle is made with the wire through the body. Light blades are recommended for such designs.

WIRE END
FLATTENED AND
ATTACHED
WITH SCREWS
OR NAILS

Some large birds look very good with wings of this type. They seem more stately in regard to wing movement. Many whirligig makers, however, prefer the versions with two double wings, because the turning wings seem more realistic and produce more of a twirling motion.

FOUR-BLADED PROPELLERS

The most useful propellers for the large whirligigs are four-bladed. This type appears on American whirligigs over 100 years old. It should be encouraging to craftspersons that very few, if any, of these classic examples were ever made in a cabinet or machine shop. They were made by people who used simple tools, odd pieces of wood, and common hardware. Some chunky old propellers do not look as if they could ever possibly turn, but they did and still do. The principle is the same as for the double-bladed propellers. Each blade must be set at the same angle in relation to the hub, and on the opposite side of the hub, this angle is reversed. The angle is easier to understand on a four-bladed propeller. If the hub is mounted upright and turned for marking at the top, it will be seen that the same angle will appear for each blade, even though it seems reversed at the bottom. The four-bladed propeller requires that the hub and the blades be made separately. There are two principal types of hubs: solid-hub and crossed-hub.

The Solid-Hub Propeller: This is a single-piece hub with holes or notches cut in to hold the blades. The size of the hub usually depends on the size and weight of the blades, but hubs 2″ square to 3″ square are sufficient for most of the mechanical types shown in this book.

The hub is measured in detail and marked before any cutting or boring is done. Drill the hole in the center for the shaft, then cut the blade slots. The latter can be done with any straight saw and the bottom can be squared off with a coping saw. Narrow slots can be trimmed with a knife, and wide slots can be filled with wedges when the blades are fitted and glued. As with a double-bladed propeller, a four-bladed one should be balanced as accurately as possible. If, when mounted, one blade is noticeably heavier than the others, it should be trimmed and lightened. The hub illustrated is 3/4″ thick; larger hubs are sometimes necessary. Blades vary in size and thickness; the ones shown are 1/4″ X 3″ X 10″. Plywood can be used for blades if it can be waterproofed or painted. However, it does not lend itself to fine finishing, and solid wood is best if it's available.

ATTACHMENT OF BLADES TO A 3″ HUB

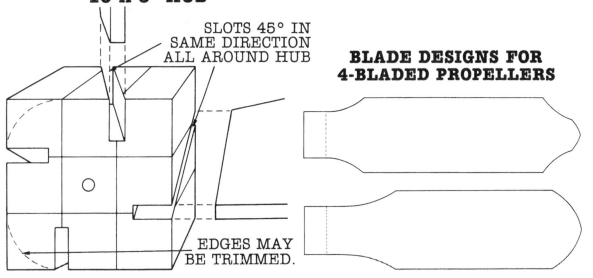

SLOTS 45° IN SAME DIRECTION ALL AROUND HUB

EDGES MAY BE TRIMMED.

BLADE DESIGNS FOR 4-BLADED PROPELLERS

The Crossed-Hub Propeller: Another type of the four-bladed propeller is the crossed-hub or cross-arm propeller, which is also found on many early whirligigs. This is made of two pieces of wood joined at the center. The arms thus produced become supports for blades of different materials and designs. The ends of the arms can be either narrowly slotted or partially cut away to take the blades, which are then inserted or nailed in place. Metal or wooden blades may be used. The prin-

33

cipal advantage of metal blades is that they are lighter than wooden ones; there-fore, for the same weight, the metal blades can be designed to present more surface area to the wind. The older whirligigs used wooden propellers, and these lend them-selves to fine craftsmanship.

CROSS-ARM PROPELLER STRUCTURE

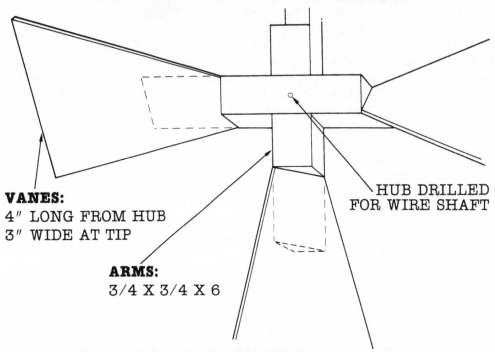

VANES:
4″ LONG FROM HUB
3″ WIDE AT TIP

ARMS:
3/4 X 3/4 X 6

HUB DRILLED
FOR WIRE SHAFT

MULTIBLADED PROPELLERS

In this section, the term multibladed propellers refers to those having more than four blades. One can have as many blades as there are spokes on a wheel. I have made a propeller out of an old bicycle wheel by using about one-third of the spokes on which to mount metal blades, and though a propeller with such a great num-ber of blades is rare, six-, eight-, and ten-bladed propellers are not uncommon on whirligigs. They are often constructed on the spoke principle. One end is whittled down to a 1/4″ or 1/2″ rod which then fits into a socket drilled into the hub.

MULTIBLADED PROPELLERS

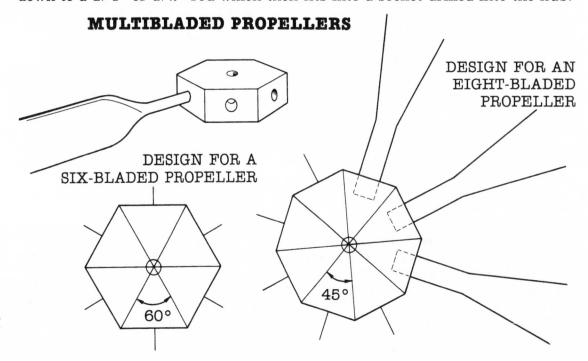

DESIGN FOR AN
EIGHT-BLADED
PROPELLER

DESIGN FOR A
SIX-BLADED PROPELLER

60°

45°

34

For propellers with six or eight blades, the hub can be cut hexagonally or octagonally, respectively, but for props with ten or more blades it's easier to cut a circular hub and then measure off the angles between the blades. (Of course, a circular hub can be used for all types of propellers.) To determine the angle between the "spokes," divide the number of blades you intend to use into 360 degrees. For example, if you want ten blades, the angle will be 36 degrees measured from the center of each spoke and can be measured by a protractor at the hub. For 12 blades, the angle is 30 degrees, and so on.

METAL PROPELLERS

All-Metal Propellers: When I first made metal propellers—mostly for decorative purposes like a ship's propeller on a weather vane whirligig—they didn't always work properly. The problem was that the hubs were not wide enough to hold them in a position perpendicular to the shaft, and they would often wobble and lie over in the wind. All-metal propellers used for power require wide hubs or must be rigidly secured to the drive shaft. They may be positioned in a wooden hub, or held in place between bolts, as illustrated. Large all-metal propellers have their limits for someone without access to a machine shop, but for those who like to work with metal, all kinds of possibilities are open.

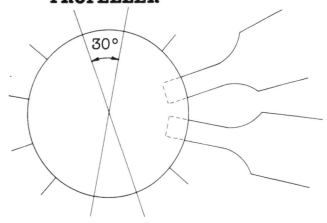

DESIGN FOR 12-BLADED PROPELLER

30°

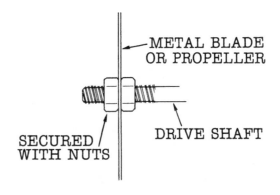

ATTACHMENT OF A METAL PROPELLER

METAL BLADE OR PROPELLER

DRIVE SHAFT

SECURED WITH NUTS

Metal-Bladed Propellers: Most whirligig makers have never bothered with all-metal propellers, but they have frequently made metal blades to fit on a wooden hub, which is convenient to use and works best on a propeller with several blades. The metal used is standard lightweight sheet metal of various thicknesses. Galvanized steel is quite rigid but may be too heavy for your purposes; aluminum sheeting is excellent in the right thickness. It is best to test the metal yourself; if it is too thin, it will be flimsy and bend too easily. If it is too thick, it will be too heavy. I found that zinc flashing material, for example, proved too heavy for my particular uses, although I would consider it for much larger blades; besides, it is more expensive than steel or aluminum sheeting. Your hardware store will cut off any size piece you wish from rolls of sheet metal, which you can examine before purchase. This comes in widths as wide as four feet, so if you purchase one running foot, you will have enough for many blades (and tail vanes). Aside from rolls, aluminum flashing comes in 5″ X 7″ pieces that are easy to cut down to size or use as is. Metal blades are attached to wooden arms with wire nails or secured in narrow slots sawed in the arms.

The propeller used for Eleanor at the Tub, shown on the following page, had 6″ crosspieces that, after being joined, were drilled for the wire drive shaft and then were slotted diagonally at the ends. The ends were trimmed neatly, and metal blades were inserted and held in place with small wire nails and glue.

METAL-BLADED CROSS-HUB PROPELLER
14 INCH DIAMETER

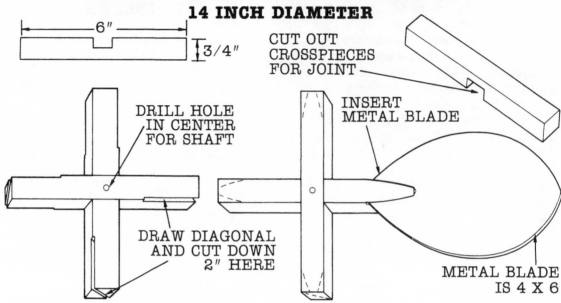

6"

3/4"

CUT OUT
CROSSPIECES
FOR JOINT

DRILL HOLE
IN CENTER
FOR SHAFT

INSERT
METAL BLADE

DRAW DIAGONAL
AND CUT DOWN
2" HERE

METAL BLADE
IS 4 X 6

To secure the end of a wire drive shaft to the propeller hub, as in the case of camshaft whirligigs, it is necessary to keep the propeller from running free. This is done by bending the wire and securing it either by means of a staple or bending it into the hub or around it. Sometimes the use of hub bracers, as described in the Too Many Chickens whirligig in chapter 12, will hold a wire shaft securely.

If the propeller is being used with a larger drive shaft, such as a 1/4" bolt, the center of the hub should be drilled with either a 7/32" or 1/4" bit. A 1/2" bit might also be used to countersink the nut.

UNUSUAL DESIGNS

The propeller designs already discussed lend themselves to a number of variations, a few of which will be described here.

Tin Can Top Propellers: One whirligig maker gained considerable fame through using tin can tops—and bottoms—for propeller blades. His work is sought by museums and collectors of modern art. While the construction of tin can top propellers is quite simple, this creative craftsman added a number of innovations that carried his work to the high level of contemporary art. He painted each blade a different color and mounted dozens of the props on rods and pipes to create a vibrant, mobile-like unit that seemed to move in many directions at once. The basic tin can top propeller begins with a square wood hub. As with other propellers, slots are cut into the hub for the can tops, and a hole is drilled in the center for the axle or shaft. When the can tops are fitted into the slots, a circular-bladed propeller is born.

TIN CAN TOP PROPELLER

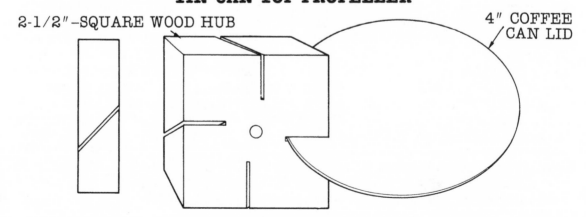

2-1/2"–SQUARE WOOD HUB

4" COFFEE
CAN LID

Can top propellers can be used to drive mechanisms, but there are a few problems about their use, one of which is that they usually are thicker at the hub than is convenient for attaching to whirligig bases. They can be mounted in relays or in sets for display purposes.

The Lollypop Propeller: This can be a decorative or a working propeller, and as with the candy, you can have small lollypops or large ones. The blades may be made of wood, metal, hardboard, plastic, or any of several other materials. After determining the size and shape of the whole propeller, make a hub appropriate to the design. A circular shape will accept many arms while a square will accommodate four. When the hub has been drilled at the center, the positions of the arms can be marked and the holes drilled for the arms. The arms are usually made of dowels, although they can be made from any square-sawn wood pieces. The thickness of the dowel or arm depends upon the size of the propeller and the vanes or blades to be supported. The ends of the arms are slotted for the blades, or they can be cut out, as shown.

LOLLYPOP PROPELLER

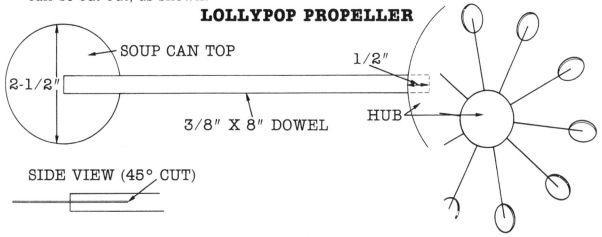

SOUP CAN TOP

2-1/2"

1/2"

3/8" X 8" DOWEL

HUB

SIDE VIEW (45° CUT)

In the illustration, the hub is 3/4" thick and 2" in diameter. The arms are made of 3/8" dowel, 8" long. The vanes are 2-1/2" soup can tops. These blades can be made of wood and of any shape, as long as the entire piece is balanced at the end. This makes a propeller about 20" in diameter. It is obvious that many other designs are possible with this type.

The Horizontal Propeller: The horizontal propeller design that will be most familiar to readers is that found on wind speed indicators. This type of propeller, found in some antique whirligigs, was used mainly to turn a platform on which some activity was taking place. It really works. To produce a strong enough force

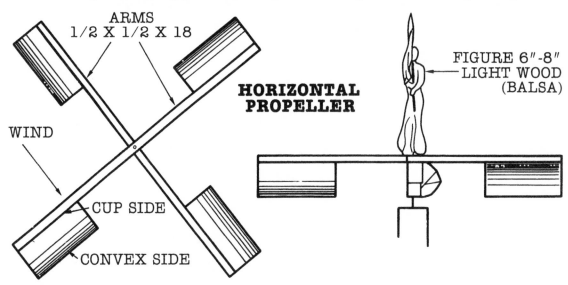

ARMS
1/2 X 1/2 X 18

HORIZONTAL
PROPELLER

FIGURE 6"-8"
LIGHT WOOD
(BALSA)

WIND

CUP SIDE

CONVEX SIDE

to make things move, it requires relatively large cups, and the whole structure must be well supported and well balanced. This design requires more planning and work than other types of propellers, but it is different and interesting to watch. If not used for driving some of the action, this type can serve as a decorative addition to a more complex whirligig.

HORIZONTAL PROPELLER

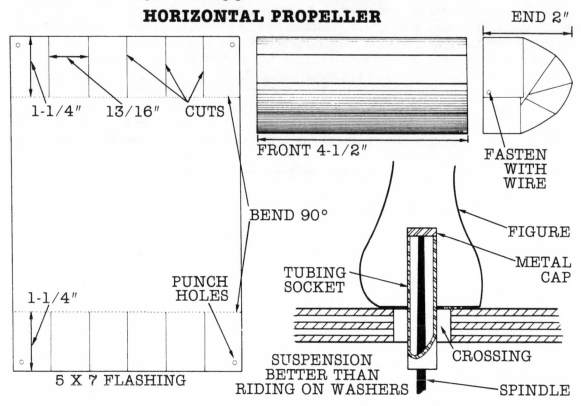

Just about any design that catches wind in a cup in back and is shaped to minimize wind resistance in the front can make a horizontal propeller. The essence of the design shown here was taken from an old whirligig.

ONLY THE BEGINNING

This chapter is only an introduction to the construction and design of propellers, of which there is no end. There can be many variations on the basic designs illustrated here. Throughout the book other propellers will be described because they worked particularly well with the whirligigs under discussion.

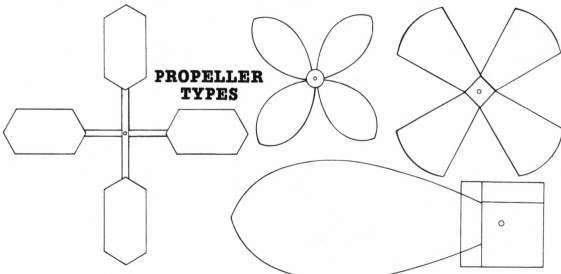

PROPELLER
TYPES

CHAPTER 5

CONSTRUCTION OF
LARGE BIRD WHIRLIGIGS

The design and construction procedures for large bird whirligigs follow the guidelines regarding the making of smaller birds as indicated in chapter 1. There are some major differences, though, and these will be discussed below. While there are any number of winged subjects for the craftsperson, this chapter will deal in detail with the construction of four large birds: the Mallard Duck, a perennial favorite of hunters and outdoor types; the Sea Gull, beloved of coastal people; the Common Loon, the lake-loving diver; and the Gooney Bird, a fowl of fantasy. The last design is provided to show that one can design anything and make a whirligig out of it. Descriptive illustrations of other bird plans are also included. It should be noted that, as with the smaller birds, the size of the large bird whirligigs should approximate life-size. In real life the sea gull and the mallard are about 24" long; therefore these whirligigs are of that length.

THE MALLARD DUCK

Materials: Wood

Body block (1) 3/4" X 4-1/2" X 24"
Wing base (2) 3/4" X 1-3/4" X 5"
Wing hub (2) 1-1/2" X 1-1/2" X 2-1/2"
Wings (4) 1/4" X 2-3/4" X 10-1/2"

Other pieces include:

(2) 1/4" carriage bolts, 8" long, with nuts and washers
(2) 1-1/4" pieces of 3/8" metal tubing
(1) 2" tension pin (3/8")
(1) 20d or 30d nail

PROCEDURE

Body: The drawing on the next page is reduced in scale. If you do not wish to draw any bird freehand, draw one-inch squares on a sheet of paper (inexpensive 18" X 24" newsprint drawing pads are handy) 24" across and 10" down and transfer the drawing by observation. It can then be traced onto the wood. The drawing can also be transferred directly to the wood.

Saw the body out in profile and sand it, taking particular care to round the edges somewhat. This gives a finished three-dimensional effect. At the appropriate place on the bottom, mark the pivot point, which should be about 8-1/2" from the tip of the tail, and drill a 3/8" hole 2" deep or slightly less. In this set a 2" tension pin of the same external diameter as the hole. Cut 1/2" off the tip of a 20d or 30d nail and drive the short piece into the socket. You can now set the body on a stand with a 20d or 30d nail as the pivot pin or spindle. An alternative to the nail tip is a round head screw that will fit inside the tension pin. It is better to put the metal socket base, or cap, in position after the socket liner is in place, and not before. NOTE: The socket can be of any diameter and need not be lined with metal tubing. Any nail of the right size can act as a spindle. The use of socket liners and metal caps, and ball bearings, is to make the whirligig operate easily and last longer. But even if no liner is used, a cap made of a nail tip or screw is highly recommended.

Wing Bases: The wing bases (3/4" X 1-3/4" X 5") are rounded off as shown in the diagram. Each is drilled through the middle with a 1/4" bit. Small holes for security nails may also be drilled in the curved sides.

The first one is then attached to the body with waterproof glue. Before gluing,

MALLARD DUCK

1 SQUARE = 1/2 INCH

BODY BLOCK:
3/4 X 5-1/2 X 24

WINGS:
1/4 X 2-3/4 X 10-1/2

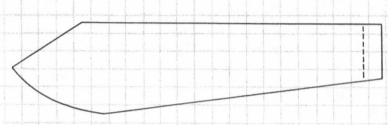

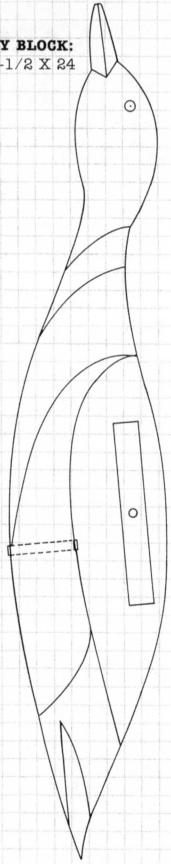

WING HUB:
1-1/2 X 1-1/2 X 2-1/2

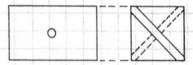

WING BASE:
3/4 X 1-3/4 X 5

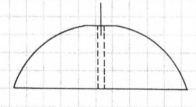

place it on the upper side of the body with the hole in the base 3/4″ to 1″ to the front of the pivot pin socket when the body is horizontal, or in flying position. Then outline the position with a pencil and complete the gluing job. While the wing base is clamped into position, the two security nails (usually 6d finishing nails) may be driven home. Let the glue dry completely before proceeding. (You can work on the wing hub or wings in the meantime.)

When the glue is thoroughly dry, drill a hole through the body with a 1/4″ bit using the hole through the wing block as a guide. Push a 1/4″ bolt through and run it through the second wing base also. The bolt, with its nut and washer attached, will hold the second wing base in position when you glue it to the body. Then secure this base with the two nails. This trick will assure that all the holes will line up with the bolt. NOTE: When attaching the second base, if you have a wide enough clamp (3-1/2″ or larger), use it. Otherwise, a 4″ bolt can be used with a washer; the nut can be tightened to draw the wing base firmly against the body.

The body is now ready with wing bases in position. The painting pattern can be drawn on. The bird's body can be painted at this time, or you can wait until after the wings are built.

Wings: For the large birds, each wing structure includes a hub and two wing sections. Cut out the wing sections before you make the hub. A pattern for 10-1/2″ wings is illustrated. The wings may be made of 1/4″ plywood, preferably of exterior grade, or of solid wood 3/8″ thick. The advantages of solid wood are that the wings may be made more shapely and that they take paint better.

Hub: The hub begins as a block of wood 1-1/2″ X 1-1/2″ X 2-1/2″. Beginning at the center of one of the 1-1/2″ X 2-1/2″ faces, drill a 3/8″ hole through the block. Then, thinking of a block as the wing itself, draw a wing slot diagonally across each end of each block. The slots on a block are the opposite diagonals of one another. They are laid out so that, corresponding to the body, the angles will be complementary. Note in the illustration that the slots in each block are opposite each other when seen from the front. They will be seen as slanted in the opposite direction from the back.

Mark the hub to make 1/2″-deep cuts for the blades to fit into, and use the wing blades to insure the proper width of the cuts. Too narrow a cut can be trimmed with a knife; too wide a cut can be made tight with small wood chips or wedges when the wing is glued into the slot. Either before the gluing process or after the glue is dried, the hub can be cut at an angle, or rounded, to make it more attractive or streamlined. When the hub is finally shaped, it is fitted with a metal sleeve. Brass tubing (3/8″) will serve. For the first ones I made, I found old cafe curtain rods excellent for the purpose. When mounted on the body, the wings should form two reverse propellers. If an error has been made, a new hub or hubs must be constructed before the wings are finally attached to the hubs. NOTE: To make sure the wings will be free of interference with the body, they should be glued so that a straight edge is formed on what will be the inside of the propeller. The back of the wing is then next to the body and the curve of the wing extends outward.

Painting the Body and Wings: At this point each part of the bird should be painted separately. Because of the variety of colors in the mallard, it is recommended that the outline of the color scheme be drawn on the wood body and wings with a pencil. This outline can then be redrawn with black paint, with a line of any width up to about 1/4″. The black paint, as well as serving as a guideline, makes an excellent border against which to paint the bright colors. If a little is left showing between different colors, it will intensify them. Waiting for the black paint to dry can be a nuisance, but if it is done when the body is finished, the work can proceed on the wings and time will be saved.

Hunters will know that the colors of the mallard drake are head, green; neckband, white; breast, chestnut; body, gray; tail, white. The back of this whirligig can be painted brown to make it stand out, and the wings of this bird should be black or brown with white tips or white outlines. Chestnut and green stripes may

41

be painted on. Different patterns, colors, stripes, etc., create striking effects when the wings are turning. A drop of black paint is suggested for the eyes, though sometimes colored tacks are used.

Attachment of Wings to Body: First, the 1/4" bolt with a washer in place is thrust through the wing hub. Another washer is put on, and the bolt is pushed through the body. The other wing is attached in a similar way. A 1/4" nut holds the whole assembly in place.

Leave considerable free play for the wing hub on both sides. The nut can be secured with a lock washer and another nut, if there is room, or with a spot of glue. Unsecured nuts sometimes wind off or tighten up. While these problems are not serious, they are a nuisance, so it is important to make sure nuts stay in place. Very rarely will a bolt move; if it does and this movement tightens a hub, it can be tapped back into place. The duck is now ready to fly.

ATTACHMENT OF WINGS TO LARGE BIRDS: DETAIL FOR SEAGULL AND DUCK

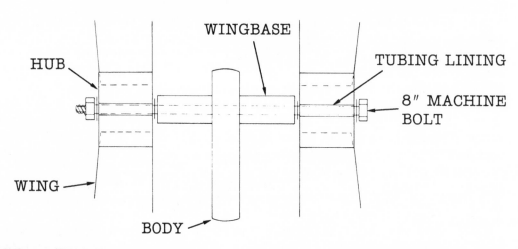

THE SEA GULL

The Sea Gull is made in the same manner as the Mallard Duck. It is advisable to read and to understand the above instructions before proceeding with the Gull, because, in general, the construction details are the same. All the instructions are not repeated for the Sea Gull or the other birds in this chapter.

Materials: Wood

Body block	(1)	3/4" X 5-1/2" X 24"
Wing base	(2)	3/4" X 1-1/4" X 5"
Wing hub	(2)	1-1/2" X 1-1/2" X 2"
Wings	(4)	1/4" X 3" X 10"

Materials: Other

- (2) 8" bolts (1/4") & washers
- (2) 8" bolts (1/4") & washers
- (1) 2" tension pin (3/8")
- (1) 20d or 30d nail & (4) 6d common nails
- (2) 1-1/4" pieces of 3/8" brass tubing

PROCEDURE

Body: The body can be transferred to a sheet of 24" paper marked with one-inch squares or can be drawn freehand. The outline is not that difficult.

After being drawn on the wood, the body can be sawed out and sanded, rounding the edges. Then paint the feature outlines and colors.

Drill the base with a 3/8" bit at the pivot point about 12" from the bottom tip of the tail. Insert a 3/8" tension pin, 2" long, in this socket. Metal tubing may be used. Drive a nail end or metal cap into the socket for the pivot pin or spindle to ride on.

SEA GULL

1 SQUARE = 1/2 INCH

BODY BLOCK:
3/4 X 5-1/2 X 24

WINGS:
1/4 X 3 X 10

WING HUB:
1-1/2 X 1-1/2 X 2

WING BASE:
3/4 X 1-3/4 X 5

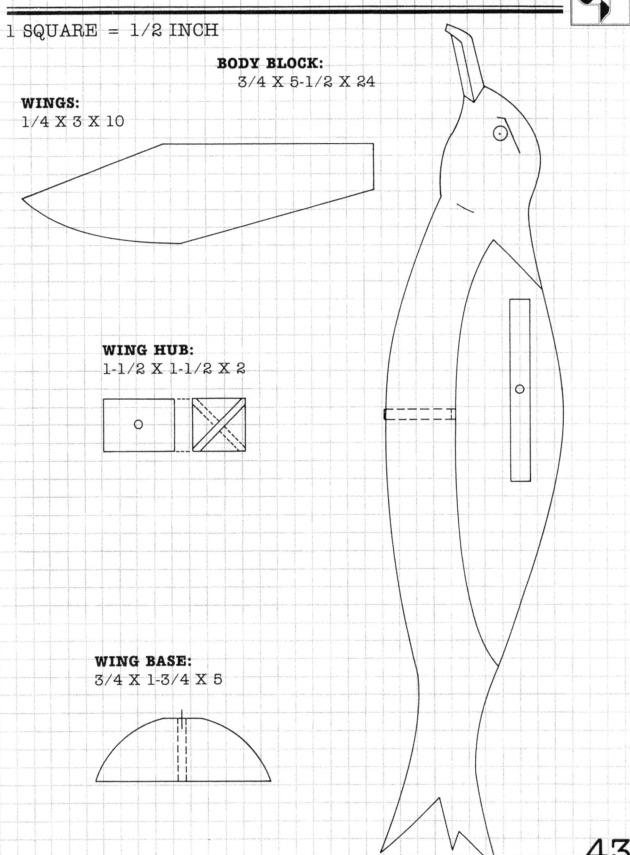

Wing Bases: Cut out these two pieces (3/4″ X 1-3/4″ X 5″) and drill a 1/4″ hole through the center of each. Smaller holes may also be drilled for security nails.

Place one base on the upper part of the body so that the hole is at least 3/4″ to 1″ in front of the pivot point when the Gull is held horizontally. Draw the outline of this position on the body, and glue the wing base to the body with waterproof glue. Drive in 6d nails for strength.

When the glue is dry, drill through the body using the hole in the wing base as a guide. Put the 1/4″ bolt through the hole and let this serve as a guide for attaching the second wing base. This should also be glued and secured with nails.

Wings: The four pieces that will serve as wings can be cut out of solid thin wood (3/16″ or 1/4″) or from 1/4″ plywood. Solid wood will be easier to shape and to make thinner and lighter.

Wing Hubs: The two wing hubs are 1-1/2″ X 1-1/2″ X 2″. Drill a 3/8″ hole from the center of one side.

At the ends, draw the angles where the wing slots will be cut, remembering that at the opposite ends, the slot angles will be in reverse so that a propeller will be formed. Cut the wing slots out, using the wings as a guide as to width. A backsaw to make the vertical cuts and a compass saw to cut the piece out are very useful for this.

Combining Wings and Hubs: Wings are glued in the hubs with waterproof glue. If the fit is too tight, the wings can be sanded down. If the fit is too loose, wooden wedges or strips may be glued in when the wing is being seated. As before, there are two things to watch out for. First, the wings must be fitted so that they form two reversed propellers when attached to the body. Second, the inner side of the wings (the parts next to the body) should form more or less a straight line. The hubs can be trimmed to form a curved or sloping design, and they should be fitted with metal sleeves made of brass or other metal tubing.

Painting: The Sea Gull has only three main colors: white for the body, breast, and wings; gray or blue-gray for the back; and yellow for the beak. Black lines outline the beak and the eyes. The painting should be done before the wings are attached to the body. It is suggested that two coats of oil-based paint be used.

Attachment of Wings: The same instructions used for the Mallard Duck apply for attaching the wings to the Sea Gull.

THE COMMON LOON

Flying, the Common Loon is a strange-looking bird. Its neck swings down, its back seems hunched, and its feet stick out in back. Nevertheless it makes a striking whirligig, and in this example demonstrates the split-propeller wing. While in real life loons can be 38″ long, this model is only about half that size.

Materials: Wood

Body	(1) 3/4″ X 3-1/2″ X 21″
Wing bases	(2) 3/4″ X 1″ X 2″
Wings	(2) 1/4″ X 2-1/2″ X 9″
Axle	(1) 3/8″ dowel 5″ long
Wing braces	(2) 3/4″ X 3/4″ X 4″
	or 3/4″ X 3/4″ X 2-1/2″

Materials: Other

Body liner: 3″ of 1/2″ brass tubing
Socket liner: 2″ tension pin (3/8″)

COMMON LOON

1 SQUARE = 1/2 INCH

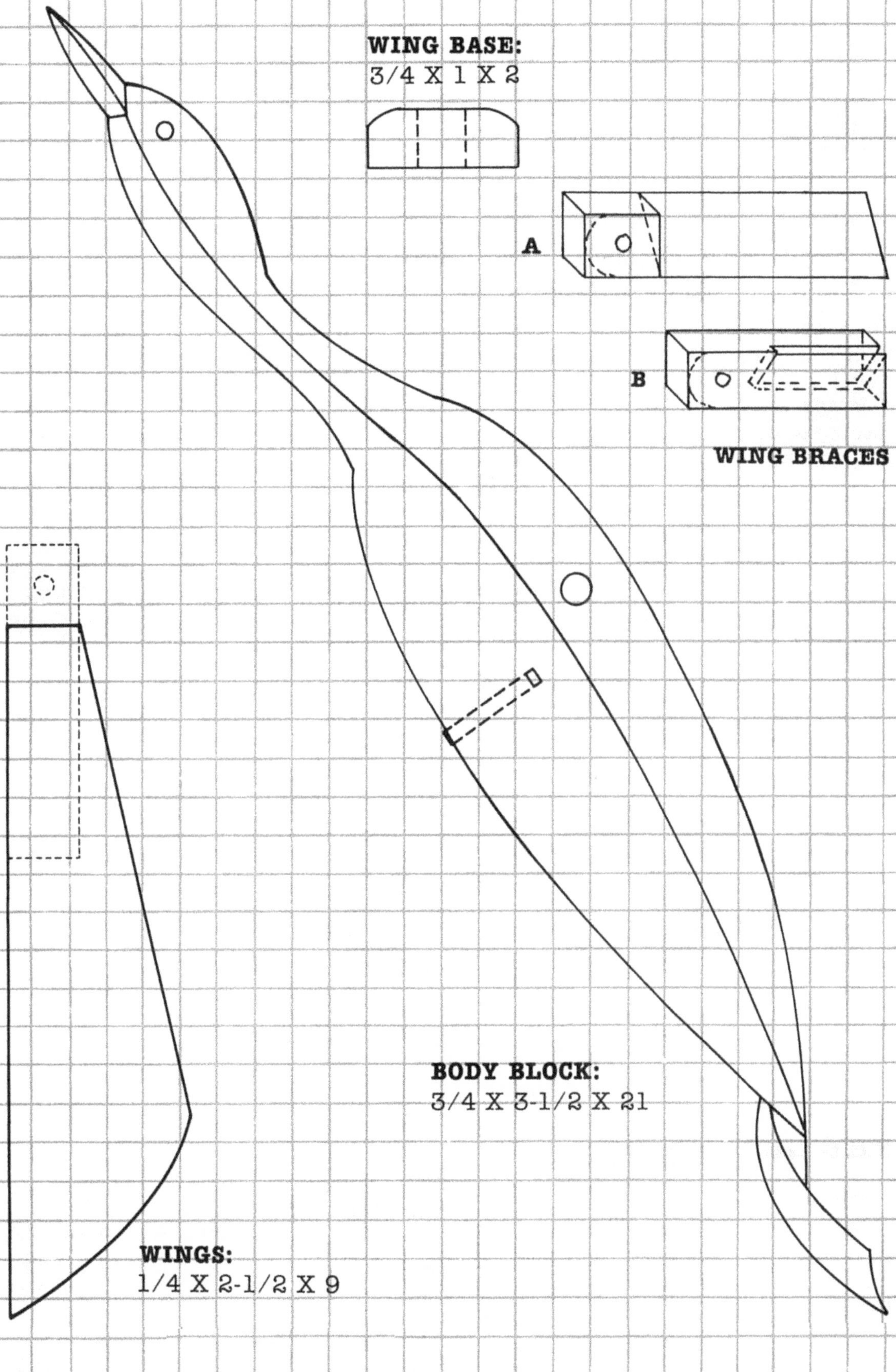

WING BASE:
3/4 X 1 X 2

A

B

WING BRACES

BODY BLOCK:
3/4 X 3-1/2 X 21

WINGS:
1/4 X 2-1/2 X 9

45

PROCEDURE

The Body: Cut out the body and round it off. Draw in the color line, the eyes, and beak. Drill the socket hole, place the tension pin in it, and cap it. Drill the wing axle hole. This must be large enough to contain a liner of metal tubing that will hold the wing axle. Get the correct tubing first and test the axle in it before proceeding.

Wing Bases: Cut out the wing bases. Drill the same size hole through both as you did through the body, and glue and nail them in place. When they are fast, put the metal liner in place. If it sticks, it is easy to redrill through the three wooden pieces.

Wing Braces: Alternate patterns (**A** and **B**) are provided. Cut out the wing braces and mark them for drilling and cutting. Hold them in position against the body to make sure you have the markings correct. Drill a 3/8″ hole for the dowel axle. Position the straight edge of the wings next to the body. If the curved edges were placed inside, the wing would strike the body when turning.

A. Cut out a 3″ diagonal section from each piece. This will position the wing at a 45-degree angle when completed. Each must be cut at an opposite angle. Check them against the body.

B. For the alternate wing brace, cut out a 1/8″ diagonal slot, 1-1/2″ deep, into which the wing can be fitted and glued.

Wings: Cut out the wings and attach them to the wing braces. Before gluing and nailing them in place, check to make sure, first, that the wings will be at opposite angles and, second, that the straight edges will be next to the body. Balance the completed wings by placing them in the axle temporarily and turning them. Trim them if necessary.

Attachment of Wings: Glue one of the wings on the dowel axle and secure it with a brad. Slip the dowel through the body, placing a washer between the body and the wing. Place another washer on the dowel and attach the other wing in alignment with the first, being certain to allow at least 1/4″ of play between the wings and the body. Lubrication of the axle from the beginning is recommended.

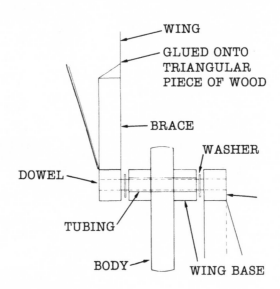

THE GOONEY BIRD

This is just a funny bird that was constructed to show that any shape will work if prepared along the same lines as the duck and the gull. As the instructions for construction are similar, they are not repeated here. Aside from the body shape and the paint patterns, and a different wing shape, the only major difference is the eye structure.

GOONEY BIRD

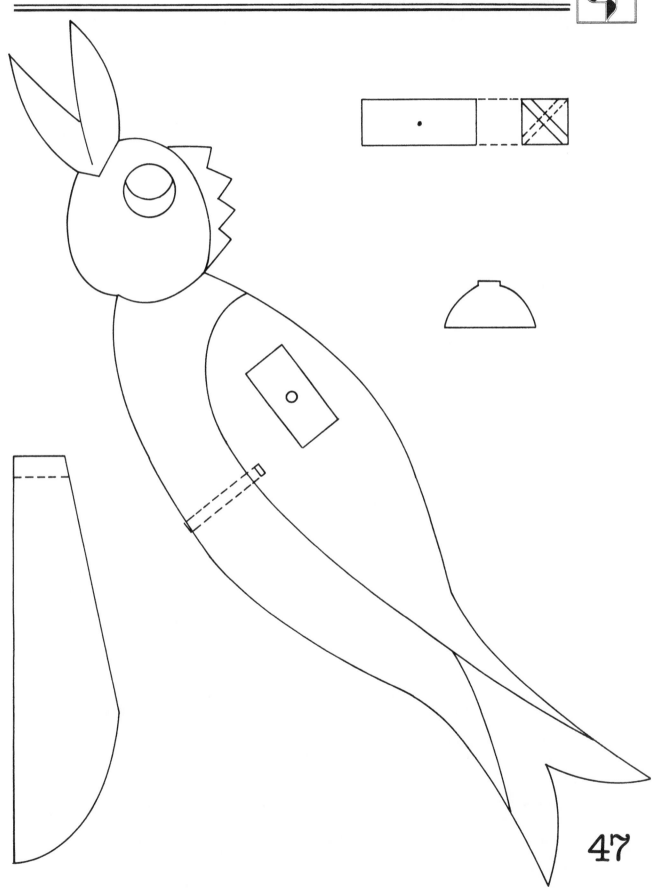

47

OTHER LARGE BIRD DESIGNS

Some sketches of other birds that may be transferred to wood blanks are also shown. While the general rule is to make the birds life-size, this may not be entirely practical for really large birds. The male wild turkey, beak to tail, is four feet long, a pelican 50″ long, and a gannet 40″ long. The largest birds can always be reproduced in proportion in smaller sizes. Nothing should stop the craftsperson from making his or her favorite bird, and the larger birds are a real challenge. Here are some examples:

American Bittern	24″–34″	Great Blue Heron	42″–48″
Double-Crested Cormorant	30″–35″	Wild Turkey	46″–48″
Bald Eagle	33″–36″	California Condor	43″–55″
Canada Goose	22″–43″	Whistling Swan	48″–55″

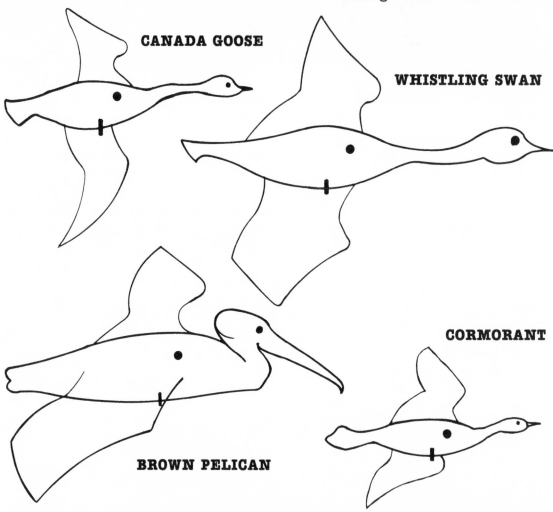

CANADA GOOSE

WHISTLING SWAN

CORMORANT

BROWN PELICAN

Books on ornithology and bird-watching provide anatomical information as well as excellent drawings of birds. Bird bodies have a similar basic structure, and once this is understood, any bird can be sketched in a basic whirligig pattern.

Mention should be made of birds carved in the round, or in three dimensions, to serve as whirligigs. If one is going to the trouble to make a bird carving, it is unlikely it will be used as a whirligig, but rather as a sculpture in its own right. A three-dimensional figure is difficult to make, and takes much more time. The body will be heavier, and the balance and the location of the pivot are more critical. Anyone using a rounded figure will find attaching the wings a little more difficult, but wing bases should not be necessary as the curve of the body will give the wings room to move.

CHAPTER 6

DIRECT DRIVE WHIRLIGIGS

Direct drive may be something of a misnomer for this classification; the Acrobat whirligig described in chapter 7 is more directly activated by the drive shaft than the models described here. Direct drive merely means that there are few elements between the drive shaft and the main movements of a mechanical whirligig; in these examples there's only a connecting rod.

More detail on construction procedures is given to The Railcar than to the other models in order to save repetition of the basic steps. It is anticipated that readers will go over The Railcar procedures before constructing Anne at the Pump or Tony with His Wheelbarrow, and the reader should review the general information in chapters 2 and 3. For example, on each of the models it is advisable to draw a plan of where the attached parts will be placed before continuing with the construction; this may not always be specified, but it is important.

THE RAILCAR

The Railcar whirligig (also called The Handcar) design remains popular because of its moving figures, and crafts people still inquire about this model. The one illustrated in this section was intended to be a humorous one, displaying a very tall conductor pumping opposite a very small miner. When the whirligig was finished, it occurred to me that a female figure operating the handcar would be funnier, so I drew a lady in Victorian dress to fit the period. Any odd couple will do for your own design. In the original the figures were carved out and partially sculpted. They can be left in outline, of course, but giving the figures a three-dimensional quality makes them much more interesting and picturesque.

Materials: Wood

Base and Support:

baseboard	3/4" X 5-1/2" X 16"
support post	2" X 4" X 5"
side braces	5" X 7" X 9"

Handcar:

base	3/4" X 1-1/2" X 4"
sides	1/4" triangles, 5-1/2" X 7"
handlebar	1/4" X 1/2" X 8-1/2"
wheels	3/4" X 4" diameter

Tail support	3/4" X 5" X 5"

Figures:

	Conductor:	**Miner:**
Leg	3/4" X 2-1/2" X 4-1/2"	3/4" X 2" X 4-1/2"
Torso	1-1/2" X 2" X 5-1/2"	1-1/2" X 2" X 4-1/2"
Arms	1/4" X 3/4" X 4"	1/4" X 1" X 4"
	Lady:	
Leg	3/4" X 2-1/2" X 4"	
Torso	1-1/2" X 2" X 4-1/4"	
Arms	1/4" X 3/4" X 3"	

Propeller:
  hub   3"-square block of 3/4" thickness
  blades   1/4" X 2-1/2" X 10"

Materials: Other

(1) 1/4" bolt, 6" long, with nut and washers
1 piece of 5/16" tubing for drive shaft, 4-1/4" long
(1) 2" tension pin (3/8")
1 piece of 5" X 9" sheet metal, for tail
(1) 3" wheel or other rotary piece and a No. 4 X 3/4" round head screw
Connecting wire and wire for axles can be 3/32" or 1/16" brass rods or
  clothes-hanger wire
Various brads, small nails, and screws, as indicated

Base: Construct the base pieces first in order to have a platform for testing the
positions of the figures and drive mechanisms. (See Foldout No. 1.) First, cut out
the baseboard, or floor, of the railcar. Make sure the front and rear are cut square.
Measure and draw the positions of all the standing and attached pieces.

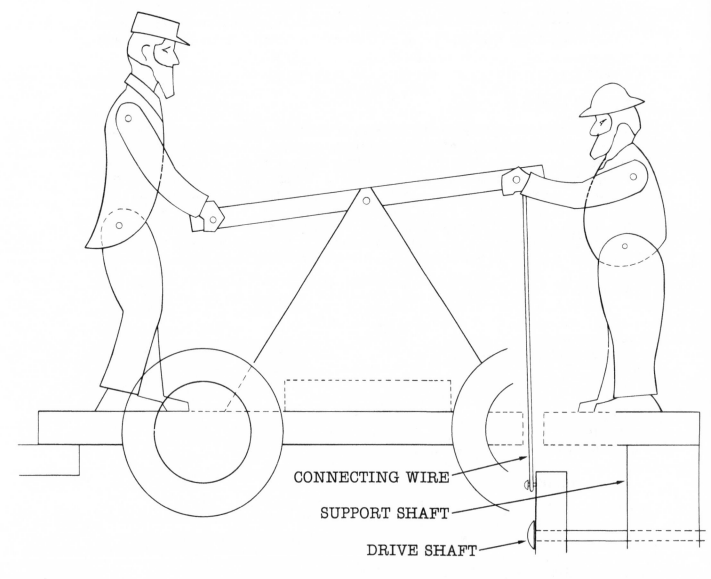

CONNECTING WIRE

SUPPORT SHAFT

DRIVE SHAFT

50

SIDE VIEW OF CAR AND FIGURES

Cut out the space for the connecting wire; this is a section 1/2" X 2-1/2" centered 4" from the front end. Where the two figures are located drill holes for the 1-1/4" screws, countersunk on the bottom side. Attach the work frame of the railcar in the position indicated, 6" from the front end of the base.

Cut out the tail support in the pattern indicated or in any similar shape. Cut the slot for the tail and drill two small holes for brads or nails that will secure the tail.

Post: For the drive shaft, drill a 5/16" hole, centered 2-7/8" from the bottom of the 2" X 4" X 5" post. For the support socket, drill a 3/8" hole in the bottom center and place a 2" tension pin in the socket. Attach the post to the front of the base with glue and screws, and attach the side braces.

DRIVE MECHANISM AND SUPPORT

TAIL SECTION

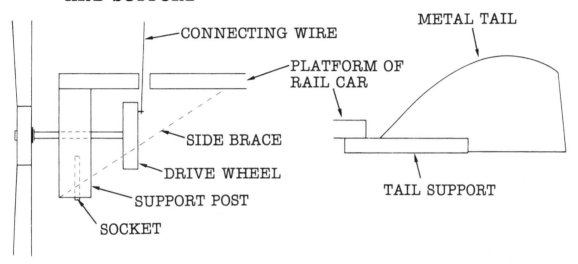

CONNECTING WIRE

PLATFORM OF RAIL CAR

SIDE BRACE

DRIVE WHEEL

SUPPORT POST

SOCKET

METAL TAIL

TAIL SUPPORT

Completing the Main Frame: Cut out the triangular sidepieces for the handcar. Drill a small matching hole in the top for a rod or axle. Glue and nail the sidepieces in place.

The wheels can be made of 3/4" wood, 4" in diameter and shaped like a train wheel as shown, or can be made of 1/4" plywood, in which case a small 2-1/2" wheel is glued over the center of a 4" wheel. The wheels are attached with nails so that the centers of the hubs are 4" from the midline of the handcar and 1/2" below the bottom of the platform. If desired, the wheels can be attached after all other work is completed.

The base is now ready to be mounted. The mounting can be a platform of 1/2" or 3/4" plywood, 12" square with a 1-1/2" square post 8" long, with a 20d or 30d nail as the spindle.

The parts that have been assembled can now be painted.

The Drive Mechanism: Cut the 5/16" tubing and place it in the hole in the post, letting it protrude from the front 1-1/4". Cut out a 3"-diameter wheel and drill a 1/4" hole in the center. Turn in a No. 4 X 3/4" round head screw about 1/4" from the edge. Place the 1/4" carriage bolt through the wheel and with washers in place, insert it in the tubing. Hold it temporarily with its nut.

Make the handlebar: Cut out a hole in the center for the axle. This can be lined with brass tubing. One-half inch (1/2") from the ends drill 1/8" holes and glue in 1-1/2" lengths of dowel or similar wood pieces. The ends should be drilled for small wire to be inserted, to hold the characters' hands in place. Place the handlebar in position with a brass rod or thick wire serving as an axle. Separate the bar from the sides, keeping the handle in the center with wood washers or pieces of brass tubing 1/2" wide. Make the connecting wire for the drive wheel. This should be strong, rigid wire about 10" long; the distance between the handlebar and screw

51

is about 8″. With the handlebar in place, see if the wire will operate easily through the floor opening.

The Figures: Construct the figures as shown in the diagrams on the opposite page. The torsos, arms, and legs are drilled for wire connections through the body and hands. Any practical rigid wire may be used. While it is not essential, brass tubing may be used to line the holes to prevent wear.

Attach the legs to the base with glue and 1-1/4″ screws. Then attach the torsos, and then the arms. To attach the hands, force strong, thin wire about the thickness of a paper clip into the ends of the handles and secure it with epoxy glue. (NOTE: If you can drill a hole all the way through the handles, without gluing, this would work best.) Insert the hand and bend the wire to hold it.

The Tail: The tail may be painted before it is attached to the drive shaft. To add realism to the whirligig, I painted a western scene on the metal. The tail is secured with a brad and a small finishing nail.

The Propeller: Any four-bladed propeller about 22″ in diameter will move this whirligig, and the accompanying design is suggested only because it works. Also, if you have never made a fully wooden propeller, this one is easy to make and, when finished, looks professional.

The center of the hub is drilled for the 1/4″ drive shaft, but it is first drilled 1/4″ deep with a 1/2″ bit to enable countersinking the nut. The blade slots are cut out as shown.

The blades are cut, shaped, and sanded, then glued in the hub slots. The propeller should be balanced; it should be turned, and if one blade is noticeably heavier than the others, that one should be trimmed.

With washers in place, attach the propeller and turn it to test all the moving parts. More washers may have to be placed between the propeller and the drive shaft liner. After some minor adjustments of this sort, the mechanism should work properly.

ANNE AT THE PUMP

In most whirligigs, activity moves in line with wind flow, but on several, a crosspiece is introduced that permits the action to take place across the wind. Anne at the Pump is a simple example of this type. As the drive wheel turns, Anne's

body and arms move the pump handle up and down. Anne can be made quite a bit larger than she is in the diagram, and if she is, the other parts should be enlarged proportionately. The basic structure (baseboard and post) with the drive shaft through the post is an old standard design used in North Carolina. A number of other whirligigs of the same type use it: The Woman Churning Butter, The Man at the Anvil, etc. It allows a straightfoward power mechanism with parts that are easy to observe, repair, or replace. It is also used with the drive shaft operating from under the platform, in which case the platform is placed higher on the post.

Materials: Wood

Base	3/4″ X 2″ X 13″
Post	1-3/4″ X 1-1/2″ X 13″
Crosspiece	1/2″ X 3″ X 9-1/2″
Pump (see diagram for details)	
Drive wheel	2″ in diameter, center hole 1/4″

1 SQUARE = 1/2 INCH

LADY

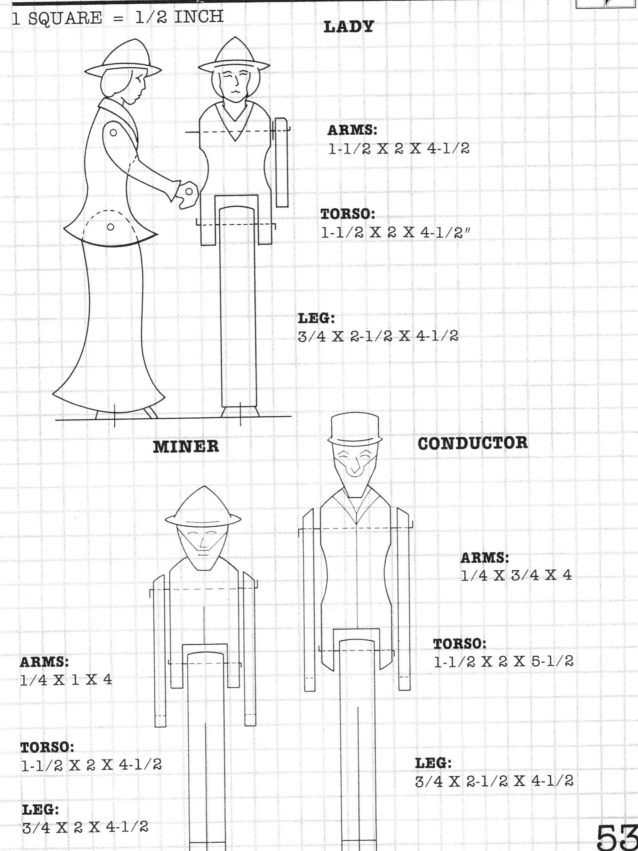

ARMS:
1-1/2 X 2 X 4-1/2

TORSO:
1-1/2 X 2 X 4-1/2"

LEG:
3/4 X 2-1/2 X 4-1/2

MINER

CONDUCTOR

ARMS:
1/4 X 3/4 X 4

ARMS:
1/4 X 1 X 4

TORSO:
1-1/2 X 2 X 5-1/2

TORSO:
1-1/2 X 2 X 4-1/2

LEG:
3/4 X 2-1/2 X 4-1/2

LEG:
3/4 X 2 X 4-1/2

53

Figure: skirt   3/4″ X 2-1/2″ X 3″
        torso   1/4″ X 1-1/2″ X 3″
        arms   1/4″ X 1″ X 2-1/2″

Propeller (see design)

Materials: Other

2″ tension pin

1/4″ carriage bolt, 7″ in length, with nut and washers

Sheet metal, 5″ X 7″, for tail

(2) No. 6 X 1-1/4″ flat head screws, (3) 1″ screws and assorted nails and
   brads for joining.

Connecting wire, wires, or rods for joints.

Procedure

Post: Make the post first. To support the drive shaft, drill a 3/8″ hole in the center, 2″ from the top. Drill another 3/8″ hole in the bottom for the support socket, drive in the tension pin, and set in a nail section for a cap. (See Foldout No. 2.)

Base: On the baseboard, cut a narrow 3″ slot for the tail. Then cut out a 1-1/2″ X 1-1/2″ slot from the front to fit onto the post. Glue and nail the baseboard 3″ up from the bottom of the post, and attach (also with glue and nails) the support piece so the base and post are at right angles. The main frame is now complete and may be painted, at least with a first coat, at this point.

Crosspiece: Prepare the crosspiece, drilling holes as indicated. Mount it on the baseboard with the leading edge 2″ from the post. Secure it with a 1″ screw and glue.

Figure: Cut out the pieces for the figure and drill the necessary holes for the joint connections. Secure the lady's skirt with a 1″ screw and glue. Then attach the torso and arms with wire.

Pump: The pump is made of several sections; cut them out and assemble them with glue and brads. The pump is then secured to the crosspiece with a 1″ screw. Drill the joint holes in the handle and shape it. Attach it to the pump and the hands with pieces of wire through the holes. Paper clips are a good source of wire for this purpose.

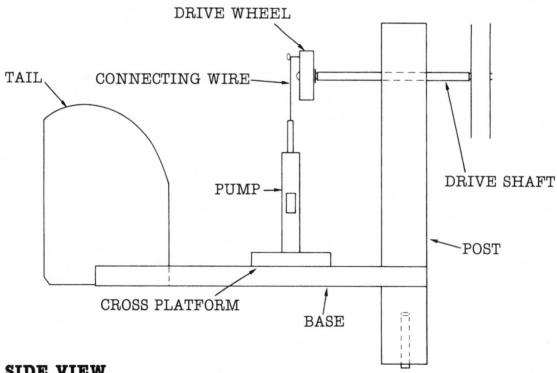

54 SIDE VIEW

Pails: Two or three pails can be made of broom handle cross sections or whittled from other wood. They are glued or nailed in place, or both.

Drive Shaft: Insert the drive shaft tubing so that it projects 2-1/2" from the back of the post. Set a small (No. 4 X 3/4" round head) screw 1/4" from the edge of the drive wheel. Then place the wheel on the drive shaft with a washer.

Propeller: Attach a four-bladed, 15"-diameter propeller to the drive shaft. The hub is first drilled 1/4" deep with a 1/2" bit, then drilled through with a 1/4" bit. The propeller is made fast with two 1/4" nuts and a washer.

Tail: The tail is cut from a 5" X 7" piece of standard sheet metal or aluminum flashing. It can be shaped in any way desired, though it should remain as large as possible.

TONY WITH HIS WHEELBARROW

This idea came from a neighbor who wanted a present for her uncle, whom she remembered as always working in his garden with his wheelbarrow. It became a "powered-from-beneath" type. A cam could have been used on the drive shaft, but a larger radius was needed. One problem was to fit a heavy gauge wire—the drive shaft—to the connecting wire, which moved the wheelbarrow and the figure. I was able to devise an effective rotary drive with a piece of wood into which the wire fitted snugly and which could not twist off the wire, as illustrated.

The second problem was related to the combined weight of the wheelbarrow and the figure. Although the propeller could move them, there seemed to be considerable pressure on the shaft and the connecting wire mechanism at the moment of lift. There were several alternatives, one of which was to make a larger propeller. Another possibility was to create a counterweight, but there was no room for placing it in front of the wheelbarrow. It was finally placed off the back of the figure by rigging a curved wire with a wooden weight on one end and the other end fixed into a small hole drilled into the figure. The wire makes the weight bob up and down and attracts attention. A steadier counterweight could be made of a 1/4" strip of curved wood. Counterbalances should be considered when heavy objects are to be moved or a disproportionate strain is placed on any mechanism.

Materials: Wood

Baseboard	3/4" X 5-1/2" X 22"
Base support sides	(2) 3/4" X 2" X 3-1/2"
Socket support	1-1/2" X 3" X 5-1/2"
Figure: torso	1-1/2" X 1-1/2" X 5"
legs	1-1/2" X 2-3/4" X 5"
arms	1/4" X 1-1/4" X 4"
Wheelbarrow: frame	1/4" X 3/8" strips
sides	1/8" X 2-3/4" X 8"
wheel	1/2" X 2-1/2" diameter
post	2-1/2" X 5/8" dowel
Rotary arm	3/4" X 3/4" X 2"
Propeller	18"–20" propeller with hub drilled for wire shaft

Materials: Other

Mechanism support	(2) 2" angle iron brackets
Drive shaft	20" heavy drapery wire
Connecting wire	10" length
Tubing and rods	Brass tubing as sleeves for arms and other moving parts. Metal rods for axles as indicated.
Screws and nails	as described

Procedure

Base: Cut out the baseboard. Mark off the centerline on the top and the bottom and mark the patterns for the front and back. Mark the following positions and cut out and drill the holes: the 1″ aperture for the connecting wire, 15″ to 16″ along the centerline, 3-1/2″ across; the location of the 5/8″ wheelbarrow-post hole 3″ from the front; the place to attach base-support side sections, measuring 3″ to 6-1/2″ from the front, and screw holes; the location of the figure, from 17″ to 19″ from the front, and screw holes 1/4″ left and right of the centerline, one 18-1/2″ from the front and the other 19″ from the front. (See Foldout No. 3.)

On the bottom of the base, locate the position of the first angle iron bracket at the edge of the front of the base and of the second with its upright end 14-1/2″ from the front and about 1/2″ from the aperture for the connecting wire.

Base Supports: Cut out the side sections, and glue and screw them in place with No. 8 X 1-1/4″ screws. Cut out the bottom section where the socket is to be, and in the middle drill a 2″-deep hole, which will hold the 3/8″ tension pin. If a heavier spindle is desired, drill for tubing that will hold a 1/4″, or larger, rod. Drill the lead holes and glue and screw the bottom to the sidepieces. Screw the angle iron brackets in place on the bottom.

Wheelbarrow: Construct the wheelbarrow, using brads and glue to hold the pieces together. The frame parts are as follows:

Handles, 15-1/2″ long
Front bar, 1-3/4″ long
Back spacer, 1-3/4″ long
Sides, 1/8″ X 2-3/4″ X 8″ (trimmed)
Legs, 2″ long
Support struts, as needed
Wheel, 1/2″ X 2-1/2″ diameter

Drill the holes for the various connecting parts: post, wheel, connecting wire, and hands. Cut out the metal rods and use them for testing the position of the wheelbarrow. If all is right, sand and paint the wheelbarrow.

Figure: Cut out the figure and arms as shown on page 57. The figure may be carved to give a more realistic appearance. Sand the parts well. Attach the parts loosely together, and then connect the figure to the wheelbarrow to see what happens when the wheelbarrow is lifted up 2″ to 3″. Both the figure and the arms should move freely. If they do, separate and paint the parts.

CONSTRUCTION OF ROTARY CAM

DRIVE SHAFT

2″

3/4″

DETAIL OF SUPPORT STRUCTURE

BASE

SUPPORT SIDES

2″

5/8″

1-1/4″

3″

SOCKET

SOCKET SUPPORT PIECE

3″

56

1 SQUARE = 1/4 INCH

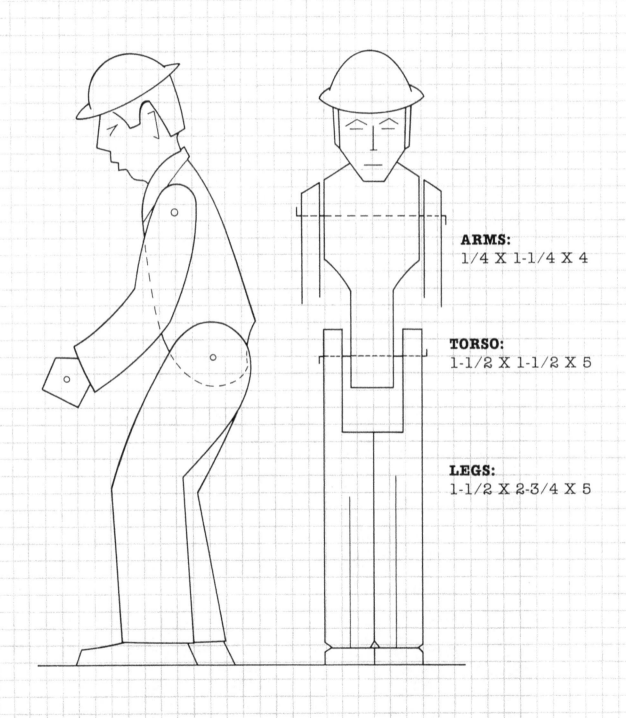

ARMS:
1/4 X 1-1/4 X 4

TORSO:
1-1/2 X 1-1/2 X 5

LEGS:
1-1/2 X 2-3/4 X 5

Attachment: Glue and screw the figure's legs to the base. Then assemble the rest of the figure. Secure the wheelbarrow to its support and attach the figure's arms. Then place the whirligig on a stand for further construction.

Drive Mechanism: Cut out the rotary arm and drill it for the drive shaft and for the connecting wire screw. Note that the bend is inside the rotary arm about 1/4" so that it cannot swing sideways. A wooden wedge can be glued in the top to make it even more secure.

Prepare the drive shaft. Bend it 1" from the back end and insert it into the rotary arm. Connect the rotor with the wheelbarrow cross rod using stiff connecting wire. Make a wooden spool (5/8" X 5/8" X 1-3/4") for this cross rod with a hole drilled through it through which the rod may rotate freely. Cut small notches in the middle to hold the connecting wire. This will keep the connecting wire from slipping around.

Turn the shaft and see how everything works together. Make any necessary adjustments to the mechanism.

Propeller: Any propeller 18" to 20" in diameter will serve. The original model had a 3" hub with 1/8" X 2" X 9-1/4" blades, each inserted 3/4". To separate the propeller from the front of the base, the model had two 1/4" washers with a 1" wooden bead in between. The drive shaft wire was bent around the front of the propeller and additionally secured with a staple.

The Counterweight: When the wheelbarrow is lifted up, there is some extra tension on the mechanism. With the propeller in place this will still be noticed. To counter this, cut a piece of stiff piano wire and bend it into a slight curve. Drill a hole in the back of the figure to hold this wire. Cut out a small wood block about 3/4" X 2" X 2" and temporarily attach it to the wire.

Test the counterweight in position. If it is too heavy its weight will tend to hold the wheelbarrow up. Trim the piece, or shorten the wire, until the movement is as well balanced as possible. Another type of counterweight is a solid piece of wood inserted into the body. This piece is 1/4" wide at the body end and 1" or more at the outer end. This type may require more testing and cutting.

Finally, secure all the parts, bend the loose ends of wires and rods, tighten screws, and complete any painting. This is a whirligig that does not require any special tail or rudder.

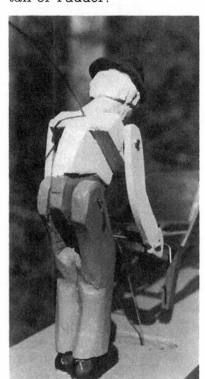

CHAPTER 7

CAMSHAFT WHIRLIGIGS

Most action-type whirligigs use camshafts for transferring power. Part of the fun of making the more complicated whirligigs lies in figuring out how to make a new mechanical movement or have a figure act in a certain way. The simple design shown here clearly illustrates the use of a bent wire cam. The Acrobat is an old American design. In the Acrobat the wire is bent into a cam which becomes a trapeze. The Acrobat's arms are fixed securely in place on the cam, and as the shaft revolves, the jointed figure swings and does tricks.

In the whirligigs demonstrated in this chapter, Bill the Fisherman and Eleanor at the Tub are single-cam whirligigs, while The Concert is a double-cam whirligig, and Waving the Flag is a triple-cam-plus whirligig.

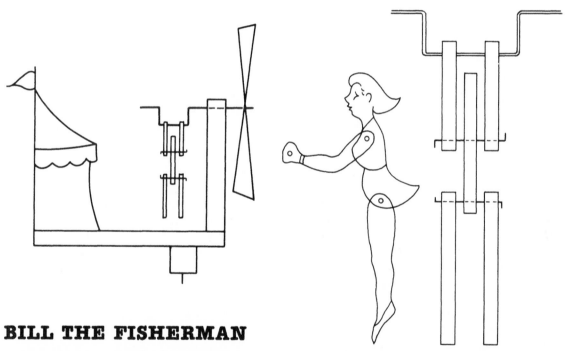

BILL THE FISHERMAN

A neighbor asked if I could make a whirligig showing her husband fishing. During summer vacations on a lake in Vermont, he loved to row out alone and just sit in the boat waiting for a bite. This whirligig is the result; it gets lots of attention.

Materials: Wood

Baseboard	3/4" X 5-1/2" X 20"
Base support block	1-1/2" X 1-1/2" X 2-1/2"
Boat:	
sides	1/8" X 2" X 14-1/2"
stern	3/4" X 2" X 4"
stem	1/2" X 3/4" X 3"
seat	1/8" X 1" X 3-1/2"

Figure (see drawing for details)

Materials: Other

(2) 1-1/2" angle (corner) irons
(1) 2" tension pin
(1) 22" heavy wire for camshaft
(4) metal blades for propeller, 3-1/2" X 6"
(1) sheet metal for tail, 5" X 7"
Rigid wire, music-wire type, for connecting joints and for fishing line
Semirigid wire for use as connecting wire from camshaft
Various brads and screws as required

PROCEDURE

Base: Cut out the baseboard and draw centerlines down the middle on the top and the bottom for guidelines. From the front, measure down 10-3/4" and 12-3/4" and draw lines through those points across the board perpendicular to the centerline. Between these lines, draw two lines parallel to and 1-1/4" from the centerline. The rectangle marked off (2" X 2" X 2-1/2") is to be cut out for the camshaft connecting wire. (See Foldout No. 4.)

Cut the two-inch tail slot in the rear. At a point 15" from the front, cut a slit 1/8" X 1-1/2" along the centerline for the fishing line. Keep in mind that later this slot may have to be widened or lengthened to accommodate the size and shape of the line. Then cut the baseboard into its final shape and sand it.

The corner angles will be the camshaft supports, but one of the ends (the upright end) will be too long, so each should have a section cut off (see diagram). One angle is placed at the top of the front end of the baseboard. The other is attached (facing in the same direction) with the upright end 12-3/4" from the front. This should place it at the edge of the cutout section.

Make the base support or mounting block. Drill a 3/8" hole in the base for a socket. Insert a 2" tension pin or any other metal liner, and set in a cap. Then glue and screw the block in place; the leading edge is 4-1/4" from the front of the base, which should make the center of the socket about 5-1/2" from the front. The whirligig frame can now be mounted on a base for easier handling.

The Boat: The boat is constructed separately and then put in position on the baseboard. The bow and stern ends of the sides are cut at angles, as illustrated. The transom is also cut at angles so the top is 4" and the bottom measures 3". The stem is shaped slightly, and a small hole is drilled through the top for the anchor line. The sides are glued to the transom first and may be held fast by small flat head nails or brads. When dry, the sides are then glued to the stem, which is shaped to fit. Holding the bow pieces together for drying is one of the tricky parts; use brads, wire, clamps, elastic bands, or whatever to do this job. Cut out the bow seat and fit it into the boat about 3-3/4" from the transom. It sits in place 1/2" below the top edge of the sides. The boat can then be painted.

The Power Mechanism: The camshaft is made of heavy wire like drapery hanger wire, about 22" to start with. At 1-1/2" from one end, which will be the stern, bend the wire to form a 3/4" cam (see drawing). Make a sleeve to hold the connecting wire securely in place (see chapter 5).

Test the camshaft position. Make allowances for the propeller and front washers, and for the extension at the rear. See if the cam with the sleeve can rotate freely in the cutout space of the baseboard. Make any necessary cuts to widen the space. Cut the rear end of the camshaft about 1/2" from the angle iron; this will be bent over later.

Make a 16"-diameter propeller. The metal-bladed type with wooden crosspieces is recommended so that it can easily clear the baseboard. If the baseboard is cut with a more or less pointed end, this may not be necessary. Test the location of the propeller, with necessary washers, on the camshaft but do not permanently attach the propeller at this point. It will only get in the way of further construction. It can be painted.

Put the boat in position. It should ride with the bow slightly in the air and a small wood strip glued in place will take care of that. File or cut the bottom of the transom so it will meet the base flatly. Mark the place where the boat is best located and drill a hole in the center where a screw will fasten the transom down. Then fix the boat in permanent position with glue and a screw. The anchor line can be glued in place.

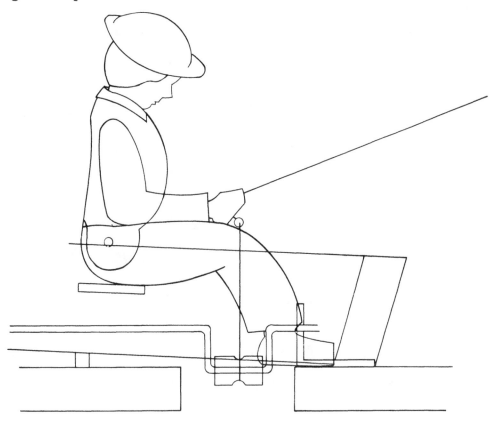

The Figure: The figure is made in two separate steps: the legs, and the upper body and arms.

The legs are two separate pieces made of 3/4" wood, 2-1/2" X 4-1/2". They fit at the outer edge of the seat, and they have to be shaped inside to accommodate the turning cam and also the moving body top. The back of the legs should fit on the seat, and the toes should touch the transom. All this will take some whittling, but it is not as difficult as it seems. Round the outside of the legs to give them shape. Glue them in position after adjustment with the torso.

While the upper body, including the arms, may be carved from one piece of wood, it will be easier to make the arms, or particularly the forearms, separately. The basic body block is 2" X 2" X 4-1/2". The main thing is to

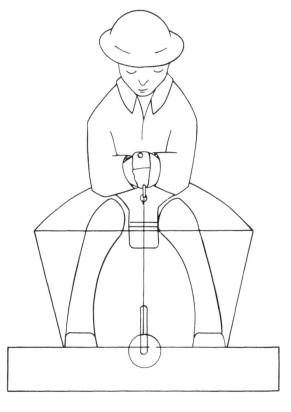

have the hands meet in front of the body in a block where they will hold a small screw eye for the connecting wire and also hold the fishing pole. The hand block should be about 5/8" square.

Fit the body into the leg sections. Drill a hole through all three pieces and hold them together with wire. Test the movement of the body by temporarily connecting it with the drive shaft to see that it works properly, trim if necessary, and paint the body parts.

Final Connections: Attach the propeller, with proper washers in place. You may wish to detach the top of the figure while you do this. Make sure the cam can turn freely in its proper place, and then bend the end of the camshaft by the transom to hold it in place.

Prepare the 12" long, thin music-type hard wire for the fishing pole. It will have to be adjusted to fit your particular measurements, but it will be bent about 4 to 4-1/2" from the handle end. After the long fishing line is inserted into the slot, the pole's other end is inserted into the hands at an angle of about 20 degrees with the hands lowered. This setup must be tested carefully, because the slightest drag, especially fore and aft, will hold up the turning camshaft.

Cut out any light metal in the shape of a small fish, and secure it tightly onto the end of the fishline.

COURTESY OF THE NORTH CAROLINA MUSEUM OF HISTORY

ELEANOR AT THE TUB

The washerwoman whirligig is an old American pattern, and antique models seem to indicate that each artisan had an individual idea of how it should be constructed. The only tricky part is making the camshaft so that it fits into the washtub and still allows room for the woman's hands. This whirligig is eye-catching, which probably accounts for its popularity.

Materials: Wood

Baseboard	3/4" X 5-1/2" X 10"
Pivot base	1-1/2" X 1-1/2" X 2-1/2"
Washtub legs	1/2" X 1/2" X 1-3/4"
Figure:	
torso	1-1/4" X 1-1/4" X 3-1/2"
lower body	1-1/2" X 1-1/2" X 4-1/2"
arms	1/4" X 1/4" X 3-3/4" or 4"
Clothes pole	1/2" X 1/2" X 7-1/2"

Materials: Other

(1) 2" tension pin
(1) 3" angle iron
(1) can for washtub: 3-3/8" diameter & 1-3/4" high, like a small tuna fish can
(1) length of heavy wire, like drapery hanger wire, about 12"–13" long, for camshaft
Rigid wire for joint connections
Screws (No. 6 X 1-1/4" flat head and No. 4 X 3/4" round head), and nails and brads as needed

PROCEDURE

Base: Cut out the baseboard and, using the drawing, measure out and mark the location of all standing parts. (See Foldouts No. 5 & 6.) Shape the baseboard as you wish, though it's helpful to cut the back end so that nails can be used to hold the tail in place. Cut the tail slot. Attach the camshaft support bracket. This will extend 1″ beyond the front of the baseboard to help clear the propeller. The pivot base can be made now. Drill a hole for the socket and insert the tension pin, or other liner, and a cap. Find the location of the pivot base on the centerline of the baseboard; it should be about 2-1/2″ from the front end. Drill holes for 1-1/4″ screws and secure the post to the baseboard with glue and screws. The whirligig base can now be mounted on a platform for easy handling.

The Washtub: Test the washtub on its legs at its location. The height should be such that the camshaft, coming through the support about 2-3/4″ up from the baseboard, will be located approximately in the middle of the can or slightly higher. Cut two holes for the shaft at opposite sides of the can, and then cut a slit down to the hole on the far side. This slit is necessary to move the camshaft into its final position. Fasten the legs to the base and to the can with glue, and drive finishing nails up from the bottom.

The Figure: The lower part is carved as shown, and then the upper part is carved and fitted into it. Drill a hole through both parts at the waist, insert a wire, and test the figure for free movement.

Cut out the arms. Drill the upper arm holes for a No. 4 X 3/4″ round head screw. Brass tubing may be placed in the holes to reduce wear.

Using a small bit, drill tiny holes in the ends of the hand sections for small wire loops. Any wire will do, but I used the ends of paper clips and secured them in place with epoxy glue. These loops will enclose the camshaft. The alternative is to make the arms longer and drill holes through the hand part to fit onto the camshaft, but these did not operate as smoothly for my model. Paint all body parts before any further assembling.

Position the lower body by the washtub, drill a hole there, and permanently attach it to the baseboard with a No. 6 X 1-1/4″ flat head screw.

The Camshaft: Measure the camshaft carefully from the front end of the baseboard, making allowances for the propeller, the washers, the collar, etc. Then measure back to the washtub and make a cam no more than 3/4″ deep and 2″ across so it will fit into the middle of the tub.

Slip the hand rings onto the shaft and into the cam. A separator sleeve should be placed between the hands to keep them apart. Since a long cylinder cannot be moved around the cam, the sleeve should be a simple one, cut from a piece of soft metal about 1″ X 1-1/4″ and folded around the camshaft. It can be preshaped beforehand by fitting it around a nail.

Thread the camshaft through the front washtub hole and into the support bracket, slipping it into the rear hole through the slit in the can.

Attach the washers, the collar, and the propeller, and test to see that all works properly.

Final Fittings: Fit the torso to the lower body with rigid wire, and attach arms to the torso with 3/4″ screws. Turn down the end of the camshaft to keep it in place.

The Tail Section: Place the tail in the slot and secure it with two finishing nails. To add to the picture, position a clothesline pole between the washtub and the tail. String a wire from the pole to the top of the tail, and hang some clothes on it. For the purpose, I fashioned a pair of men's shorts (painted white with blue polka dots) and a pair of lady's pink lace panties out of aluminum flashing.

THE CONCERT

The Concert whirligig was designed as the result of an order I could not fill. A patron of the arts wanted to present a gift to a noted violinist who had generously contributed to a special program at the North Carolina School of the Arts in Winston-

Salem. To the patron's surprise, the maestro asked if he could have a whirligig for his farm. I was asked about my whirligigs but had none available at the time. Later, I began to think about the musician and his request and designed a whirligig involving a violinist and an accompanist. The Concert is the result.

The Concert whirligig has the same mechanical system as the Bill the Fisherman whirligig; this consists of a double-cam drive shaft mounted above the baseboard. One cam provides the up-and-down motion for the pianist's arms, and the other provides the motion for the thrust of the violinist's bow. The pianist was easy to make; the parts worked well from the first. The violinist's arm was more difficult. I made several curved arms, but they didn't work properly and became stuck against the body. I finally settled on a flat arm cut from a piece of 1/4" wood and moved the figure around, relative to the cam and the connecting wire, until the arm moved freely. The illusion of motion (violin playing) does not require a completely sculpted arm. See page 67 for illustration.

Materials: Wood

Baseboard	3/4" X 5-1/2" X 18-1/2"
Base pivot	1-1/2" X 1-1/2" X 2"
Piano:	
block	3/4" X 4-3/4" X 7"
legs	1/2" X 1" X 2"
top	1/4" X 1" X 6"
	1/4" X 4-3/4" X 6"
Pianist:	
block	1-1/2" X 2-1/2" X 5-1/2"
arms	1/4" X 1-1/4" X 3-1/2"
Violinist:	
block	1-1/4" X 1-1/2" X 7"
arm, left	1/4" X 1-1/2" X 3"
arm, right	1/4" X 1-3/4" X 2-1/4"
violin	1/4" X 1" X 3"

Materials: Other

(1) large-width tension pin, 2" long
(2) inside corner irons, 1-1/2", with screws
(1) heavy wire (drapery hanger type), 17"–20"
Connecting wire, 20" or so
Materials for wood spool (see illustrations)
Screws and nails as indicated

PROCEDURE

Base: Cut out the baseboard and use it as a planning guide. Measure out the locations of the hardware and figures, and make pencil notations on the board. Shape the baseboard to its final form and sand it down. Then secure the 1-1/2" angle irons in place, as shown in the diagram.

Make the pivot base. Drill a hole for the tension pin and insert it, with a cap. With glue, nails, or screws, fasten it to the bottom of the baseboard. The whirligig platform can be mounted on a stand at this point.

The Camshaft: A heavy drapery hanger wire 18" or so in length should be long enough to allow for mistakes or imprecision of measurement. Allowing 3" for the propeller end, mark off another 3"; it is here that you make the first right-angle bend in the wire for the cam. This can be done with a pair of pliers or in a vise if greater precision is needed. Measure 3/4" and make the second bend. At this point a spool is introduced. This will insure the proper fitting of the connecting

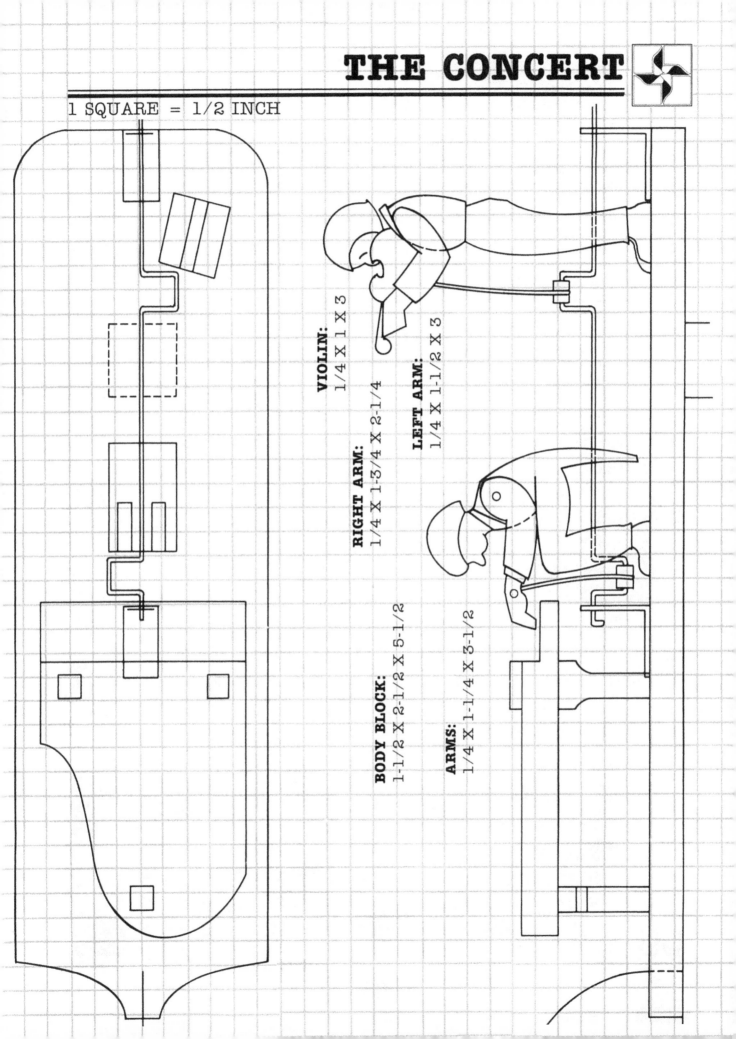

THE CONCERT

1 SQUARE = 1/2 INCH

VIOLIN:
1/4 X 1 X 3

RIGHT ARM:
1/4 X 1-3/4 X 2-1/4

LEFT ARM:
1/4 X 1-1/2 X 3

BODY BLOCK:
1-1/2 X 2-1/2 X 5-1/2

ARMS:
1/4 X 1-1/4 X 3-1/2

of the connecting rod or wire and aid in guiding rotation of the shaft and rod.

The Spool: There are several ways to make a spool or sleeve. The first is to cut a piece of 3/16" brass tubing to something less than 3/4" to fit into the cam. Take a piece of wood 1/2" X 1/2" X 1" and drill a 3/16" hole through it. Trim it the length of the brass tubing and insert the tubing. This makes an excellent sleeve on which the connecting wire can be fastened. A groove may be cut out of the middle to facilitate this. Place the spool on the cam before making the third bend in the cam. This can be awkward, but it's necessary. To make it easier, the third bend may be started before slipping the tubing in place. Then make the fourth bend.

A second method involves making the spool in two stages. The brass tubing is first placed on the cam and the bending is completed. Second, the wood segment is drilled, split in half along its length, and then glued in place over the tubing.

For one more way, the spool may be made entirely of wood. This will work well if the hole is made large enough so the spool will not bind on the cam. The brass tubing is used mainly to prevent wear.

When the first cam is fitted with its spool and is complete, make the second cam, beginning 8" from the front angle support. Insert the second spool in the same manner as the first.

The Piano: The piano is built first so the pianist can be adjusted to it. Cut out the basic piano pattern as shown. Glue the front piece above the keyboard. Cut out the legs and attach them with glue. One-inch brads can be used to secure them.

The Pianist: Make the pianist figure, fashion his head to look as real as possible, cut out the arms, and shape and sand the parts. Drill small holes through the hands for the No. 4 X 3/4" round head screws which hold the arms. The arms are then temporarily put in position. Insert the cross wire and move the arms up and down. Trim the body and the head to assure free movement.

Temporarily place the camshaft and the piano in position. See how the pianist's hands fit on the keyboard. In the down position they should be 1/4" or so above the keys. Attach a connecting wire to the camshaft and see how it all works. Make whatever adjustments are necessary and remove the pieces.

The Violinist: The violinist is carved and sculpted. Note that the left shoulder is up and the head leans to the left to hug the violin.

After the figure is completed, cut out the violin. Notch out space for it between the shoulder and the head, and glue the violin into this notch, making sure it's parallel to the base and at an angle to the body.

Cut out the left arm and glue it to the left shoulder and to the neck of the violin. The shoulder may have to be trimmed for a perfect fit.

Cut out the right arm. A small piece of brass tubing may be inserted in this arm. Drill the hand to receive a small screw eye. When the left arm and violin are glued fast, try the right arm out. The hand should move up to the body of the violin. Trim the shoulder to adjust for this movement before drilling the shoulder hole for the right arm screw.

Place the violinist in position, and attach a connecting wire to the camshaft and try out the motion of the arm. The violinist may have to be moved somewhat to

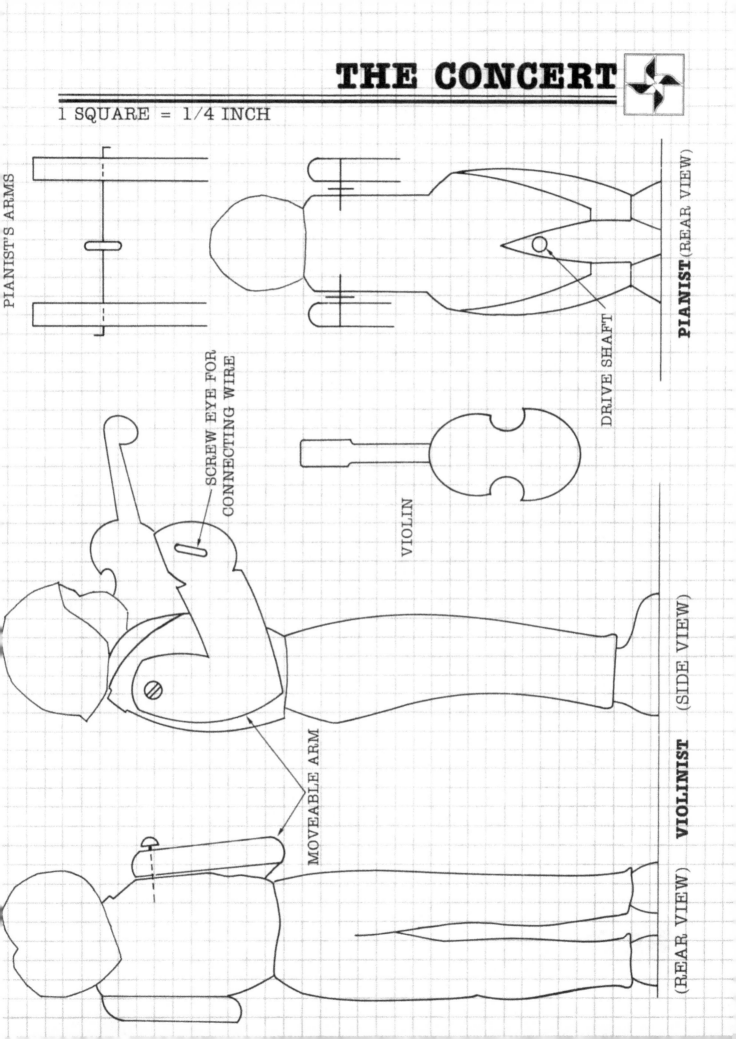

THE CONCERT

1 SQUARE = 1/4 INCH

PIANIST'S ARMS

PIANIST (REAR VIEW)

DRIVE SHAFT

SCREW EYE FOR
CONNECTING WIRE

VIOLIN

MOVEABLE ARM

VIOLINIST (SIDE VIEW)

(REAR VIEW)

allow for the free movement of the right arm and the camshaft.

The bow is made of a semirigid piece of wire, such as the connecting wire, and a small hole is drilled in the top of the hand to hold it. Put in a wire loop or staple on top of the violin; this can be done with two small drilled holes with a cut paper clip end inserted. The loop should be secured with glue.

When all movements have been tested successfully, the pieces may be painted—at least with a first coat. Any combinations of colors may be used; some suggestions are indicated in the drawings.

The Propeller: Any 12″ to 15″ four-bladed propeller can be used for this whirligig. The propeller should be fixed in place before all the moving parts of the whirligig are permanently in place. There is always some heavy handling of the base when the camshaft is being turned into the hub of the propeller, and this must be kept in mind as the whirligig is being constructed. The best time to fit the propeller is after the final positions of the standing figures are determined and the exact places of the completed cams have been located. This is before the connecting wires have been attached.

REMARKS

In testing the camshaft and the moving parts, it's best to turn the camshaft in one direction (clockwise or counterclockwise) every time. When the moving parts are adjusted to move in one direction, they may not move so well in another direction. So be consistent in this regard. Also, this means that when you make the propeller, it must turn in the direction in which you wish the shaft to turn.

WAVING THE FLAG

This whirligig is an example of serendipity. It was designed to have a monkey jumping up and down on a stick, but the chump continued to get stuck on the stick. I cut back the camshaft and thought of having a waving stick instead of a vertical one. The idea of the flag came next, and a problem turned into a prize. Often in the course of whirligig-making, a person must not only improvise but also change plans and designs. Waving the Flag demonstrates how to handle problems related to double-cam devices. It will include fitting various parts (arms, flagpole, etc.) to the camshaft while at the same time positioning the propeller and the supporting pieces. It all takes a bit of juggling, and you may find that you can improve on the steps in construction mentioned here. Note that while the camshaft can be constructed according to the plan, it cannot be permanently positioned until all the moving parts of the whirligig are either attached to it or planned for. Final fitting involves attaching the propeller before securing the rear angle iron bracket. When this whirligig is finished you may breathe a sigh of relief, but you will have a very satisfying whirligig.

Materials: Wood

Baseboard	1″ X 5-1/2″ X 15″	
Pivot base	1-1/2″ X 1-1/2″ X 2″	
Flagpole base	1″ X 1″ X 3″	
Flagpole	1/2″ X 1/2″ X 6″	
Figure blocks	Man	Woman
legs	1/2″ X 3/4″ X 3″	1/2″ X 3/4″ X 1-3/4″
torso	3/4″ X 1″ X 3-1/2″	3/4″ X 1-1/4″ X 4-1/2″
arms	1/4″ X 1/2″ X 3-1/4″	1/4″ X 1/2″ X 2-1/2″

Spools or beads (2) 3/4″ width, drilled 1/8″ to 3/16″, for separating hands
Propeller (see instructions)

Materials: Other

Aluminum flashing or sheet metal, 5″ X 7″, for tail

1 SQUARE = 1/2 INCH

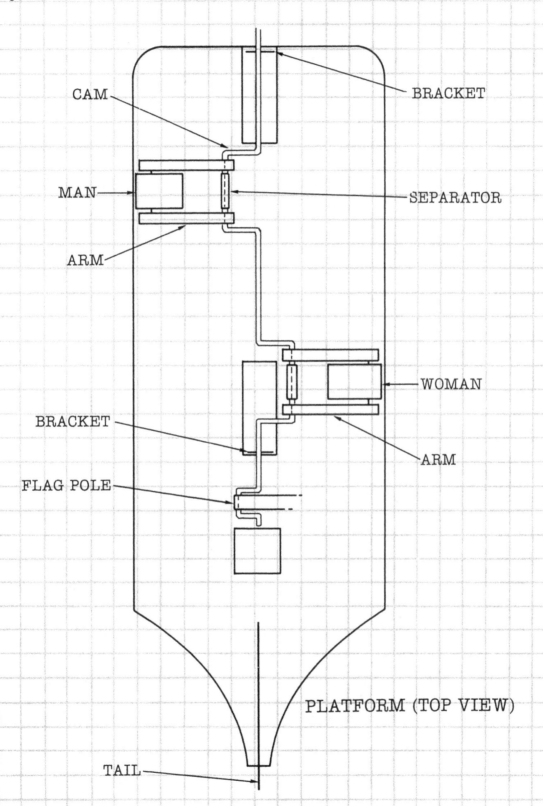

CAM

BRACKET

MAN

SEPARATOR

ARM

WOMAN

BRACKET

ARM

FLAG POLE

PLATFORM (TOP VIEW)

TAIL

(2) 2″ angle corner irons
1 piece heavy drapery wire for camshaft, 18″–20″
1 piece heavy wire for flagpole holder, 6″
1 piece .078 wire for small pole, 4″
1 piece .078 wire for pole top, 7″–8″
1/8″ brass tubing for figure axles
Odd pieces of wire for attaching arms and legs
1 piece open brass tubing, for shaft collar, 2″ long
NOTE: All separate parts should be painted before final attachment

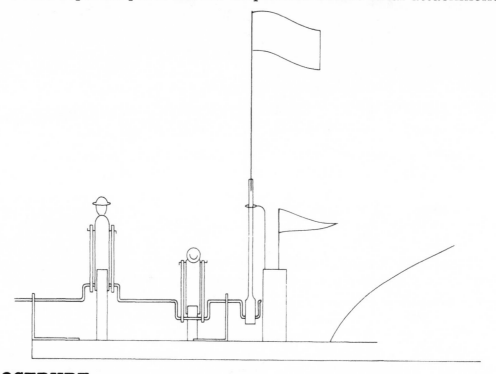

PROCEDURE

Preparing the Base: Laying out the plan on the baseboard is a most important aspect of this construction. The board, with the tail slot cut out, should be trimmed and sanded. Then the position of each standing part should be plotted and marked on it, though some points, such as the exact location of the figures, are not final.

Make the pivot post next. Drill the base for the 3/8″ socket and insert the tension pin or socket liner, or cap. With glue and 1-1/4″ screws, fasten the post to the bottom of the board. The frame can now be placed on a mounting to facilitate the work. Affix the front angle iron, and temporarily position the rear iron.

The Camshaft: Make the camshaft according to the plan shown, leaving a sufficient lead for the propeller. There are two 3/4″-deep cams followed by one 1/2″ deep. The first cam is 1-1/2″ wide and starts 2-1/4″ from the front support iron. The second, which projects in the opposite direction, starts 6″ from the front and also is 1-1/2″ wide. The third starts about 9-1/8″ from the front angle iron, or 3/4″ from the rear iron. It is 1/2″ wide and 1/2″ deep and can be bent in any direction. When the last cam is complete, the shaft can be cut off after the last bend.

The Propeller: Make a four-bladed propeller about 16″ in diameter. It can be made with a solid hub or a cross hub, but it must clear the baseboard. Drill the hub for a wire camshaft.

Cut a collar to be placed on the shaft between the propeller and the front corner iron to insure that the blades will clear the base. Place the collar on the shaft, with washers, and insert the shaft into the front support. Put the shaft through the propeller hub, and with pliers, make a hook on the shaft. Be sure to allow proper

WAVING THE FLAG

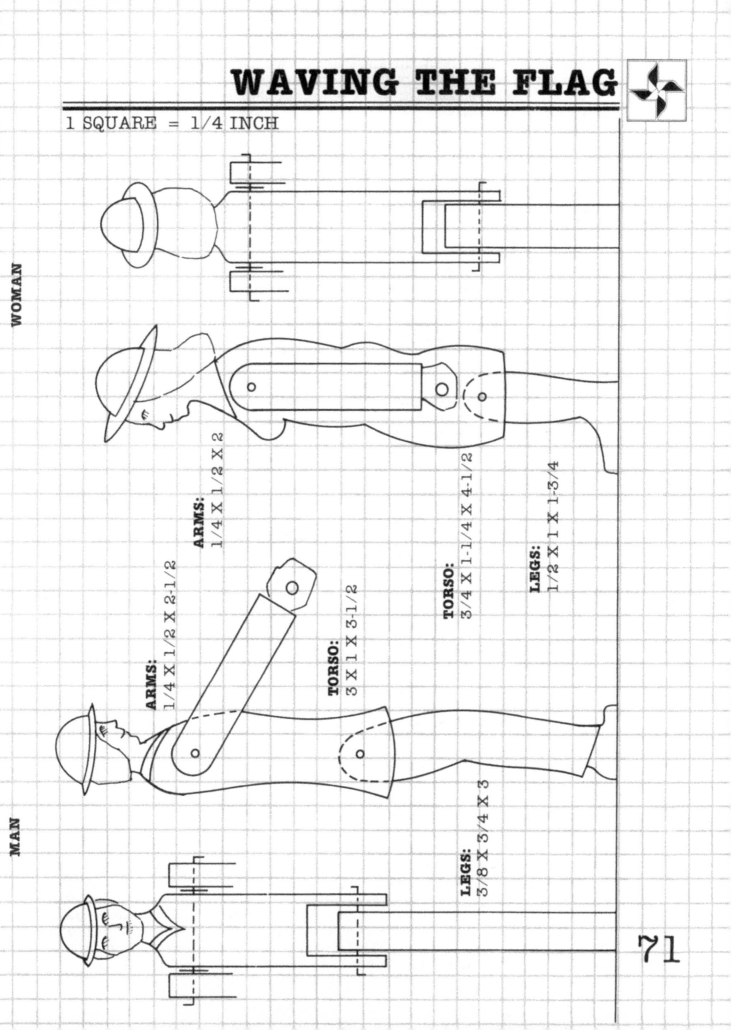

1 SQUARE = 1/4 INCH

WOMAN

ARMS:
1/4 X 1/2 X 2

TORSO:
3/4 X 1-1/4 X 4-1/2

LEGS:
1/2 X 1 X 1-3/4

MAN

ARMS:
1/4 X 1/2 X 2-1/2

TORSO:
3 X 1 X 3-1/2

LEGS:
3/8 X 3/4 X 3

spacing for the propeller width and the collar washer. Force the point of the hook into the propeller hub, wrap it around the hub, or fasten it with a staple.

On the baseboard, measure off the centers of the cams. Also locate the position of the rear corner iron.

Prepare and Set the Figures: Cut and shape the parts of the figures: legs, torsos, and arms. Drill the proper holes for the axles and for joint wires. If desired, line the holes with brass tubing to save wear. For example, lining in the hands where they ride on the camshaft is important. It may also be placed in the leg holes.

Position the man in line with the first cam. Drill a hole there and attach the man's legs with glue and with a 1-1/4″ wood screw from the bottom. The reason for not drilling the hole in the beginning is to provide for adjusting the man's position to the cam. Attach the woman's legs to the baseboard in a similar manner.

Attach the wood flag block, as indicated, with a screw and glue. This is centered about 10″ from the front of the base.

When the characters' legs are in place, remove the rear angle iron and pull the man's and woman's arms along the camshaft to their position in the cams. Replace the angle iron. Attach the torsos to the legs, then the arms to the torsos, with wire. Bend the ends to hold the pieces together.

Prepare two wooden washers, or spools, 3/4″ wide to hold the hands apart on the cams. These can be ready-made beads, or 1/2″ square strips drilled through the center. To attach them, they must be cut in two, separated lengthwise, and then joined and glued over the camshaft. Test the movement of the camshaft and the figures, and make any necessary adjustments.

The Flag Apparatus: Using heavy wire about 6″ long, make the flagpole holder with a loop extending over the camshaft, 3″ higher than the 3″ block. The loop should be about 1″ in diameter, but it may be necessary to make it smaller.

Make the flagpole itself from a wood stick 1/2″ X 1/2″ X 6″; this can be rounded to 1/4″ in diameter, but it must retain the wider base. Drill a 3/16″ hole for the camshaft and cut out a tight slot to receive it. The camshaft should revolve freely within it, but the pole should not drop off. In the other end, drill a hole for a small-gauge wire, 7″ to 8″ long, which will serve as the top of the flagpole.

The American flag is made of aluminum flashing or other metal. It is 1-1/2″ X 2-1/2″ and is bent around the wire.

The flagpole is placed through the loop and the slot slipped over the camshaft. If the pole slips out, it can be rigged securely with wire, or a wooden wedge can be glued into the slot. The apparatus should move freely with the flagpole in place.

The second flag can be any other; the one illustrated is a triangular 1″ X 3″

WIRE POLE

FLAGPOLE HOLDER

MAIN FLAGPOLE

CONNECTION WITH CAMSHAFT

POLE BASE

BRACKET

FLAGPOLE DETAILS

pennant. It is on a 4″ wire flagpole which is fitted into a small hole in the flag base.

Attaching the Rudder: The rudder may be attached before the figures and flag are mounted, but it's best done at this stage so it can't interfere with those construction steps. The rudder shown is made from a piece of 5″ X 7″ aluminum flashing, but it can be made of any size and shape within reason. If the tail is to be painted, that should be done before it's put in place. Slip the finished rudder into the slot on the base and secure it with two small finishing nails.

CHAPTER 8

SILHOUETTE WHIRLIGIGS

Of all the silhouette-type whirligigs, one of the most popular today is one of a man sawing wood. It was popular over a century ago; quite a few nineteenth century models survive. The mechanisms and basic movements of most silhouette types are similar. Learning about this type through reading this chapter or constructing Pete Sawing Wood will provide the information necessary to make other models, such as the one that follows Pete: Erik Chopping Wood.

While the mechanisms are the same in these whirligigs, there remain several choices regarding the construction of the base and the figure. The support for the propeller and drive mechanism can be mounted below or above the base or main frame. The figure can be mounted with legs outside or inside the main frame. A person may even want to consider going a step further and using a baseboard with a three-dimensional figure mounted on it. All these variations have been constructed in the past. Our models will follow the basic patterns of old American whirligigs. The main frame is narrow, the figure and objects are affixed outside the frame, and the mechanism is mounted on top of the frame.

Sketches of two models are reproduced below. The first was made in Boston about 50 years ago, and the second was made in Pennsylvania over 100 years ago. Note the similarities between our models and these older ones.

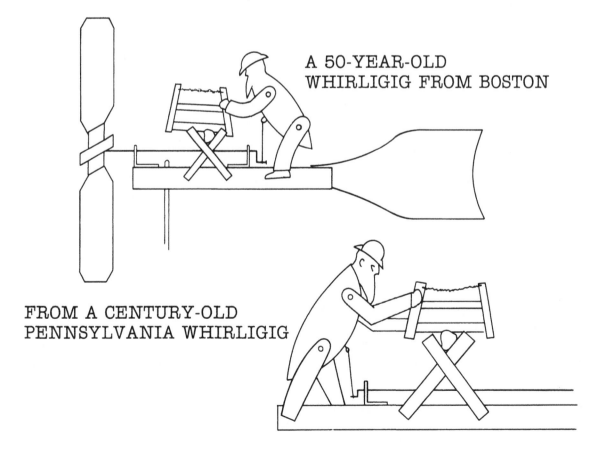

A 50-YEAR-OLD
WHIRLIGIG FROM BOSTON

FROM A CENTURY-OLD
PENNSYLVANIA WHIRLIGIG

PETE SAWING WOOD

Materials: Wood

Platform	3/4" X 1" X 20"
Pivot base	3/4" X 1" X 4"
Figure: legs	(2) 1/4" X 2" X 5-1/2"
torso	1/4" X 2-1/2" X 6-1/2"
arms	(2) 1/4" X 1-1/2" X 4"
Saw	1/4" X 3" X 5"
Sawhorse	1/4" X 3-3/4" X 4"
Log	3/4" dowel, 2" long
Tail	1/4" X 6" X 8"

Materials: Other

(1) metal bracket (1/2" or 5/8" X 8") or (2) 1-1/2" angle irons
(1) 3/8" tension pin, 2" long
(1) 1/4" carriage bolt, 6" long
(1) 6" to 8" connecting rod wire
(1) Small screw eye
Small length of 3/16" brass tubing, or other tubing for lining holes
Assorted brads, screws, and nails, as called for.

PROCEDURE

The Frame: Cut the base frame (3/4" X 1" X 20") and mark off the positions of the objects and figure as illustrated. Cut out the pivot base, and nail and glue it in position 4" from the front of the base frame. Drill a socket hole in the center of this piece. This will place the socket about 6" from the front end. The socket can be lined with metal tubing or a 2" tension pin, and a metal cap should be inserted. Make a tail slot extending 3" or so from the rear of the base frame. The size of the slot will depend upon the type of tail. A metal tail requires a narrow saw cut, while one of 1/4" plywood needs a slot 1/4" wide. The length of the cut also depends upon the design.

Make a metal bracket or screw 1-1/2" corner angles into position on top of the frame. The holes in the bracket or the corner angles must be large enough for the 1/4" bolt to revolve easily in them. In the case of corner angles it may be necessary to redrill or file the holes. Cut out and shape the bolt for the drive shaft, following the method shown in chapter 3.

As construction continues, parts of the whirligig—and particularly the figure—can be painted when they are ready to be assembled but before they are permanently attached to the frame and other parts.

The Sawhorse and Log: The sawhorse can be made in two ways. To fashion a one-piece sawhorse, cut it out of a single piece of 3/4" wood as shown in the pattern. Cut a 1/2" notch at a top end, and glue and nail the sawhorse with 1" brads to the main frame. The log is a 3/4"-diameter piece (or a section of broom handle) 2" long. A 1/2" notch is cut into it, 3/8" deep (for the saw). When attached to the sawhorse, the notches match.

The two-piece sawhorse is mounted with its legs on the outside of the frame. The pieces are cut from 1/4" plywood and attached as shown. A piece 3/4" X 3/4" is glued and nailed into position at the cross. The log may be attached to this before nailing. The log is 3/4" in diameter and 2" long with a 3/8" X 1/2" slot. This is secured in the middle of the sawhorse.

The Figure: The legs (1/4" X 2" X 5-1/2") are glued and nailed into place with the pivot holes lined up. The pivot holes can be drilled after the legs are in place. The torso (1/4" X 2-1/2" X 6-1/2") is attached to the legs with a bolt or a rod.

PETE SAWING WOOD

1 SQUARE = 1/2 INCH

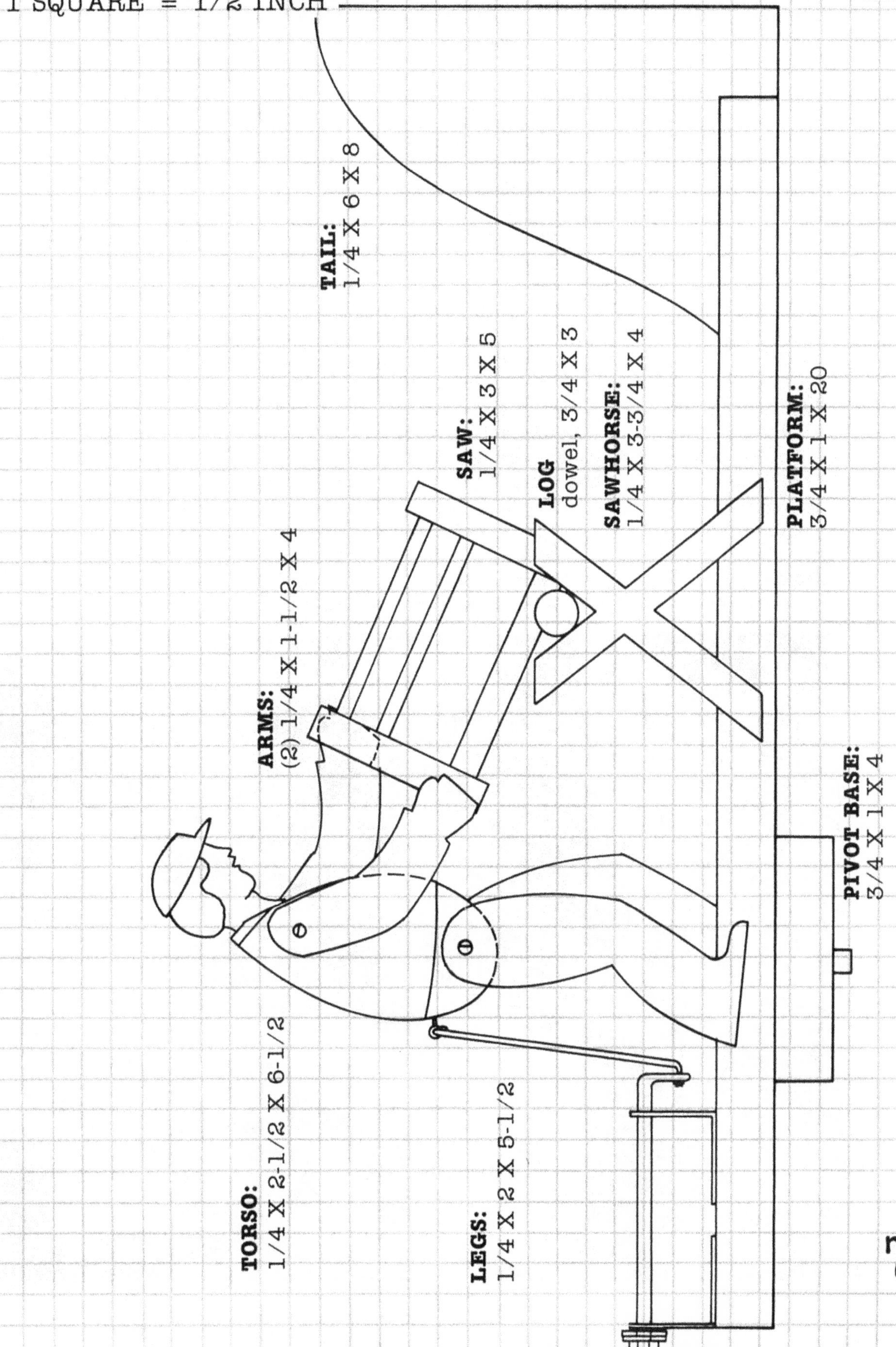

TAIL:
1/4 X 6 X 8

SAW:
1/4 X 3 X 5

LOG
dowel, 3/4 X 3

SAWHORSE:
1/4 X 3-3/4 X 4

PLATFORM:
3/4 X 1 X 20

ARMS:
(2) 1/4 X 1-1/2 X 4

TORSO:
1/4 X 2-1/2 X 6-1/2

LEGS:
1/4 X 2 X 5-1/2

PIVOT BASE:
3/4 X 1 X 4

75

The arms may be made alike, in which case they will be attached to the saw at the same place. On the other hand, they may be made slightly different so that the hands are more realistically placed at separate locations on the handle. Attach the arms to the torso with small washers in between, using a bolt or rod.

The Saw: The saw can be cut out of one piece, as shown below. Old models often have a realistic saw, as illustrated.

Place the saw in the log slots and hold the figure's hands in position. See if the arms, torso, and saw move properly, make any necessary adjustments, and fasten the hands to the saw. Place a wide staple over the saw in the log slot, or use a wire to keep the blade in place.

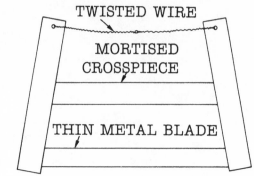

The Tail: The design of the tail can vary and distinctively suit the activity taking place on the frame. It can be a barn or a house—as if logs were being cut in the backyard—or it can be a tree or trees or clouds or whatever. It can be fashioned from metal of sufficient thickness to remain firmly in position and not bend easily. It can be made of solid wood that's as thin as practical, or of 1/4″ plywood. Cut out the design and fasten the tail in the tail slot. This usually requires two or three small nails or brads driven through the frame and the tailpiece.

The Propeller: Instructions for constructing the propellers for both Pete and Erik Chopping Wood are given on page 80. When the propeller is completed, it should be painted before being turned onto the bolt. Secure it with a 1/4″ nut on both sides.

Secure the connecting rod to the figure and the back of the drive shaft. Two means may be used to connect the wire or rod to the bent shaft. The end of the connecting rod can be cut into and then split after it passes through the hole in the shaft, or a small bolt may be placed in the hole and the connecting rod attached to it.

ERIK CHOPPING WOOD

The woodchopper whirligig demonstrates the fact that most of the bent-bolt models operate in much the same fashion. Some of the details of construction are the same as in Pete Sawing Wood and will not be repeated. The construction is relatively simple, although the final assembly of the working parts may require adjustments.

Materials: Wood

Platform	3/4" X 1" X 18"
Pivot base	3/4" X 1" X 4"
Figure:	
legs	(2) 1/4" X 2-1/2" X 5"
torso	1/4" X 3-1/2" x 6-1/4"
waist	(see diagram)
arms	(2) 1/4" X 2-1/2" X 5"
axe	1/4" X 1-1/4" X 4"
Chopping block	1-1/2" X 1-1/2" X 4"
Tail	1/4" X 6" X 8"

Materials: Other

Metal brackets 1/2" or 5/8" X 8" or (2) 1-1/2" angle irons
(1) 2" tension pin (3/16")
(1) 6" carriage bolt, with nuts and washers
(1) No. 8 X 1-1/2" machine screw, with nuts and washers
(1) 6" to 8" connecting rod material (coat hanger wire)
(1) screw eye, small
Small piece of 3/16" brass tubing for lining holes.
Assorted brads, nails and screws as needed for securing assembly, such as
   3/4" screws for the angle irons, 1-1/2" nails for the pivot base, etc.

PROCEDURE

The Platform: Cut out the platform piece (3/4" X 1" X 18") and mark off the points for the various parts and the figure. (See the diagram on the following page.) Remember that the positions are relative and all the parts will not be permanently attached until the movement of the entire whirligig is tested.

Attach the drive shaft supports (either the metal strip drilled and bent into shape or the two angle irons). If angle irons are used, the support holes may have to be redrilled or filed to accept the 1/4" bolt. The back angle of the support should be 4" from the front of the platform. Fashion the drive shaft from the 6" bolt and see how it fits in the support bracket.

Cut out the pivot base (3/4" X 1" X 4") and drill it through in the center for a 3/8" socket. Glue and nail this piece to the underside of the platform so that the socket is 6" from the front. When it is in place, drill another 1/2" or so into the bottom of the platform through the socket hole. Then insert metal tubing or a 2" tension pin. (A 20d or 30d nail or a 3/16" steel rod can serve as a spindle for this size pin.)

The Figure: Cut out the parts of the figure. Glue the arms to the body as shown in the drawing; the upper parts of the arms follow the lines of the torso.

Trace the bottom of the torso on 1/4" wood to about where the belt line would be, and cut out two "waists." Glue these to each side of the torso; they enable the body to fit closely between the legs. Drill a hole in the torso for the leg connection and insert brass tubing (3/16") to prevent wear.

Place one of the legs in position about 4-1/2" from the front end and check to

ERIK CHOPPING WOOD

1 SQUARE = 1/2 INCH

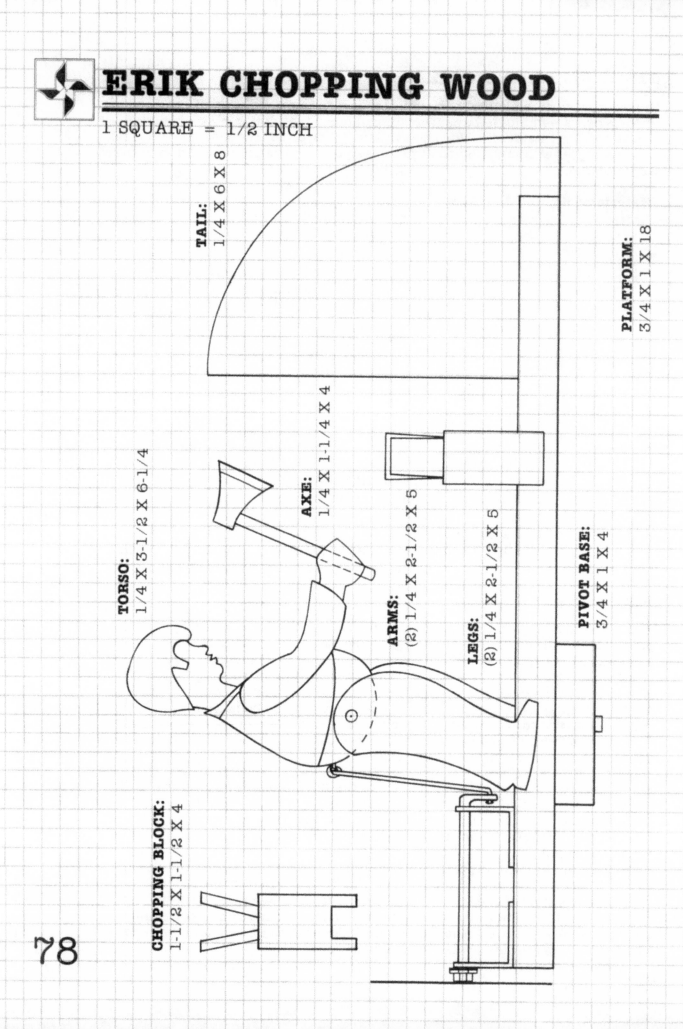

TAIL:
1/4 X 6 X 8

PLATFORM:
3/4 X 1 X 18

TORSO:
1/4 X 3-1/2 X 6-1/4

AXE:
1/4 X 1-1/4 X 4

ARMS:
(2) 1/4 X 2-1/2 X 5

LEGS:
(2) 1/4 X 2-1/2 X 5

PIVOT BASE:
3/4 X 1 X 4

CHOPPING BLOCK:
1-1/2 X 1-1/2 X 4

see if it will be clear of the turning drive shaft and the connecting rod. Try the torso in place and see if the end of the drive shaft and the back of the torso will be in proper alignment. Glue and nail it in place. Do the same with the other leg, making sure to match up the drilled holes.

Put the torso in position with the machine screw through the legs. Screw a small eye into the rear of the figure as shown. Cut out the connecting rod and temporarily attach it so you can test the movement of the drive shaft and body.

Chopping Block and Axe: Cut a 1-1/2″ X 1-1/2″ block, 4″ long, and at one end cut a 3/4″ notch, 3/4″ deep. At the other end, cut out a 1-1/2″-deep V in line with the notch above, then cut around it and trim it so that it looks like a piece of wood being split. (If you prefer, the piece can be squared off at 2-3/4″, and two pieces of wood can be glued in place on top to simulate the split wood.) Cut the corners down and round off the wood roughly so that it resembles a log block. Place the block in position about 12″ from the front.

Cut out the axe and place it between the hands. Test it as the body swings toward the block. The axe should go about halfway into the split wood. Adjust the block and the axe. When they are in proper relation to each other, mark their location and glue them in place.

The Tail: The tail is cut out, in any desired shape, of metal or wood. The one illustrated is of 1/4″ plywood (6″ X 8″) and is painted to show the corner of a log cabin. It is attached with glue and nails after the other parts are operative.

The Propeller: The long-arm propeller for this model is described on page 80. When the propeller is finished, it is advisable to paint it before attaching it to the drive shaft. As in the case of Pete Sawing Wood, place washers between the back nut and the drive shaft support bracket, and secure the propeller with another nut. Secure the connecting rod to the figure and to the drive shaft.

REMARKS

While Erik Chopping Wood is associated with the Pacific Northwest and Pete Sawing Wood is from the East, the character on either of these whirligigs can be from any part of the country. He can be a Midwest farmer, a bayou shrimper, or a Western rancher. In other words, the character that best suits you and your environment can be created. The figure need not be male; a slight change in clothes, figure, and hairstyle will create a woman hard at work.

PROPELLERS AND STANDS FOR SILHOUETTE MODELS

The structure of these models requires strong propellers that will clear the platform. Also, supporting stands must be high enough for clearance and wide enough at the base to hold the whirligig steady. The following are suggestions for such propellers and mounts.

The Propeller: Build a cross frame, joined at the center, of two pieces of wood 3/4" X 3/4" X 11". Out 3" from the center of the hub, cut the remaining length of the arms diagonally (45 degrees) to hold the blades at a consistent angle. The model requires a minimum clearance of 2-1/2". At the center of the hub, drill a 3/16" or 1/4" hole for the drive shaft bolt. A 1/2" hole may be slightly countersunk for the 1/4" holding nut, but this may not be necessary if the bolt is long enough. Cut the blades to any desired pattern. Those illustrated are 1/8" or 1/4" thick, 3-1/2" wide, and 7" long. Fasten the blades to the arms with glue and brads, or wire nails.

LARGE PROPELLER DESIGN
FOR SILHOUETTE WHIRLIGIGS

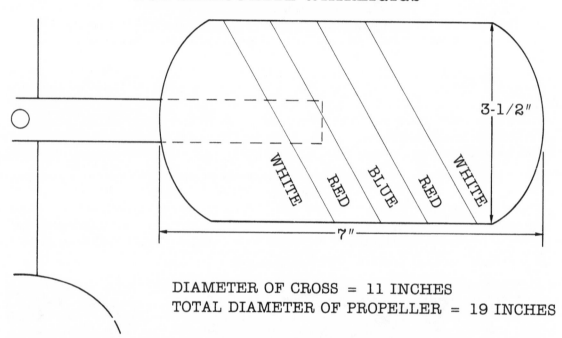

3-1/2"

7"

DIAMETER OF CROSS = 11 INCHES
TOTAL DIAMETER OF PROPELLER = 19 INCHES

The Stands: Two stands that will provide stability and clearance are illustrated on the facing page. For the first, the base is 3/4" X 9" X 13" and is cut curved, and the post is 1-1/2" X 1-1/2" X 10". The symmetrically cut curve makes an attractive base. The post is set in the middle and attached with a No. 8 X 1-1/2" flat head screw and two finishing nails through the base, and it is also glued. The pivot spindle can be a 20d nail, rounded on top.

For the second stand, the base consists of two pieces: one 1/4" X 11" X 11" and the second 3/4" X 5-1/2" X 7". The post is 1-1/2" X 1-1/2" X 9-1/2". The second base piece sits on the first and is glued on top. However, before the base pieces are joined, the post is secured to the second base with a No. 8 X 1-1/2" flat head screw, glue, and holding nails. Then the larger base piece is added. Incidentally, the post need not be set even with the sides; it can be turned diagonally for effect. Also the base pieces can be left squared, or they can be rounded. These stands look very good when painted white, especially if the whirligig frame and the propeller are also white. This sets off the bright colors of the whirligig's objects and figures. Much more elaborate stands may be designed, and of variation in propeller design, there is no end.

TWO STANDS FOR
SILHOUETTE WHIRLIGIGS

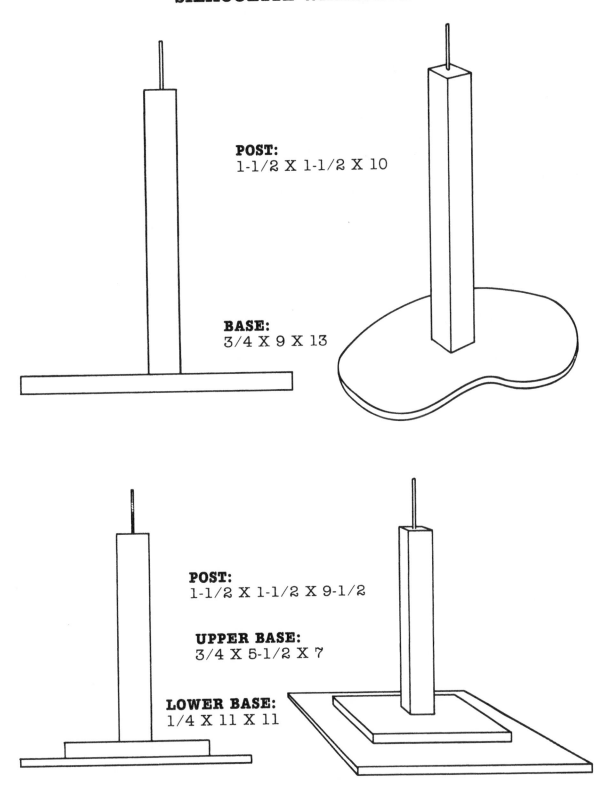

POST:
1-1/2 X 1-1/2 X 10

BASE:
3/4 X 9 X 13

POST:
1-1/2 X 1-1/2 X 9-1/2

UPPER BASE:
3/4 X 5-1/2 X 7

LOWER BASE:
1/4 X 11 X 11

CHAPTER 9

THE LARGE-ARM WHIRLIGIGS

One of the most satisfying whirligigs to make is the large-arm type. When properly balanced, one will move in a relatively light wind with steady and stately motion. In a high wind the motion increases, but there is no spinning, whirling effect, and the arms always appear to be under control. This type is relatively easy to make and should last a very long time. I have had one on a post in the yard for about two years; it hasn't given out yet and is always in motion except in a dead calm.

The first model illustrated is a standard; the others are versions of it. Note that the arms are of differing lengths so that there will be a variance in their turning. Also, consider each arm a propeller and keep in mind that the blades on each arm must be placed at opposite angles. Likewise, each arm must turn opposite to the other arm, as in the winged whirligigs. The large-arm whirligig works so well that I have toyed with the idea of making one with arms eight or ten feet long. One would be easy to make and would look truly splendid mounted on a high pole—a real eye-catcher.

CAROUSEL I

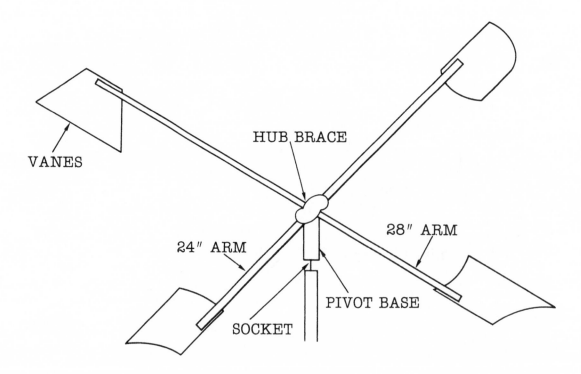

CAROUSEL I

Materials: Wood

Arm 1	3/8" X 3/8" X 24"
Arm 2	3/8" X 3/8" X 28"
Hub braces (2)	1/8" 1-1/4" X 3-1/2"
	1/8" X 2" X 3-1/4"
Blades (4)	1/8" X 2-1/2" X 5"
	1/8" X 3" X 5-1/2"
	1/8" X 2-1/2" X 5"
	1/8" X 3" X 6"
Platform	1" X 1-1/2" X 6"
Pivot base	1" X 1-1/2" X 2"

Materials: Other

Tension pin	3/8" X 2"
Screws	No. 6 X 1-1/2" brass round head and washers

Brass tubing

PROCEDURE

The Arms and Blades: Cut the two arms to length, then cut out the four blades, making them of different shapes. Sample shapes are shown here. Hold the arms together, and thinking of them as opposite propellers, draw the angles to be cut at the ends. When you are sure you have it right, cut a section 2-1/2" from each end. If you want a better fit, you can hold the blades to the arms and draw a more precise cut. For some blade designs or positions, you may wish to cut the arm only 2" back and for others, perhaps as much as 4" back.

DETAILS OF VANES

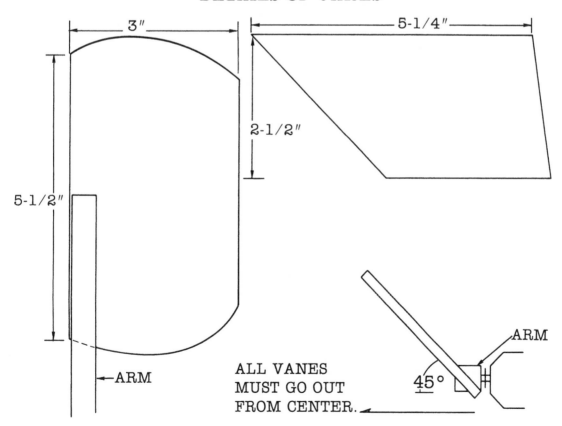

3"

5-1/4"

2-1/2"

5-1/2"

ARM

ARM

ALL VANES MUST GO OUT FROM CENTER.

45°

83

You are now ready to glue the blades in place. Lay the arms on the worktable side by side in the positions in which they will be mounted. Make sure the angles, etc., are correct. Then glue the blades in place, making sure that they extend <u>out</u> from the center. If a wide blade extends inside, it will strike the other arm or a blade on that arm.

After the blades are glued to the arms, balance them and mark their balance points. Glue the hub braces to the outsides of the arms at the point of balance, and try to place the hub braces so the balance point will not be changed. Then drill the hub holes at that point, and line these holes with brass tubing.

The Platform and Pivot: Make the platform section, and curve or point the ends so the arms can move freely. You may want to drill a small hole as a guide hole in each end for the hub screws.

Cut out the pivot base and drill a 3/8″ socket hole in it. The socket can be fitted with a 2″ tension pin or lined with metal tubing. A metal cap should be also inserted. The pivot base can then be attached with glue and nails or screws to the center of the platform.

Mounting: The completed arms are attached to the platform with No. 6 X 1-1/2″ screws with washers on both sides of the arms.

The whirligig should be mounted on a long pole or post high enough to keep the arms clear when they turn. A 3/4″-square pole 3 to 4 feet long with a 30d nail in the top is sufficient; this can be fixed to a larger post or fence to get it up in the air, or it can be mounted on a building.

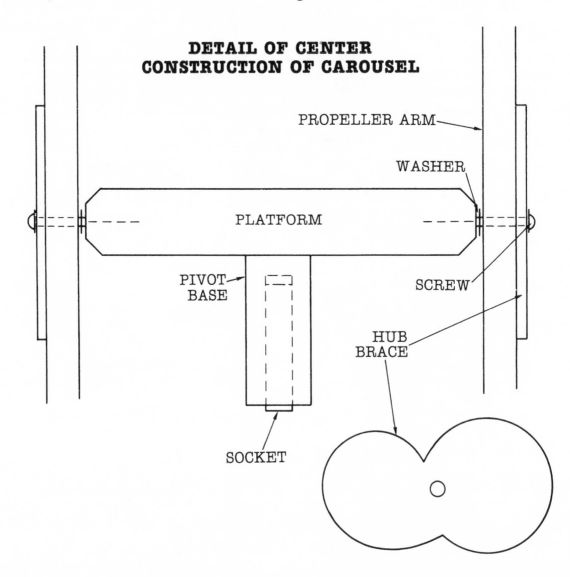

**DETAIL OF CENTER
CONSTRUCTION OF CAROUSEL**

PROPELLER ARM

WASHER

PLATFORM

PIVOT BASE

SCREW

HUB BRACE

SOCKET

CAROUSEL II

This is a slightly larger version of Carousel I; the construction is the same. I needed a larger model for a demonstration and enlarged all the parts to the sizes indicated below. It worked perfectly, except that I had to be careful about setting the hub screws at right angles to the platform. Because of the length of the arms, when the angle was slightly off, an arm could strike either the mount or the other arm. The measurements of Carousel II are shown here:

Arm 1   3/8" X 3/8" X 34"
Arm 2   3/8" X 3/8" X 44"
Hub braces (2)   1/8" X 2" X 4"
                   1/8" X 2-1/2" X 3-1/2"
Blades (4)   1/4" X 3" X 6"
                   1/8" X 3" X 7"
                   1/8" X 2" X 4"
                   1/8" X 2" X 6"
Platform   2-1/2" X 3" X 6"
Pivot base   1-1/2" X 1-1/2" X 2"

COSMOS

This is similar to the Carousel whirligigs, except that it is intended for the space age, as indicated by the blades and the hub platform. Although the illustrations are not provided full-size, the reader will get the idea if he wishes to make Cosmos. The blades are designed as planets or stars. The platform is designed as Earth or any other planet.

COSMOS

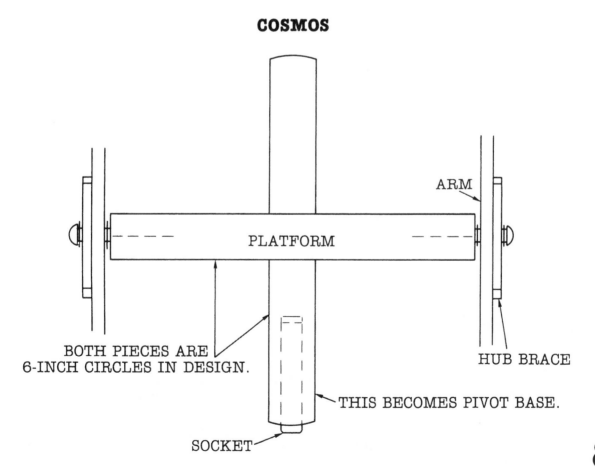

BOTH PIECES ARE 6-INCH CIRCLES IN DESIGN.

ARM

PLATFORM

HUB BRACE

THIS BECOMES PIVOT BASE.

SOCKET

85

COSMOS

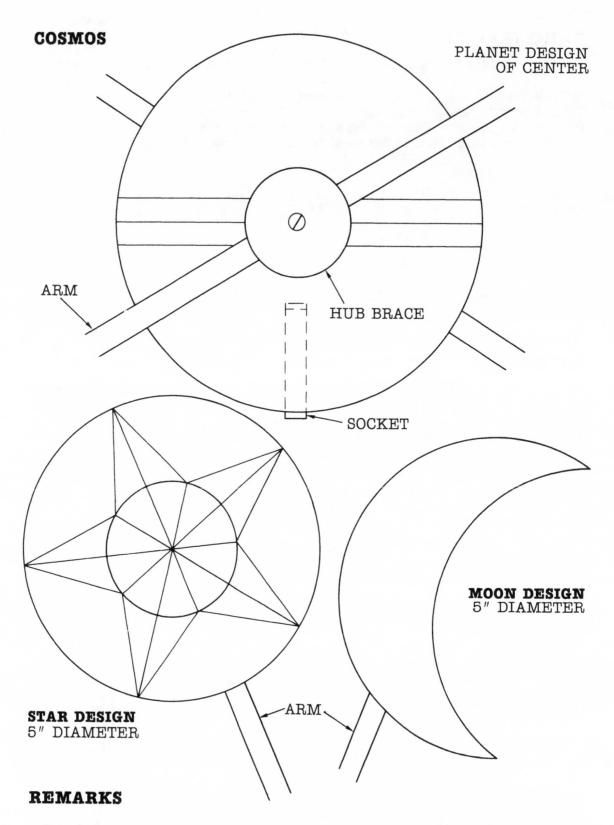

PLANET DESIGN
OF CENTER

HUB BRACE

ARM

SOCKET

STAR DESIGN
5″ DIAMETER

MOON DESIGN
5″ DIAMETER

ARM

REMARKS

On one Carousel, I used different woods which were interesting enough in their color variation to be kept natural. Most large-arm whirligigs lend themselves to varicolored arms. They are bright and flashy, and you can take your choice of colors.

The platform can have a piece of sculpture on it if the piece is not too heavy, or the whirligig itself can be a piece of sculpture: an Atlas or a circus man holding the waving arms, for example.

CHAPTER 10
WEATHER VANE
WHIRLIGIGS

The principal feature of the weather vane whirligig is that it indicates wind direction. Most whirligigs perform in this way, but their principal function is not to act as a vane. In fact, some whirligigs operate off the wind, such as the winged types and certain arm-waving models. The real question is, What is the difference between a weather vane and a weather vane whirligig? Sometimes it may be only a matter of designation, but a proper whirligig should have more wind-moved parts than a simple vane. If a craftsperson puts a direction-finding whirligig on a pole with a letter indicating North, or all four major points of the compass, that could be called a weather vane whirligig. Also, if a relatively long object obviously designed for the purpose of indicating wind direction has other wind-related objects attached, it, too, could be called a weather vane whirligig. The models described in this chapter have been designed to serve primarily as wind indicators; the propellers add action and make them whirligigs.

It is highly recommended that a full-scale drawing of the weather vane whirligig be the first step in construction. With some other types, a small-scale drawing may suffice, but with weather vanes, a life-size drawing is almost imperative. You need to see it as it will actually appear on a post or rooftop to judge the size it should properly be. The whole job is made easier if you make a full-size drawing, pin it to the wall, stand back from it, and see if it is exactly what you want. This process increases in importance as size increases. You can explode a 10" drawing to a six-foot weather vane, but you can never be sure it's what you want until you see it full-size. Such drawings can be made on newsprint, available in large pads in arts and crafts shops or at newspaper offices, or on wrapping paper, obtainable at many stores. Pin the paper to a wall or tape it to a tabletop. Using charcoal or a soft pencil or crayon, draw a baseline near the bottom of the paper; this will be the horizon line, or bottom of the vane. Then proceed to lay out the figure. Charcoal is preferred, because, lightly applied, it is easy to brush off and correct.

When the drawing is finished to your liking, either cut out the pattern and draw the outline on the wood or trace it with carbon paper. All the details should be transferred. Saw out the figure. Find the balance point and, allowing for the weight of the propeller, establish a pivot point somewhere between the balance point and the front end. Drill the pivot socket, line the hole with metal tubing, and insert a socket cap.

Some thin figures (like The Bathing Beauty) lend themselves to a bit of bas-relief wood carving, while other, more realistic, figures (rounded fish, for instance) may take detailed carving. If this is planned, it should be done at this stage. Otherwise, the whirligig should be smoothed down and the edges rounded off with sandpaper. The figure can then be painted or stained.

The propeller is added last, and since it is nonfunctional, it should be kept within artistic limits. A huge propeller will make a weather vane whirligig seem front-heavy; a tiny one will make it look silly. The propellers indicated for each of the models in this section have been designed for appropriate size. However, this should not limit people or restrict them from doing what they want regarding propellers!

If, for any reason, the whirligig does not act like a vane in the wind, which is unlikely if all points have been covered in planning, consider moving the pivot socket forward a bit, enlarging the long end, or adding a tail. Careful location of the pivot point in relation to the balance point should prevent any such problems.

THE BATHING BEAUTY

Materials
Pine board 3/4" X 7" X 48"
Materials for propeller (see below)
3" piece of 5/16" metal tubing
8"–12" length of 1/4" steel for spindle
No. 6 X 1-1/2" round head screw with (2) No. 6 washers
Small length of 3/16" brass tubing for propeller hub

The Figure: Draw the figure on a four-foot sheet of paper, or trace the enlarged sketch in the diagram by the comparison method. (See Foldout No. 7.) Put in all the details. Transfer the detailed drawing to the board, then cut out the pattern. Find the balance point and determine the pivot point. Drill a hole for the pivot socket 3" deep. Line it with 5/16" tubing (curtain rods of that size are good) and place a cap inside.

If sculpting is planned, carve out the necessary details, but keep the cuts shallow. Trim, file, and sand the figure. Then stain or paint it. One idea is to waterproof the body portions with varnish to provide a natural flesh tone. The hair and eyebrows can be painted black and a bikini red.

The Propeller: The hub is made of pine or fir 1/2" thick and 2" square. Drill a 3/16" hole in the center and line it with brass tubing. The blade slots are cut in the four centers at 45 degrees, 1/2" deep. The four propeller blades are 1/8" X 1-1/2" X 4-1/2", also of clear pine or fir. The boards are rounded at the tops and cut back to about 1" at the base. These are glued in place and sanded down to a neat final fit. Attach the propeller to the pointed finger with a No. 6 X 1-1/2" brass round head screw.

The Mounting: When fixed into a sturdy pole or pipe, the 1/2" steel pivot rod, slightly rounded off on top, will hold the weather vane whirligig steadily in the wind. If a wood post is used, drill a 1/2" hole, 6" deep. If a metal cap has been inserted, a 1/2" ball bearing placed in the socket will keep the whirligig turning freely, but this addition isn't strictly necessary.

THE WHALE

Whale weather vanes were very popular in old New England, and many of the old ones were made of wood. In Eastham, Massachusetts, a small whale rides over the oldest windmill in the United States. When early artisans added a propeller on the snout for decoration or fun, they had a weather vane whirligig.

When I started to make a whale whirligig, I found that most of the old patterns and drawings were exaggerations; real whales don't quite look like the whales in standard designs. I kept to the standard image of a right whale—a huge head, inseparable from the torso, and a huge tail. This is the one shown in Figure 1 of Foldout No. 8. Unsatisfied with this, I also made a "modern" design (Figure 2). You can design your own, or a dolphin, if you wish.

Materials
Pine board 3/4" X 7-1/4" X 28"
Materials for propeller (see below)
2" tension pin (3/8")
5/8" dowel, 2" long
No. 6 X 1-1/2" brass round head screw, with (2) No. 6 washers
Small length of 3/16" brass tubing for propeller hub.

The Body: Draw the whale on a large sheet of paper or enlarge the sketch in Fold-

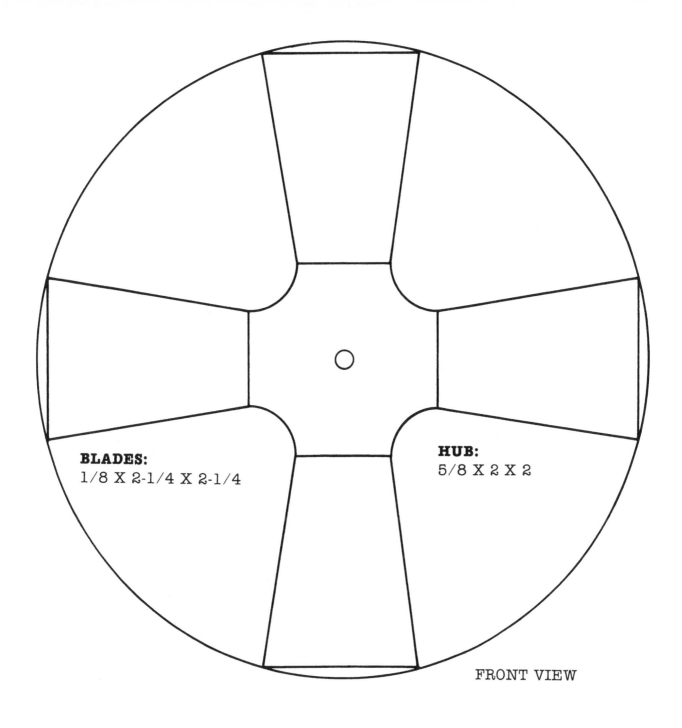

BLADES:
1/8 X 2-1/4 X 2-1/4

HUB:
5/8 X 2 X 2

FRONT VIEW

DESIGN OF PROPELLER FOR WHALE

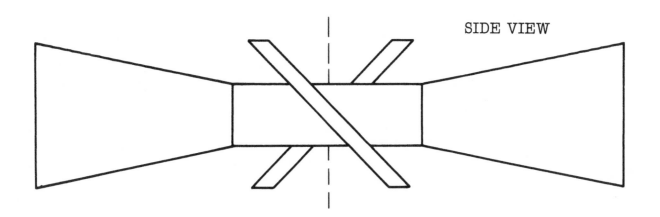

SIDE VIEW

out No. 8, and transfer it to the board. Cut out the whale. If you have made your own or a larger or smaller pattern, you may wish to check out the balance point and determine a new pivot point. Otherwise, drill a 3/8″ hole, 2″ deep, at the pivot point, which, in the illustration, is 6″ from the front of the whale. Insert a tension pin and a cap. Then drill a 5/8″ hole, 3/4″ deep, in the nose, 2″ up from the base. Drill a lead hole in the dowel for the propeller screw and glue the dowel in place in the nose. Round the body with a file or knife and give the tail some shape, thinning it appropriately. Sand it down, mark the position of the mouth and eyes, and paint the figure. Whale color seems to be black or dark blue, shading down to a lighter color on the belly, but any colors will do.

The Propeller: The hub is 5/8″ X 2″ X 2″. Drill a 3/16″ hole in the center for the propeller screw and insert the brass tubing. The blade slots should be 1/2″ deep and are cut across the centers of the hub at 45 degrees. The blades are 1/8″ X 2-1/4″ X 2-1/4″. Glue these into the slots, and trim and sand them.

The Mounting: A 30d nail with the head removed will fit into the 3/8″ tension pin used as a socket, or a 1/4″ steel rod may be used.

THE COD FISH

The Cod Fish can be made as a silhouette like The Whale, and there is nothing further to add to that. However, it can also be made rounded and streamlined and as realistic as you wish to make it. The model illustrated in Foldout No. 7 was designed from photographs and drawings of a cod. If you wish to make another fish, visit the library and do some research so you can first make a portrait, accurate down to the location of the fins and the details of the scales, if you want to go that far. Unless you are making an imaginary fish, real fishermen will know if your model is accurate or not. It need not be perfect, but it should have the main characteristics of the fish you are copying.

Materials:
Clear fir block, 2″ X 5″ X 24″
The 2″ X 5″ block will provide a streamlined body sufficiently curved to look real, although the 2″ standard lumber will be milled to 1-1/2″. A larger body can be made of a 4″ X 4″ block (3-1/2″ X 3-1/2″ milled) or a 4″ X 6″ block, of any length.
Propeller material (see below)
3/8″ steel tubing
1/4″ steel rod, 12″ long

The Body: Draw the fish in detail on a large sheet of paper. Trace this onto the wood block and cut out the main outline on the block. Locate the pivot point and drill a 3/8″ hole, 3″ deep. Line this with metal tubing and insert a cap. Rough out the fish shape with tapering curves on top and bottom. A rough rasp will shape fir nicely. If you are using carving tools, remember that while fir cuts well, it splinters easily, so guard your cuts. Finish the job with a finer wood file and sandpaper.

Next, work on the details you wish to include. Many old-timers even carved scales on the fish on these vanes. A few hints of detail are often enough; tail striations may also be suggested. Mouth lines and eyes should be emphasized. Using wood 1/8″-3/16″ in thickness, cut out dorsal and other fins that project from the body. Glue them in notches cut 1/4″ deep into the body at the proper locations. Paint the body in appropriate colors.

The Propeller: The propeller for this size fish can be the same as that for the whale. It can also be a 6″ or 8″ simple double-bladed propeller carved out of one piece of wood. If painted pink, it may look like a worm.

The Mounting: A 30d nail with the head removed will fit into the tension pin used as a socket, or a 1/4″ steel rod may be used.

CHAPTER 11

SPECIAL DESIGNS

There is a wide variety of special designs, but for the most part they fall into two categories: functional and decorative. The functional types have some practical application, such as chasing moles from a garden, while the decorative types seem to serve no purpose at all, other than being interesting to look at. The focus of the decorative whirligig is in the distinctive or unique propeller; that of the functional whirligig is in the effect that it has.

FUNCTIONAL TYPES

THE MOLE CHASER

A popular, as well as useful, whirligig is The Mole Chaser (or mole control windmill as it is called in some areas). This is essentially a noisemaker or an earth vibrator. The object is to scare moles away by creating a vibrating movement in the ground. There are many mole chaser designs, and new ones will continue to be produced as long as there are moles in the garden or under the lawn. There is a continuing argument over which is the best, most effective design, but most of them must work, or whirligig makers would not continue to make them or customers to ask for them.

The simplest whirligig of this type consists of a multibladed propeller mounted close to the ground on a broad base. As the relatively large propeller spins around, it makes the mounting shake. This, in turn, makes the base vibrate. The blades

also make a noticeable noise, which, added to the trembling movement of the base, creates a disturbance in the area around the whirligig. The mole chaser pictured on page 91 was a gift from a friend who found it in a country antique shop. The distinguishing feature of this whirligig is that the post sits loosely in a box and provides movement to the base as the propeller turns.

Materials

Base platform	
(plywood)	3/8" X 16" X 16"
Box sides	(2) 3/4" X 1-1/2" X 6"
	(2) 3/4" X 3" X 6"
Post	1-1/2" X 1-1/2" X 24"
Arm	3/4" X 1-1/2" X 24"
Propeller Hub	1-1/2" X 3" diameter
Stock	3/4" X 7/8" X 12"
Blades (metal)	4" X 7"
Tail	1/4" X 10" X 24"
Braces	1/4" X 1-1/2" X 22"

The Base: Cut out the base platform and the box sides. Then fit the box tightly together with glue and nails or screws.

Fasten the box in the middle of the platform with glue and screws. It must be firmly secured.

The Post and Arm: Cut the post and fit it into the box. Move it; it should rattle around a bit. Trim it if necessary. Cut off the head of a 20d nail and place it in the top of the post as a spindle. Cut out the cross arm. Saw a tail slot in one end, 3" to 4" deep. Drill a guide hole for the propeller screw or nail in the other end. Shape the tail, giving it some kind of unusual shape, and attach it to the slot with glue, brads, or wire nails.

The Propeller: Make a multibladed propeller of at least 20" in diameter and with at least eight vanes. The propeller described here has a diameter of about 26". Drill the hub at the center with a 3/16" bit, and line this center hole with tubing. This size hole can take a 20d nail or a large screw. Also drill 3/8" holes around the outside at the necessary intervals for the blade stocks (see chapter 4).

Trim down the ends of the stocks to fit into the 3/8" holes. Attach the blades to the wide side of these stocks with wire nails. Then glue the stocks into the hub with the blades angled 30 degrees off the hub plane. Drive in brads for additional security.

Blades can also be made of wood 1/8" or 1/4" X 4" X 7", but the propeller will be somewhat heavier in this case. They can also be made of wood shingles (shakes). The thick outer end of the shake can be cut and trimmed to fit into the 3/8" hole, and the inner, thinner end will make a good blade.

Balance: Locate the balance point with the tail and the propeller in place. Then mark a point 1" to 2" toward the propeller from the balance point and drill the spindle hole with a 3/16" bit. This point may be near the center of the crosspiece or support arm. Line the spindle hole with tubing and set the whirligig on the post with washers. It should swing easily. A little grease will help.

The whirligig comes apart in three pieces so it can easily be moved from one place to another. It will work as a whirligig, but more research is needed to determine its effectiveness as a mole chaser.

There are other types of mole chasers; some make more noise than others. One makes a clacking sound and another makes a cracking noise. The clacker type adds clappers to the whirligig propeller stocks near the hub. These loose wood pieces make a banging or slapping noise as the propeller turns. The clacker whirligig can be mounted on a base similar to the simple one above, or it can be placed on a pole.

The cracker type is similar to the noisemakers whirled at New Year's parties.

THE MOLE CHASER

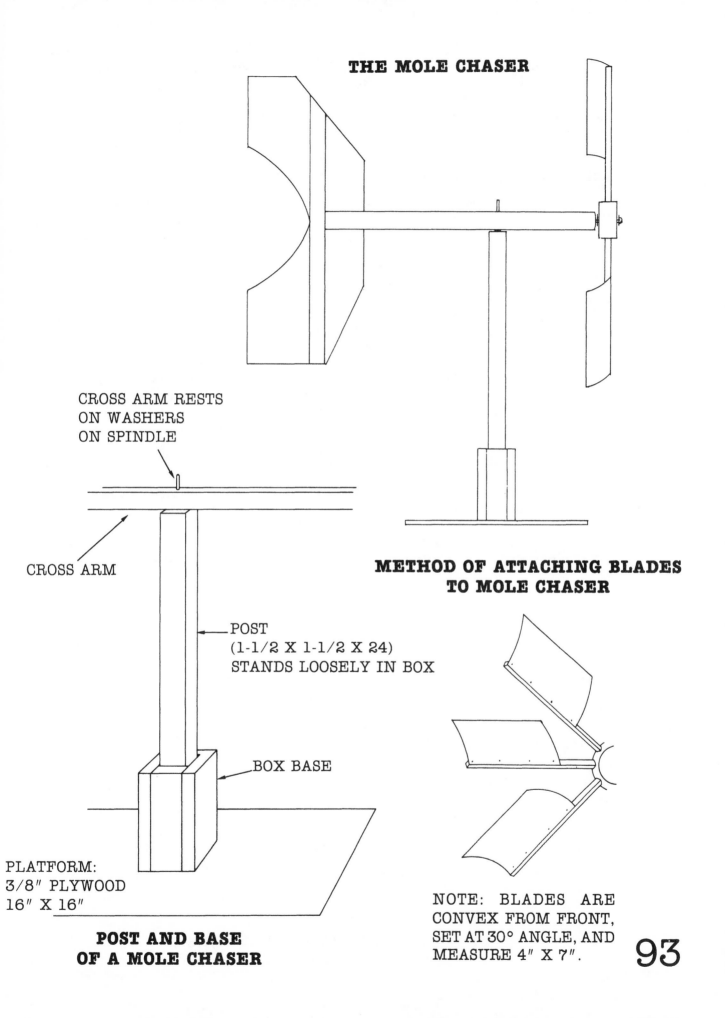

CROSS ARM RESTS
ON WASHERS
ON SPINDLE

CROSS ARM

**METHOD OF ATTACHING BLADES
TO MOLE CHASER**

POST
(1-1/2 X 1-1/2 X 24)
STANDS LOOSELY IN BOX

BOX BASE

PLATFORM:
3/8" PLYWOOD
16" X 16"

**POST AND BASE
OF A MOLE CHASER**

NOTE: BLADES ARE
CONVEX FROM FRONT,
SET AT 30° ANGLE, AND
MEASURE 4" X 7".

93

The drive shaft moves a hub wheel into which are cut four gear teeth which move past a fixed wooden blade. After a gear has passed, the blade snaps back to hit the next tooth. This makes a very loud crackling sound but has two disadvantages. First, it takes a powerful propeller and a strong wind to move a geared wheel past an obstruction like a fixed blade, and second, the blade will wear out fast. However, it can always be replaced!

THE BIRD SCARER

While mole chasers are located near ground level and have their effect there, bird scarers are usually mounted at eye level or above. The focus is not on ground vibration but on light and visual changes, and motion in the air. There is no need to make The Bird Scarer whirligig look like an enemy of birds, such as an owl or a pussycat. These objects fool no one, least of all birds. You can use any whirligig body design that suits your taste, as long as you don't assume that birds think as you do.

The simplest bird scarer is one that includes a large propeller that can create considerable disturbance in the air and develop a flashing light effect. It should be multibladed; the blades can be brightly painted or made of shiny metal. It is essential that the propeller be finely balanced and light so that it will spin with considerable speed. A fast-moving, flashing propeller will keep birds at a distance. Perhaps it isn't so much that the whirligig gives a bird an illusion of danger as it is that if a bird has ever been crowned by a moving object, he will be wary of such things. Actually it seems that birds like slow-moving propellers, such as the big arms of the Carousel whirligig. They fly around the large one in my yard as if they are playing games with it, and when there is no wind, they perch on it.

While a bird scarer can be made quickly on the Lollypop design with tuna can or coffee can lids, a more effective propeller is shown here. The whirligig as a whole is a simple vane type with a tail, not unlike The Mole Chaser in general appearance, and with the pivot point placed some inches in front of the balance point. The main thing is to get a light propeller turning fast. The one described here has a diameter of some 31″; it need not be that large. The big aluminum blades should provide a desirable flashing effect.

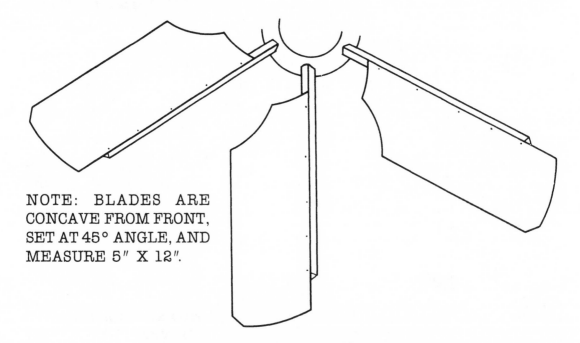

NOTE: BLADES ARE CONCAVE FROM FRONT, SET AT 45° ANGLE, AND MEASURE 5″ X 12″.

METHOD OF ATTACHING BLADES TO BIRD SCARER

Materials

Cross arm	3/4" X 1-1/2" X 24"
Propeller hub	3/4" X 3-1/2" diameter
Stocks	1/2" X 3/4" X 12"
Blades (light aluminum)	(8) measuring 5" X 12"
Tail	1/4" X 10" X 11"
Post	see details

MOUNTING A SPINDLE IN A PIPE

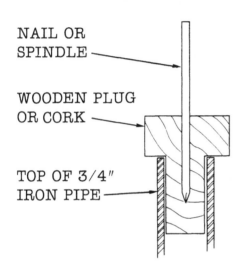

NAIL OR SPINDLE

WOODEN PLUG OR CORK

TOP OF 3/4" IRON PIPE

The whirligig is assembled like The Mole Chaser. The cross arm is slotted about 2" deep for the 1/4" tail. The tail is shaped in some unique way and is attached with glue and brads. Note that the propeller hub is only 3/4" thick; a 1-1/4" piece of brass tubing should be used as lining, to give it some additional strength. The propeller can be attached to the cross arm with a 20d nail or a large 3" brass round head screw. The post can be of wood or metal and hold the whirligig some five or six feet above ground level. If a metal pipe is used, it is easy to make a wooden or cork plug to fit into the top of the pipe. This can be drilled for the spindle.

DECORATIVE TYPES

THE WINDMILL WHIRLIGIG

There are many styles of windmills, and perhaps the first decision to make is which style to produce. There are some excellent books on old windmills in most libraries, and perhaps the best thing to do is to study them and select the windmill that most appeals to you. The second decision about building a windmill whirligig is how detailed to make it. There are some around that have gears, men and women at work, and flags flying. The third decision is how big to make it. The one here is relatively simple to construct and can lead, if one wishes to follow through, to the design of larger and more complex models.

Materials

Main building block	3" X 3" X 6"
Cap block	1" X 2" X 2"
Vanes	
arms	(2) 1/2" X 1/2" X 7"
sails	(4) 1/8" X 1-1/2" X 3"
Tail	
tailpiece	1/2" X 1/2" X 6"
tail	3" X 5" (metal) or 1/8" X 3" X 5" (wood)
Base	3/4" X 4" X 4"
Flange	3/4" X 3" diameter
Brass screws	(1) No. 10 brass X 3" round head
	(1) No. 8 brass X 2-1/2" round head
Brass tubing	small lengths as indicated.

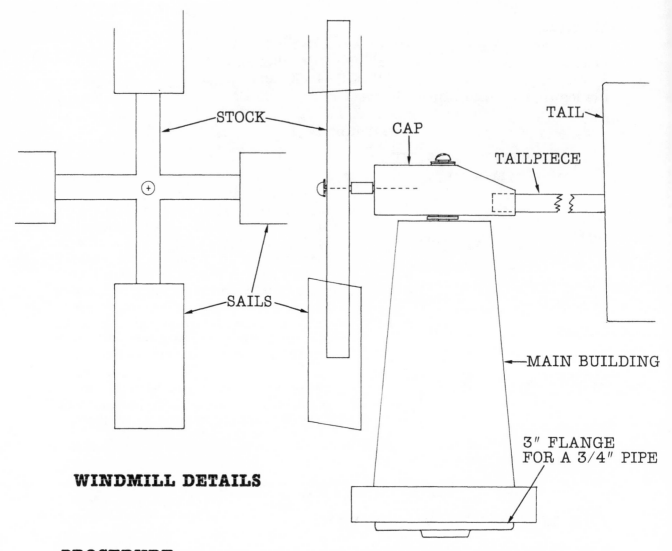

WINDMILL DETAILS

PROCEDURE

The Main Building: The mill building is a six-sided, sloped 6″ structure that is 3″ in diameter at the base and 2″ in diameter at the top. Make it out of a piece of wood 3″ X 3″ X 6″ or glue two pieces of 2″ X 4″ X 6″ together.

Make two patterns of a 3″ and a 2″ hexagon and trace them, centered, on the bottom and the top, respectively, of the block. Make sure the edges are lined up. Start by cutting the base in the hexagonal shape, keeping the edges straight. This will permit the base to be held firmly in a vise while you are shaping the sides. Then cut the sides away; each side will be about 1-1/2″ at the base and 1″ at the top. Note here that the sides may be of any pattern. The mill may be four-sided, eight-sided, or entirely round. Real mills varied widely in architectural style.

The cap is cut from a piece 1″ X 2-1/2″ X 3″ as indicated in the illustration. After preliminary shaping, three holes will be drilled. The first, in front, is a guide for the No. 8 screw that will go through the vane hub. The second is a 3/8″ hole that will go into the center of the back, opposite the first one; this will hold the tailpiece. The third is a 1/4″ hole through the top, which will act as the hub of the cap. After the holes are drilled, the cap can be shaped further and curved. A taller cap may be made similar in appearance to those on some older operating mills; the caps were quite high to make room for the main drive gear, which rotated with the drive shaft. Again, reference to a book on windmills will give you approximate dimensions.

The Tail: The tailpiece is 1/2″ X 1/2″ X 6″ if cut square. A 3/8″ dowel may also be used. This is inserted 1″ into the rear of the cap. If square cut, the 1″ section

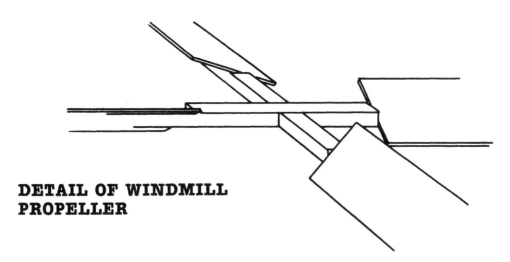

**DETAIL OF WINDMILL
PROPELLER**

must be trimmed with a knife. Before gluing it to the cap, make a 1″ cut into the piece for the insertion of the metal or wood tail. The width of this cut depends upon the width of the metal or wood used. For security, drill two small holes into the tailpiece. After inserting the tail vane with glue, drive two brads through the tail. Many types of tailpieces can be found in old windmills.

The Propeller: The four-bladed propeller is cut and assembled as shown in the illustration. The 1″ crosspieces (forming the stocks) are each cut out at the center to form a mortise joint. When they are in position, mark the four ends for the angular cuts for fitting the sails. This is easy to do, as the 1/2″ square end will make a 45-degree angle from corner to corner. Measure 1-1/2″ from the hub center and mark that point. The 45-degree cut will extend there. With a scroll saw, cut down to the angle depth and, with a knife, cut out the section. Do this with all four ends. Check to make sure the cuts are at the same angle as the propeller is turned.

The sails, so called because canvas was spread over frames in olden days, are made of thin pieces, 1/8″ (or less) X 1-1/2″ X 3″. These are glued in place on the arms. When these are dry, the arms and sails can further be trimmed to look attractive and make a light-as-possible propeller.

Drill the hub with a 3/16″ bit and test the propeller for balance by revolving it at the hub. Trim where necessary to achieve balance.

Assembling the Parts: The parts may be painted before assembly. Attach the 4″ X 4″ base to the bottom of the mill after drilling holes in it for the screws of the flange, which will be secured later. Mark the center of the top of the mill and drill a small guide hole in it. Insert a No. 10 X 3″ round head brass screw through the cap with brass washers on top and bottom. Place the propeller in front and secure it with a No. 8 X 2-1/2″ brass round head screw, with washers fore and aft. Place a 1″ piece of 3/16″ brass tubing between the propeller and the cap, separated with another washer. This sleeve keeps the sails from striking the mill. If the pieces have not been painted, they should be disassembled and painted now.

When the mill is completed, the pipe flange is screwed on. A six-foot or longer section of 3/4″ pipe can be set into the ground and the windmill fixed on it.

REMARKS

The simple windmill demonstrates the essentials of a whirligig. Driven by the wind, it moves its sails and at the same time turns as the wind shifts. From this simple model, a person can move on to more complex whirligig design.

A somewhat larger windmill can be made in which the propeller is not free-flying, as on the one illustrated here, but is attached to a drive shaft. This drive shaft can, in a hollow mill, drive a gear or series of gears to make things happen. One will then have a mechanical whirligig. Or the action can be more limited. A simple shaft can be extended through the cap to turn a wheel or cams to make figures move on an extended platform. There are as many possibilities in developing windmills as your imagination can come up with.

THE AIRPLANE WHIRLIGIG

The airplane—the one with propellers, not the one with unseen jet propulsion—was a great favorite before the space age. Biplanes and triplanes made excellent whirligigs, as did trimotors. There are many pictures of historical airplanes in books, and if anyone has any doubt about size and appearance, scale models are often available in hobby shops. Two airplanes are shown here, one an early single-engine plane and the other a trimotor. Both are constructed according to the same principles, and other plane whirligigs can be built on the same basis. Unlike other structures, planes require lateral stability in order to operate properly; therefore wing balance is important. Plane whirligigs have a tendency to fly away in a high wind, so special precautions have to be taken. The plane can be made heavy; some have had iron braces screwed to the bottom. In others, the pivot socket is made deeper than normal, or the pivot pin is screwed on the plane and a socket is made in the support pole. In these models, the sockets go through the airplanes so they can either be placed on long spindles or be secured to the support post with bolts as spindles.

THE FLYING JENNY

The Curtiss JN-4D was produced during World War I, and immediately after, it became the principal American civilian airplane. It was the favorite of the men and women who were the barnstormers of the early twenties, the wing-walkers and the stunt pilots. Some 10,000 were manufactured. They could land at 45 miles per hour, and their ceiling was about 5,000 feet. The Flying Jenny Whirligig is an approximate copy, and the body can be made in either of two ways. It can be a silhouette cut out of 1″ lumber (A), or it can have more of a shape, fashioned out of a 2 X 4 (B). It can also be made completely realistic if the builder has the interest to research its specifications. The craftsperson may also wish to add details such as wires, wing skids, etc., which are not included here. The plane here can be made larger or smaller, to suit your interests (see Foldout No. 9).

Materials

Body (A)	3/4″ X 3″ X 18″
(B)	1-1/2″ X 3″ X 18″
Rudder	1/4″ X 4″ X 4-1/2″
Stabilizer	1/4″ X 4-1/2″ X 6″
Wing:	
upper	1/4″ X 3″ X 20″
lower	1/4″ X 3″ X 16″
Struts	1/4″ X 3/8″ X 3-3/4″ to 4″
braces	1/4″ X 3/8″ X 8″
Undercarriage	(4) 3/8″ X 3/8″ X 3-3/4″ to 4″
wheels	1/4″ X 3/4″ diameter

| axle | 1/8″ rod |
| Propeller | 3/4″ X 3/4″ X 6″ or 8″ |

PROCEDURE

The Body: Cut out the body. If the thicker wood (B) is used, shape it as shown; if (A) is used, shape only the rear somewhat. The top of the body is rounded, except where the stabilizer will be attached. The rest of the body remains flat. The bottom of the body should be cut out for the wing. Drill a 3/8″ hole vertically through the body 5″ from the front for the spindle. Line this with tubing.

Rudder and Stabilizer: Cut these items to shape and round them off with sandpaper. Fasten the rudder to the stabilizer with brads and glue, and when the glue is dry, attach the piece to the body.

Wings: Cut out the wings and round them off. The original Jenny wings were relatively thin, but it is not necessary to be too realistic. Mark the bottom wing where the wing struts will go, and then mark the related points on the upper wing. At the appropriate angle, either drill tiny holes through the wings to facilitate the placement of brads or drive brads through the selected points to hold the struts. Glue the lower wing in place and secure it with brads.

Struts: The Jenny had four long struts and four short ones attached to the body on each side. While the rudder and wings may be of plywood, the struts should be made of solid wood.

Make four long struts of equal length. Nail and glue two on the outer wing surfaces on each side. Temporarily brace two of them upright; this is done by pinning a thin strip of wood to the strut and body at an angle. Place the upper wing on the four struts and tack and glue it in place. Then cut the short struts to size, and tack and glue them in place. Let the glue dry before continuing. Cut each of the four remaining struts exactly to size, and tack and glue them in place.

Finally, cut a piece that will fit diagonally between the upper corner of the outer wing strut and the lower corner or the inner wing strut of each side, and glue it in place. This will serve as a brace to hold the wings in position. Remove the temporary braces.

Undercarriage: The craftsperson will have to decide whether to make the undercarriage true to scale and whether to use separate pieces of wood or to simplify the part by cutting it out of a single piece of plywood. Either way, the pieces are trimmed to fit the body and are nailed and glued in place. Drill small holes for fitting in any small rod as an axle, and attach the wheels to the axle.

The Propeller: The Jenny's propeller was a standard single propeller, and for this model, according to scale, it should be 6″ long. But whirligigs are whirligigs, and for fun the propeller can be made of any length. The hub can be drilled with a 7/32″ bit and lined with brass tubing. It is held in place by a No. 6 X 1-1/4″ round head brass screw, with washers.

The Mounting: The pivot hole has been drilled 5″ from the front of the model. One way to support the whirligig is to construct a 1-1/2″ X 1-1/2″ (or 2″ X 2″) support post of any appropriate length. Drill a lead hole 3″ to 4″ in the top to hold a 1/4″ steel rod. Tap in an 8″ rod, slip on several 1/4″ washers, and place the plane on it. The support post can be attached to a fence post, a building, or another post. An alternative post, to be placed in the ground, can be made from any 3/4″ or 1″ pipe. For this, make a stopper from a piece of wood measuring 1″ X 1″ X 4″. Mark off 1″ for a top, and whittle down the rest to fit into the top of the pipe. Drill a lead hole 3″ into the "cork" and set the steel rod in it. Place washers and the plane on top. If your plane is quite large, you will have to make heavier support posts.

Painting: Individual Jenny owners painted them as they liked, and you can do the same. A painting of a wartime Jenny shows it with a red, white, and blue vertically striped rudder, a yellow body from the wings aft, and a black body forward, including the rounded seat cowling area. The wooden propeller was varnished.

THE TIN GOOSE

In 1926 three young engineers from M.I.T. designed, at Henry Ford's request, the 4-AT, a trimotor airplane. It was made entirely of metal and cruised at about 100 miles per hour. Some 200 were built; one is in the Air and Space Museum in Washington, D.C., and some are still flying.

The overall size of the whirligig is the same as the Jenny, but the design is different, and it requires three propellers. It can also be made to more exact specifications and be larger or smaller than the model shown here (see Foldout No. 10).

Materials

Body	1-1/2" X 2-1/2" X 17-1/2"
Wing	3/4" X 4-1/2" X 24"
Engines	(3) 1/2" X 1-3/4" diameter
Landing gear & engine supports	
struts	1/4" X 1/2" X 4-3/4"
braces	1/4" X 1/2" X 6"
engine mounts	(2) 1" X 1-1/4" X 2-3/4"
wheel cover	(2)1/2" X 1" X 1-3/4"
Rudder	1/4" X 2-3/4" X 4-3/4"
Stabilizer	1/4" X 3-1/2" X 6"

PROCEDURE

Body: Cut the 17-1/2" body from a 2 X 4. The shape is flat on all sides but can be rounded in front of the cockpit to the point where the engine is mounted. Cut out the space for the wing. Between 5" and 6" back from the nose of the plane, drill a 3/8" hole 2-1/4" deep in the center of the body as a spindle socket. Line it with tubing, but be sure to test the tubing to make sure that a 1/4" steel rod will pass through it. Cap the hole with a screw or nail end. Attach one engine to the nose of the plane after drilling a lead hole through the center for a No. 6 screw.

Wing: The wing could be made of plywood, but it's best shaped out of 3/4" pine so it can maintain its rigidity. It can have an aerodynamic form, but this is not essential; it should be rounded off, sanded, and glued and nailed in place.

Rudder and Stabilizer: Cut out both items and round them off. The rudder should be attached to the stabilizer first, and then the unit should be attached to the body.

Landing Gear and Engine Supports: These were all together on the Ford Trimotor. Make the parts for the landing gear and the engine mountings. Attach the engines to the mountings. Then attach the mountings to the struts. When these are dry or secured, attach the brace to the body, then the strut to the wing, with glue and nails. When the glue is dry or the strut is firm, attach the wheel covers. These include the wheels, which can be whittled from the same piece to show beneath the covers.

Propellers: The trouble with attaching propellers to multimotored airplanes is that they cannot be made too large. In this model the side propellers cannot be more than 6" in diameter. The front one should be the same size, but it can be made larger. The hubs are fitted with metal tubing and the propellers are attached with No. 6 X 1-1/2" round head brass screws.

Painting: The entire plane, including the propellers, is silver or aluminum in color with the exception of the motors, which are black. The cockpit windows and the row of windows along either side may be painted in blue or black.

Mounting: Any support post should be drilled at least 4" deep for a 1/4" steel rod at least 10" long which will operate as the spindle. The rod should be slightly rounded on the top to facilitate turning.

CHAPTER 12
MULTIPLE ACTIVITY WHIRLIGIGS

Anyone who has seen a large, complex whirligig is astonished, if not somewhat overwhelmed, by the great variety of activities going on—or intended to go on—at the same time. The secret of comprehending them is to avoid looking at the entire apparatus all at once and to look for and identify each separate and distinct movement or activity. Such a whirligig is made up of many parts, all cleverly put together into a single whole. The movements are sometimes individual, but frequently they are linked so that one action leads to another in a Rube Goldberg series of episodes. The whirligigs in this section become increasingly complicated, but none are as complicated as those seen in some collections. Each one demonstrates a different way of turning circular motion into a different movement. The Moon Ship whirligig illustrates a double-cam device; Too Many Chickens shows how bent-wire cams work in a series with another activity; and The Nothing Factory demonstrates how different wheels and mechanical devices work together.

THE MOON SHIP

"Whimsical" is the description frequently given whirligigs, and this word aptly describes The Moon Ship model. A man and woman operate a strange flying machine that takes them into space. Technically this model also illustrates the operation of a double cam, a very useful mechanism in multiple activity whirligigs. In traditional whirligigs, there is usually one figure or object per cam, and some simple whirligigs have an acrobat or monkey swinging from the trapeze formed by the cam. If two or more figures are to operate from a single shaft, it is best to place the cams in sequence, or series, or at different angles to each other. For example, if two figures are used, as in Waving the Flag, then the cams should be opposite one another. In this model, I started with a single cam, but at one point, when the figures were being lifted together, there was too much weight on the shaft and the motion was not smooth. Rather than planning for a larger propeller, I made the double cam, and the opposing weights balance each other.

Materials: Wood

Frame	Baseboard	3/4″ X 5-1/2″ X 7″	
	Support ends	(2) 3/4″ X 1-3/4″ X 8″	
	Pivot base	3/4″ X 1-1/2″ X 7″	
	Top piece	3/4″ X 1-1/4″ X 7″	
	Tail	1/4″ X 6″ X 6″ (or larger)	

		Woman	Man
Figures			
	Leg	1/2″ X 1″ X 2-1/4″	1/2″ X 1″ X 2-3/4″
	Body	3/4″ X 1-1/4″ X 4″	3/4″ X 1-1/2″ X 4-1/2″
	Arms	(2) 1/4″ X 1″ X 3″	(2) 1/4″ X 1-1/4″ X 2-1/4″

Materials: Other

Tension pin 3/8″ X 2″, or other socket liner
14″ heavy wire for drive shaft
Some 6d finishing nails, (2) No. 6 X 1-1/4″ flat head screws for legs, (4) No. 4 X 3/4″ round head screws for arms, and some tubing as indicated.

ACTUAL SIZE

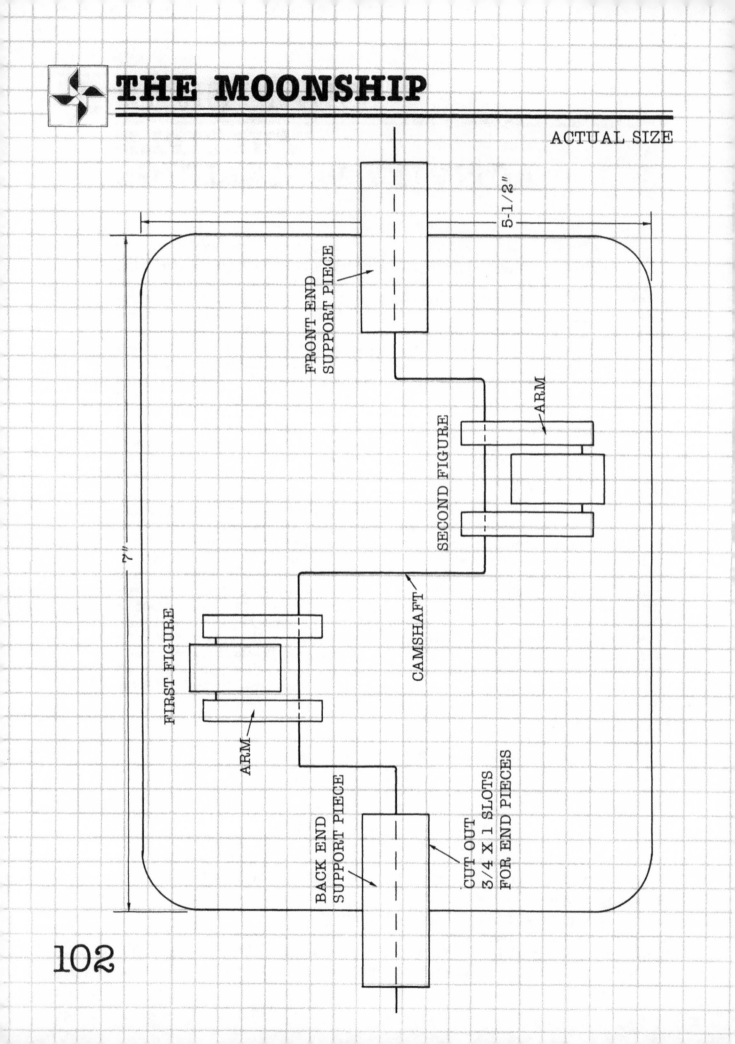

5-1/2"

FRONT END
SUPPORT PIECE

ARM

SECOND FIGURE

7"

CAMSHAFT

FIRST FIGURE

ARM

BACK END
SUPPORT PIECE

CUT OUT
3/4 X 1 SLOTS
FOR END PIECES

PROCEDURE

Frame: Cut out the baseboard, lay out the location of the figures, and make the cuts for the wood. Drill the holes for the legs only when you are sure of the final positions of the figures. Cut the pivot base. Drill the hole for the socket and secure it to the baseboard with nails and glue. The tension pin or some other socket liner, with cap, can be put in place. If desired, the frame can be mounted on a stand for further work.

Cut the front support piece and drill the hole for the drive shaft. This will be 4″ from the top of the baseboard and can be lined with brass tubing to reduce wear. The hole (and the tubing) must be wide enough to permit the shaft to move loosely and freely within it. Secure the front support piece with glue and a nail, making sure that it stands perpendicular to the base and that the drive shaft hole lies in a straight line down the center of the base.

Cut out the rear support piece and drill a hole to correspond with the one at the front. In the back of the piece, cut out a 1/4″ slot, 1/4″ to 3/8″ deep, to hold the tail. Do not glue the rear support piece in place at this time.

THE MOON SHIP
SIDE VIEW
1/2 SIZE

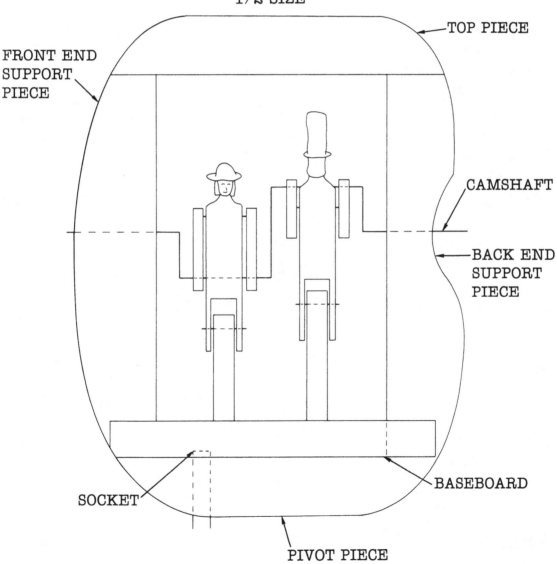

TOP PIECE

FRONT END
SUPPORT
PIECE

CAMSHAFT

BACK END
SUPPORT
PIECE

BASEBOARD

SOCKET

PIVOT PIECE

103

The Drive Shaft: Beginning at the back, bend the heavy wire to conform to the illustration. Make a right-angle bend 3-1/4″ from the end. Then make another at 1″ and the next at 2″, and so on along the line of the shaft. Try to keep everything even, making especially sure that the cam sections that will hold the hands will be in line with the sides of the baseboard where the figures will stand. Place the shaft in the front support piece, then through the back support piece while sliding that piece into position. If it is not too bent out of line, it should work freely. If you have trouble with this, first try bending the shaft into better alignment. If problems persist, enlarge the drilled holes.

The Figures: Cut out the bodies and legs. Leave them as silhouettes or carve them as much as you like, with facial features, etc. The main thing is to have the bodies and legs move without friction, so cut or file them down for free movement. Drill the holes, insert a rod or nail, and test the movement. Cut out the arms and drill the holes in the shoulders and hands. Tubing can be placed in the shoulder holes, but, unless the hand holes are quite large, tubing placed there will not pass around the bends of the camshaft. Mark the location of the shoulder holes on the bodies and start the screw holes there.

MOONSHIP FIGURES

ACTUAL SIZE

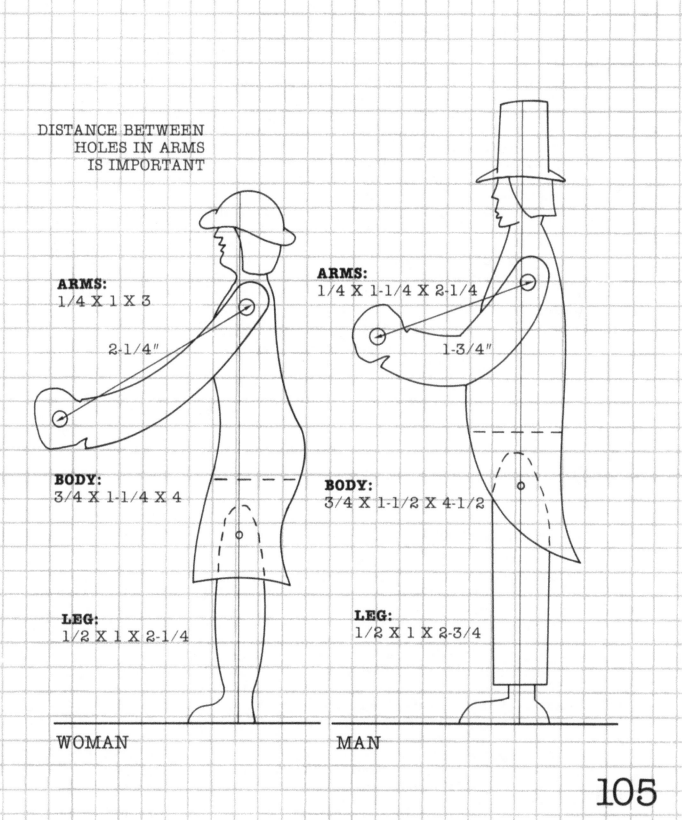

DISTANCE BETWEEN
HOLES IN ARMS
IS IMPORTANT

ARMS:
1/4 X 1 X 3

2-1/4"

BODY:
3/4 X 1-1/4 X 4

LEG:
1/2 X 1 X 2-1/4

WOMAN

ARMS:
1/4 X 1-1/4 X 2-1/4

1-3/4"

BODY:
3/4 X 1-1/2 X 4-1/2

LEG:
1/2 X 1 X 2-3/4

MAN

105

Test the figures and their positions. Slide the arms along the drive shaft, place the rear support piece in place, and attach the figures temporarily with 3/4" screws. Turn the drive shaft to see that all the parts work together properly. (This takes six hands!) Continued testing may be necessary, and adjustments may have to be made. Such testing is particularly necessary if the cams are not equal or are shallower or deeper than shown on the plan. I had to make three sets of the woman's arms before they were right. When everything is checked out, the position of the legs—in the center of the cams—should be marked.

Remove the shaft and drill the leg screw holes in the baseboard. Glue and screw the legs permanently to the base. They can be painted first, along with all parts of the figures.

Finishing the Frame: Place the rear support piece in position and square it to the base. Place the top piece in position and mark it for cutting, following the lines of the upright pieces. Cut it out for later attachment. All pieces can now be trimmed down into final shape, sanded, and painted when the tail is in place.

The Tail: Cut the tailpiece of 1/4" plywood (6" X 6" or 7"). It can be shaped differently than illustrated and may be made larger. Fasten it in the rear piece slot with glue and brads. Test the entire piece in position on the base. The rear end of the drive shaft may have to be trimmed off.

The Propeller: The propeller can be of any design and should be at least 12" in diameter. Clearance of the frame must be a prime consideration.

The four-bladed wood propeller illustrated here has 3/4" X 3/4" X 7" arms with attached blades measuring 1/8" X 2-1/2" X 6". It is drilled for a wire shaft. For an area of light wind, somewhat longer blades are suggested. Test it on the drive shaft and figure out how the washers and sleeves will be placed to allow the cams to be in proper position. Then paint it.

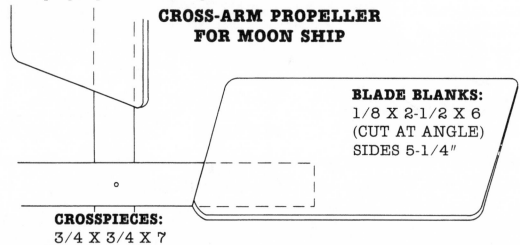

CROSS-ARM PROPELLER
FOR MOON SHIP

BLADE BLANKS:
1/8 X 2-1/2 X 6
(CUT AT ANGLE)
SIDES 5-1/4"

CROSSPIECES:
3/4 X 3/4 X 7

Final Assembly: Insert the drive shaft in the front support, then slip on the arms. Secure the rear support piece with glue and a nail at a right angle to the base, making sure that the camshaft turns easily. Secure the top piece with glue and nails. Some trimming, sanding, and repainting may be necessary here. Place the propeller on the drive shaft with washers and spacers, and secure it by bending the shaft and holding the end in place with a staple or nails.

Attach the figures, with washers between the shoulders and the arms.

NOTES: For more visual interest, drill a hole in the top near the rear and insert a flagpole, with a streamer flying back from the top.

If the whirligig does not respond quickly to wind direction, add some decorative light metal to the tail area.

If the propeller doesn't move readily, check to see that the holes are not binding and that the camshaft is not bent in the supports. Any sticking may be relieved by a drop of oil. If the movement continues to be sluggish, a larger propeller is recommended.

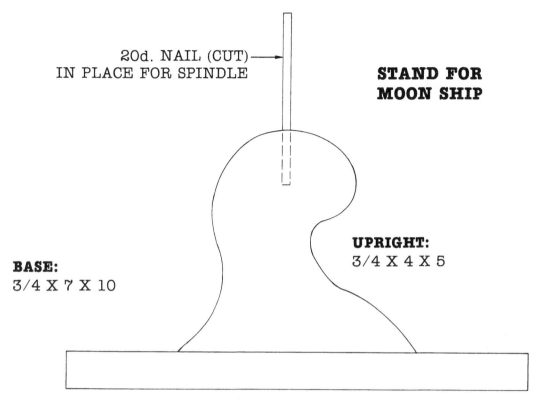

20d. NAIL (CUT)
IN PLACE FOR SPINDLE

**STAND FOR
MOON SHIP**

UPRIGHT:
3/4 X 4 X 5

BASE:
3/4 X 7 X 10

TOO MANY CHICKENS

The Too Many Chickens whirligig is an example of a multiple-cam operation. Not only do the four chickens move from a camshaft, but an extra circular cam operates a farmer endlessly throwing feed. When complex whirligigs of this type are built, special attention must be paid to timing the painting of the various parts. It would be most efficient to paint the parts as they are completed and their operation tested. However, many whirligig makers will prefer to see how the whole thing works before they paint any of the parts, which means disassembling some of the whirligig. Also, timing of nailing and gluing parts is important. No piece should be permanently fastened until all the parts that are associated with it are in final shape or position.

Materials: Wood

Platform or floor	3/4" X 5" X 15"
Front end	3/4" X 5" X 7"
Back end	3/4" X 5" X 6"
Pivot support piece	1-1/2" X 1-3/4" X 3"
Dowels (roosts)	(2) 1/4" X 17"
Cross supports	(2) 3/4" X 3/4" X 15"
Wheel (cam)	3/4" X 2" diameter
Back platform (farmer)	3/4" X 2" X 5"
Roof trim	(2) 1/4" X 1" X 5"
Farmer: body	1/4" X 4" X 9"
legs	3/4" X 2" X 5-3/4"
arms	(2) 1/4" X 2" X 4-1/2"
shoulders	(2) 3/4" X 3/4" X 2"
Wooden washer	3/4" X 1-1/4" diameter
Wood hub braces	(2) 3/4" X 3/4" X 1-1/4"
Chickens	(4) 3/4" X 2-1/2" X 7"

Materials: Other

Socket lining	metal tubing or 2" tension pin
Camshaft	heavy drapery wire, 28"
Screw eyes	5 small
Chicken legs	(8) 6d finishing nails
Figure joint	(1) small bolt or 1-1/4" machine screw
Other	3' relatively thick and firm connecting wire
	(2) No. 4 X 3/4" round head screws, for arms
	brads, nails, & screws as needed
	(2) steel washers, 1/4"

PROCEDURE

The Chicken House: (See Foldout No. 11.) Cut out the floor first. Drill the holes for the pivot support piece 3" back from the front end and 1" to the left and right of the centerline.

Prepare the pivot support. In the center, drill a hole for the spindle socket and put the socket liner in place with a socket cap. Screw the pivot support to the floor. The base can now be mounted on a stand for further work. A short stand with a 12"-square plywood base will support this work to completion. To clear a 24" to 26" propeller, the mounting post must be at least 10" high.

Cut out the front and back ends. Drill holes for the drive shaft in the center, 2-1/2" from the bottom of each piece. The front end hole can be lined with metal tubing. Cut a slot in the back end to permit sliding the drive shaft into the hole. This must be kept open until the whirligig is completed.

Drill the holes for the 1/4" dowel chicken supports. They are placed 5" from the end pieces and are 1/2" from the sides.

Nail and glue, or screw, the front and back ends in place. Then nail and glue the cross support pieces up 3" from the bottom of the base. Nail the front roofline in place. The piece may be painted at this point.

The Camshaft: Using the heavy wire, bend the camshaft as indicated with each cam in a different direction. Beginning at the back end, first make a 1/2" right-angle bend to hold the wheel in place. Then measure off another 2": this marks the inside of the chicken house "wall." Use this as a checkpoint. Measure off 2-1/2" more and make the first cam; it will be 3/4" deep and 1" across. Then allow for 2" of straight wire and make another cam, but make it in a direction different from the first. Proceed another 2" and repeat the process until four cams are made. There will be about 2-1/2" remaining inside the structure and 4" or more on the outside, or propeller, end. Try to keep the camshaft as straight as possible. If the cams are lopsided, square them off.

The front end of the camshaft will go through the hole in the front, and the rear end will slip into the back end slot. Put the shaft in position and carefully mark the centers of the cams on the cross support pieces. This will show where the chickens will be positioned.

Prepare spools for the connecting wire for each of the cams (see chapter 2). They will measure 1/2" X 1/2" X 3/4", and each will be drilled through the center. Cut them in half lengthwise and glue them around the camshaft. If they are to be lined, first cut a 3/4" length of tubing and saw that in half lengthwise on one side. Pry it around the camshaft and glue the wooden spool over it. The drilled holes must allow for the thickness of the camshaft and the dimensions of the tubing.

On the 2" wheel, cut out a slot, at least as deep as the drive shaft is thick, 1/2" out from the hub. Attach the wheel to the drive shaft, countersinking the bent end into the slot. A small staple or a brad bent over it will secure it, or a wooden wedge can be glued over it. About 1/4" in from the rim, screw a No. 4 X 3/4" round head screw about halfway in. This is for the connecting wire to the farmer.

The Chickens: Cut out the four chickens. At a point of approximate balance or center of gravity, drill a 5/16" hole and insert 5/16" tubing for lining. (NOTE: The chicken must fit loosely, but firmly, on a 1/4" dowel.) Shape the chickens somewhat and sand them down. Put the 1/4" dowels in position with two chickens on each of them in alternate positions on opposite sides, facing out. Again, mark their locations vis-à-vis the centers of the cams.

Place a small screw eye in the bottom of each chicken at the base of the tail. Attach connecting wire from the cams to the chickens and test out the mechanism. The chickens should dive for feed at different intervals.

Secure the chickens so they won't move sideways by placing 6d finishing nails (legs) into the cross support pieces alongside the chickens. It is advisable to mark their location and drill lead holes first. Do not drive these in permanently until final assembly.

The Farmer—Can Be a Woman or Man: Cut out the parts of the farmer and glue the shoulder pieces on the torso. Drill the joint holes. If desired, both the farmer's body and the arm holes can be drilled with a 3/16″ bit and lined with brass tubing. Turn a small screw eye into the bottom of the tailcoat for the connecting rod to the wheel.

Construct the back platform and secure the farmer's legs to it with a screw from the bottom. The back of the legs will be at the back of the platform. Position the platform on the back end of the whirligig so the screw eye will be just over the cam wheel screw. Attach the body to the legs with a bolt or rod. When the platform is in the best position, nail and glue it to the top of the back end.

Attach the farmer's arms to the projecting shoulder pieces with 3/4″ screws and washers. They are kept loose so, as the body moves back and forth, the arms also swing, throwing feed. If the action is not correct, check the shape of the arms and the position of the screws. At this point consider painting the parts before the final assembly.

The Propeller: Make a multibladed propeller 24″ to 26″ in diameter, drilled in the center for a wire shaft. Make sure your design will permit the blades to clear the chicken house. For constructing a six-bladed propeller for this whirligig, make the hub 3/4″ thick and 3″ in diameter, drilled in the center with a small hole. With a 3/8″ bit drill six holes, 3/4″ deep, in the rim. Make six arms, 1/2″ X 1/2″ X 10-1/2″. Trim one end of each to fit into a hub hole. Shape light aluminum blades, 4″ X 8″, tapered to narrow at the bottom. Tack the centered blades on the arms, down 6″ from the outer ends, with 1/2″ wire nails. Glue the arm ends into the holes at the same angle (35 to 45 degrees). Secure the bases of the arms by driving 3/4″ brads through the hub.

With the camshaft in proper position, measure the front end of the wire. Allow for washers, a sleeve or spool-type wooden washer to keep the propeller clear, the propeller itself, and the end needed for securing the propeller. Prepare all parts for final assembly.

ASSEMBLY OF FRONT END WASHERS AND PROPELLER

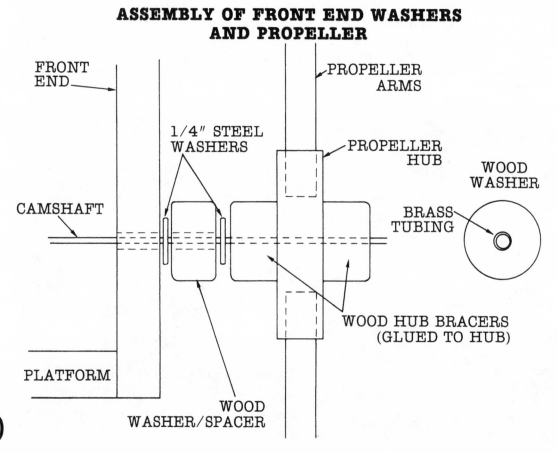

FRONT END

PROPELLER ARMS

1/4″ STEEL WASHERS

PROPELLER HUB

WOOD WASHER

CAMSHAFT

BRASS TUBING

PLATFORM

WOOD HUB BRACERS (GLUED TO HUB)

WOOD WASHER/SPACER

TOO MANY CHICKENS

1 SQUARE = 1/2 INCH

**CHICKEN HOUSE
FRONT END**

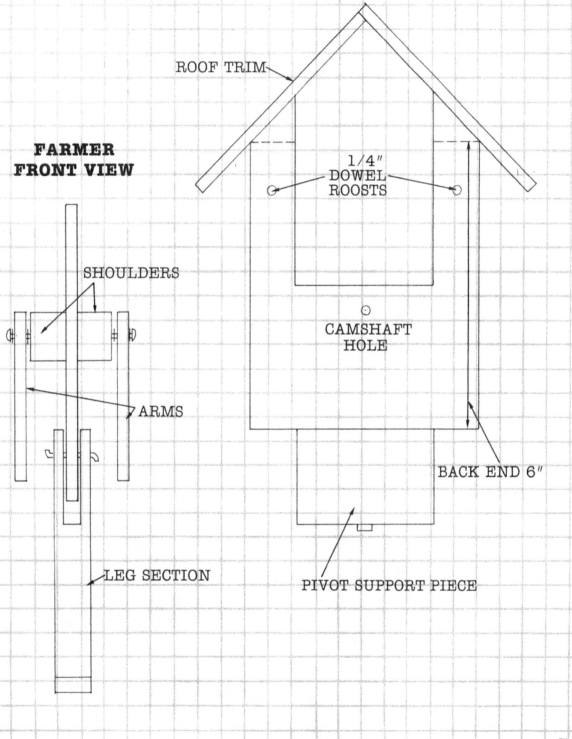

ROOF TRIM

1/4"
DOWEL
ROOSTS

**FARMER
FRONT VIEW**

SHOULDERS

CAMSHAFT
HOLE

ARMS

BACK END 6"

LEG SECTION

PIVOT SUPPORT PIECE

111

Final Assembly: When all the mechanisms operate satisfactorily, glue the dowels in place, if this has not been done already. Position the chickens and drive in the "legs." Make all final connecting wire adjustments. Where the camshaft rests in the rear slot, bend a piece of metal to fit around it to serve as a sleeve. Place a wooden wedge in the slot to keep the shaft in place.

Using two steel washers and a wood washer between it and the front, connect the propeller. One way of securing a propeller of the type described above is to make two 1-1/4"-diameter wooden hub braces with small holes drilled in the center. (Wooden washers will have holes that are larger than the diameter of the shaft.) The hub braces are glued fore and aft of the propeller hub while it is in position on the shaft. If epoxy or similar glue is used to secure all parts on the camshaft, it may not be necessary to bend the tip of the shaft over the hub and tie it down.

The mechanisms in this whirligig can be used for many other activities. Also, the various activities need not have been limited to positions above the camshaft; they could have been moved to another "floor" or to the sides. It's important to remember that when long camshafts are used, the weight of objects moved by each cam can be kept at a minimum through proper balancing and alteration of movement. For example, when one piece moves up, another should move down, and so on. Objects or bodies to be placed in motion should rest in equilibrium; the chickens are perfectly balanced on the dowels. The farmer was dressed in a protruding tailcoat because when he was dressed only in a shirt, he fell heavily forward, and his weight had to be counterbalanced.

THE NOTHING FACTORY

Now and then a whirligig maker just wants to see what he or she can do with mechanical contrivances. The title of this whirligig suggests that it is a factory, but while things go round, and up and down, and back and forth, and there is a lot of action, nothing is actually accomplished. Its distinguishing feature is that it is made entirely of wood except for some small nuts, bolts, washers, and tubing. As a last resort, some inside corner irons were added for rigidity, but these braces could have been made of wood too. The use of different wheels on the drive shaft is illustrated in this model. There are four main wheels, and each powers a different activity.

As complicated whirligigs are best understood in terms of their units, each area of activity is described separately, along with a list of materials. Some of these units may be made as whirligig objects independent of the larger structure. The base is also discussed separately, as it serves as a platform for all the activity, which must be planned and executed step by step by unit. This is a whirligig that will take time to construct. Improvements can be made in the design, and new ideas will come to the builder as the work proceeds. For example, when the whirligig was in the last stages of construction, my wife asked, referring to the man at the machine, "Will he have another arm?" I said, "Yes, I'll tack one on later." Then it suddenly occurred to me that, instead of attaching separate arms with screws, I could have joined the arms on a common axle, balanced so that both could move easily and give more action to the figure. Well, there's always a next time!

Materials

Baseboard	3/4″ X 10″ X 24″
Pivot base	1-1/2″ X 2-1/2″ X 6″
Front sides	(2) 3/4″ X 1″ X 6″
Top piece	3/4″ X 2″ X 10″
Center (cut out)	3/4″ X 6″ X 8″

The Platform: (See Foldout No. 12.) Cut out the baseboard, either of solid stock or 3/4″ exterior plywood. Use the top as a drawing board. Draw the centerline first. From the front end, mark off 18″; this will be the "factory" area. Draw a tail slot 4″ in from the rear end. Then, in the "factory" area, mark off the drive shaft and the wheel locations; use a square for accurate measurements. Locate all the additional parts; check their sizes in the sections that follow before locating them on the platform. The drive shaft and wheel locations will be permanent; the location of related parts may require slight adjustment as you proceed.

Locate the pivot base, and drill the holes for the screws that will hold it. Do not attach the pivot base to the platform until the whirligig is practically finished. You will need a steady platform to work on. Prepare the pivot base with a socket that will take either a 1/4″ or 3/8″ steel rod, at least 2″ deep. Note that the pivot base piece can run lengthwise along the bottom of the platform rather than across it, if you wish. In that case, make an adjustment for the screw holes. The socket will be in the same position, 6″ back from the front edge of the whirligig.

Read the section about the paddle wheel and decide if you want to cut a hole in the platform for a swinging piece that will hang beneath the whirligig with a monkey or something on it. If so, cut the hole now.

Cut out the tail slot. This will be a thin line if a metal tail is used and a wider slot if the tail is of wood. Trim the rear end by cutting out corresponding curves on each side of the slot. A vertical tail shaped from a piece 10″ X 10″ is suggested, but do not add a tail until the whirligig is almost finished; it may get in your way.

Put the front section in place with nails and glue. The reason for having it in pieces and the middle piece cut out is to permit viewing of the interior as well as for a decorative effect. Drill a 1/2″ hole, 3-1/2″ up from the bottom, in the middle of the center piece. This will be for the drive shaft and will place the center of the shaft 2-3/4" above the platform floor. To hold the front "wall" at right angles, I put two 2" corner braces at the edges of the front end.

Materials

Shaft	3/8" dowel, 20" long
Wheels	(4) 3/4" X 2" diameter
Paddles	(4) 1/8" X 3/4" X 1"
Wood washers	(2) 3/4" X 1" diameter
Support posts	3/4" X 3" X 3-1/2"
Nails	1" brads
Washers	(2) 3/8"

The Drive Shaft: The drive shaft must be set in place first. On it mark the exact location of each part. To begin with, it will extend back exactly 15" from inside the front. Mark off each wheel location; they are 3-1/4" apart for the first three wheels, and the last one is 2-1/4" from the third. To make sure I had everything uniform, I simply marked off every four inches and backed up the wheels to those points.

Construct the six 2" wheels. A hole saw will do this readily, although some door drill sets will cut the wheels 1-7/8" in diameter. If you use a hole saw, enlarge the center holes with a 3/8" bit to fit the drive shaft—with the exception of wheel No. 1, that is, as it is an eccentric. Drill this 3/8" off-centered hub hole in 1/2" from the outer edge of the wheel. Wheel No. 2 needs to be made into a spool or pulley type; a 1/4" groove can be made with a rat-tail file. Cut four 1/4" slots in wheel No. 3 and glue in the paddles. Wheel No. 4 needs only a small hole drilled through it about 1/4" in from the outer edge. Put the two other wheels aside until construction for the second unit is under way. With a small bit, drill a lead hole for a 1" brad from the middle of the rim of each wheel to the center. This will be used to make the wheel rigid to the drive shaft.

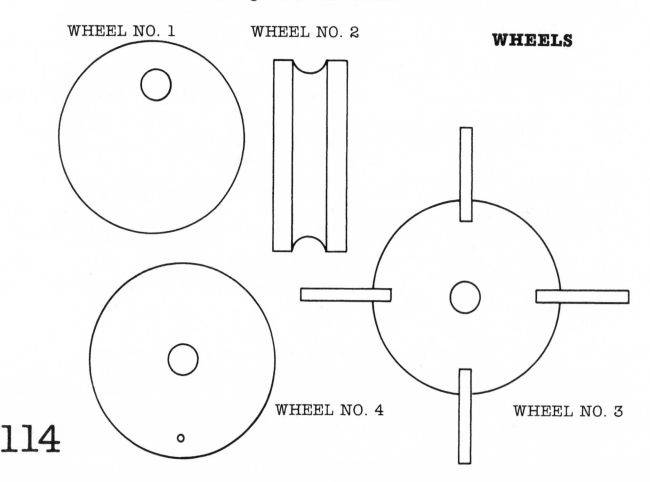

WHEEL NO. 1   WHEEL NO. 2   **WHEELS**

WHEEL NO. 4   WHEEL NO. 3

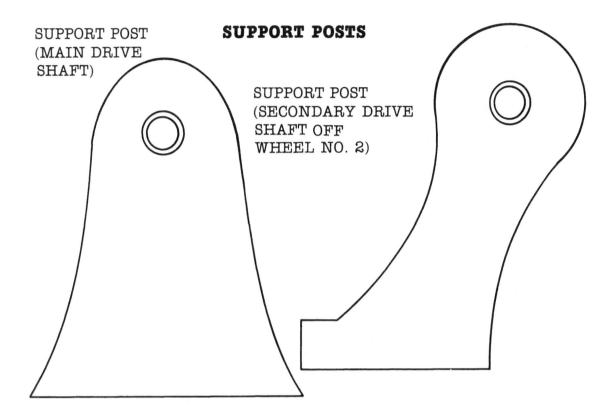

SUPPORT POST
(MAIN DRIVE
SHAFT)

SUPPORT POSTS

SUPPORT POST
(SECONDARY DRIVE
SHAFT OFF
WHEEL NO. 2)

Make the support posts. Drill a 1/2" hole in the top center, 2-3/4" from the bottom. Drill holes for screws in the platform where they will be located.

Make the wooden washers, drilled with a 3/8" hole.

Begin gluing on the wheels with the fourth wheel (at the end) first. Drive in a long brad to hold it firmly to the drive shaft. The next piece is a support post; keep that loose. Then glue the third wheel in position, and slide on the next support post. Affix the second and the first wheels. At this point, with a wooden washer on the inside, slide the drive shaft into the front hole. The support posts can now be glued and nailed in place and secured with 1-1/4" flat head screws. Next, place the drive shaft in position with its 15" inside length marked. Place two 3/8" steel washers in front and slide on a wooden washer. Glue the wooden washer in place snugly against the front and secure it with a brad into the drive shaft. Then, leaving a little room, or "play," secure the back wooden washer. The front washer will tend to keep the wheels in position; the back washer acts to keep the drive shaft in its proper place in case the wind backs up on the propeller.

The First Wheel: Wheel No. 1 is an eccentric cam, and its odd circular movement makes a vertical post move up and down, which in turn moves a lever.

Materials

Wheel	3/8" hub drilled off center, 1/2" from outside edge of wheel
Support tower	3/4" X 2" X 4-3/4"
top	3/4" X 1-1/4" X 4-1/2"
pole	1/4" dowel, 10" long
block	3/4" X 1" X 2"
Rocker (lever) arm	1/8" X 1/2" X 8"
Rider wheels	1/4" steel washers, with No. 6 X 3/4" machine bolt axle
Other	1/16" brass rods, 1-1/2" brass tubing (3/8"), machine bolts

115

SUPPORT TOWER

WHEEL NO. 1

ACTUAL SIZE

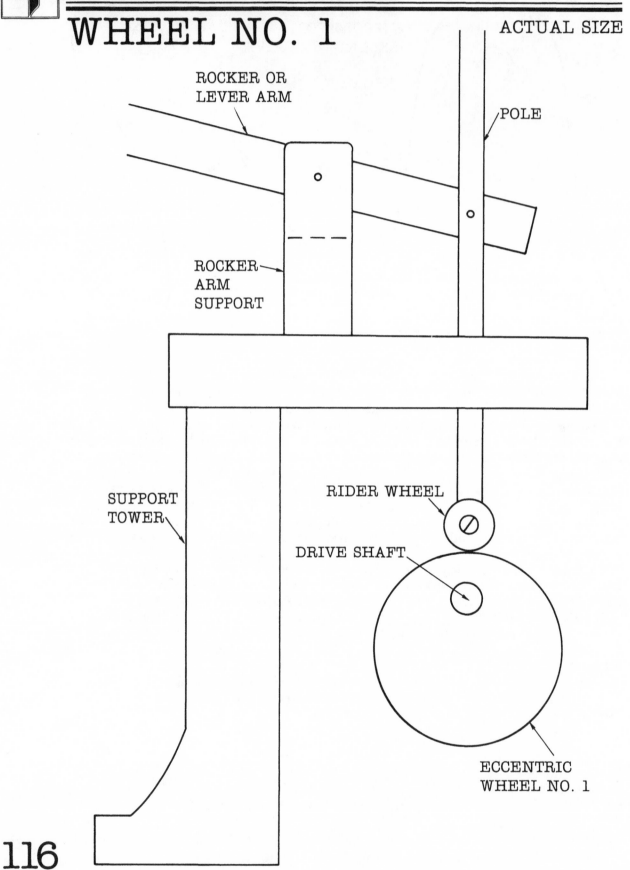

ROCKER OR
LEVER ARM

POLE

ROCKER
ARM
SUPPORT

SUPPORT
TOWER

RIDER WHEEL

DRIVE SHAFT

ECCENTRIC
WHEEL NO. 1

Make the support tower. Drill the hole for the tubing so it will be right over the center of the drive shaft when the tower is in position. Check the base location, drill a hole in the platform, and secure the tower to the platform. Insert the tubing in the top hole.

Drill a small hole through the dowel near one end for a No. 6 machine bolt. Slide the dowel through the tubing onto the wheel. Put the washers in place on either side of the rod with the machine bolt as an axle. As the drive wheel turns, mark the clearance of the pole on top of the tubing. About 1/2" above the top mark, drill a small hole through the dowel parallel to the bolt/axle for the rider wheels.

Cut out the lever block and the off-side slot for the lever or rocker arm. Drill a hole for the brass rod axle and glue it in position. Cut out the lever rocker arm, and drill holes to line up with the axle on the lever block and the hole on the pole. Secure the end of the rocker arm to the pole with a machine bolt and test the movement.

The Second Wheel: Wheel No. 2 is a pulley type and will have a similar wheel connected to it with a belt. To construct the second mechanism, shape the support posts to look like machinery and drill 1/2" holes with centers 2" above the platform level. Mark their location with the drive wheel temporarily in place on the drive shaft; that wheel must be directly in line with wheel No. 2 and similarly cut or filed with a 1/4" groove. Drill holes in the platform for screws to hold the posts firmly, and attach the posts to the platform with glue and additional nails.

Materials

Drive shaft	3/8" diameter, 6" long
Wheels	(2) 3/4" X 2" diameter
Wood washers	3/4" X 3/4" diameter
Metal washers	(2) 3/8"
Support posts	3/4" X 2-3/4" X 3"
Figures	
Woman: block	3/4" X 1-1/2" X 3"
leg	1/2" X 1" X 1-1/4"
arms	(2) 1/8" X 1" X 2-1/4"
Man: block	3/4" X 1-1/2" X 4-1/2"
arms	(2) 1/8" X 1-1/2" X 4-1/2"
Other	brass rods and tubing, screws

Begin with the other wheel. Drill a small hole through it 1/4" from the outer edge. Then glue and nail it to the end of the shaft. Glue a wooden washer next to it, place a steel washer next to that, and insert it in the support posts with the connecting wheel in position. Glue that wheel in place and secure it with a brad through to the shaft. Place another steel washer on the shaft, then glue a wooden washer next to that, allowing for some free play.

Test the entire movement by tying heavy string or a cord around the wheels and turning the drive shaft. Note that the final belt should be completely smooth; a knot or bulge may cause the movement to stop. Any thick cord will do for a belt; I used a 1/4" braided nylon rope. Either sew the ends together edgewise or, in the case of artificial cords, melt them together.

The figures may now be made and fixed in place. The man figure and the woman's leg section are glued and held in place with screws. Their positions first should be checked with the wheels turning. A narrow 2" rod is placed in the solid wheel and through the woman's hands. She should move back and forth without hindrance. In the other end of the shaft, a 1/16" hole is drilled through the side of the shaft and a 1" brass rod inserted. The right arm of the man holding the hammer is lifted by this bar and then is allowed to drop. Proper balancing with the left arm (connected on a common axle through the shoulder) is required for this action, and testing is necessary. Sometimes weights (small screws turned into the hand or arm will do) are needed; sometimes a heavier arm or a heavier hammer will do the trick. It may be necessary to drive in a brad to act as a stop, to prevent the arm from flying too far back. On the figures themselves, arm sockets and hand holes may have brass tubing in them to reduce wear.

FIGURES OFF WHEEL NO. 2

ACTUAL SIZE

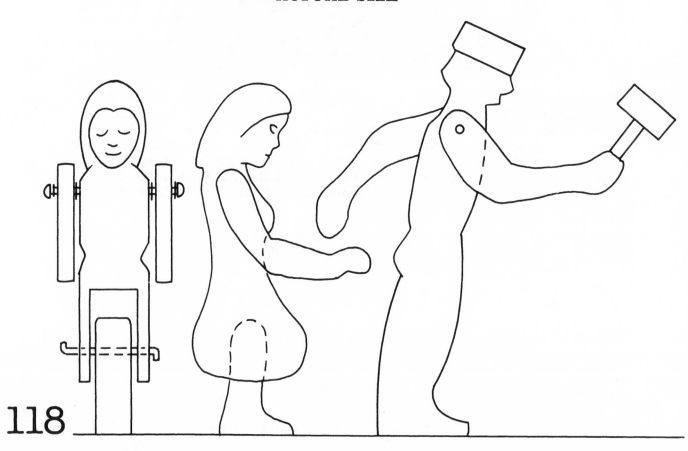

The Third Wheel: This is the paddle wheel designed to tap a balanced arm so that it swings sideways or up and down, depending on its relation to the center of rotation. In this case, an arm is suspended from above. An arm may also be suspended below, with the top projecting through a hole cut in the platform.

Materials

Post	1/2" X 1" X 9"
Crosspieces	(2) 3/8" X 1/2" X 6"
Side supports	1/2" X 1/2" X 1"
Arm	1/2" X 1/4" X 6"

Construct the upright post with crosspieces reaching over the drive shaft 7" above the platform. Drill holes for the 1/16" rod, 1" from the end of the crosspiece. Check the position of the post; the holes should be directly above the center of the drive shaft. Secure the post with glue and a screw through the platform. To make sure the post is perpendicular to the platform, check it with a square and fix the side supports with nails and glue.

Cut out the hanging arm piece and drill the hole for the rod about 3-1/4" from one end. This should clear the drive wheel but allow the paddles to strike it as the wheel turns. If an arm swinging from beneath is desired, it can be suspended on a rod stapled across the hole at the bottom or at the top. Testing the rod and arm should be done before the rod is secured in place. Such a swinging arm can be made more intriguing if an acrobat or a monkey can be swinging from it.

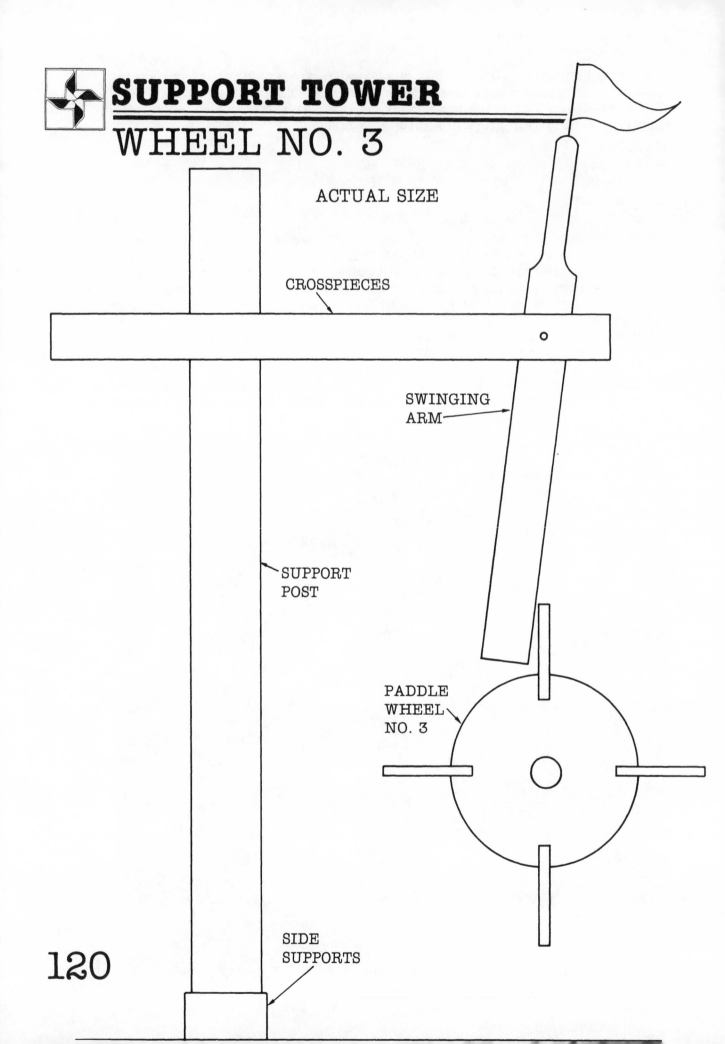

SUPPORT TOWER
WHEEL NO. 3

ACTUAL SIZE

CROSSPIECES

SWINGING
ARM

SUPPORT
POST

PADDLE
WHEEL
NO. 3

120

SIDE
SUPPORTS

The Fourth Wheel: Wheel No. 4 is an end cam which supports two human figures at work: a woman turning the handle and a man operating a machine. All are attached with wooden arms and connecting rods.

Materials

Machine block (can be made of two pieces of 3/4″ lumber)	1-1/2″ X 3″ X 3-1/2″
Tool arm	1/8″ X 1/2″ X 7-1/2″
Connecting rod	1/8″ X 1/2″ X 3-1/4″
Figures	
Woman: block	3/4″ X 1-1/2″ X 4-1/2″
arms	(2) 1/8″ X 1″ X 2″
leg block	1/2″ X 1″ X 2″
Man: block	3/4″ X 3″ X 6″
shoulders	(2) 3/8″ X 3/4″ X 1″
arm (bent)	1/8″ X 2-1/4″ X 2-1/2″
Other	screws, rods for axles, and bolts for connections; two pieces of thin stiff wire, 3″ long

Make the various pieces first because the main job will be to connect the different parts at the same time. Holes in the arms and rods are drilled with a 3/16″ bit and may be lined with brass tubing. Axle holes, such as in legs, are 3/32″ or small enough to allow 1/16″ brass rods—or similar rods or nails—a stable fit. The bottom of the woman is cut out to allow access to the pedestal-type leg piece. The man has shoulder pieces added to permit room for the movements of the tool arm and the connecting rod.

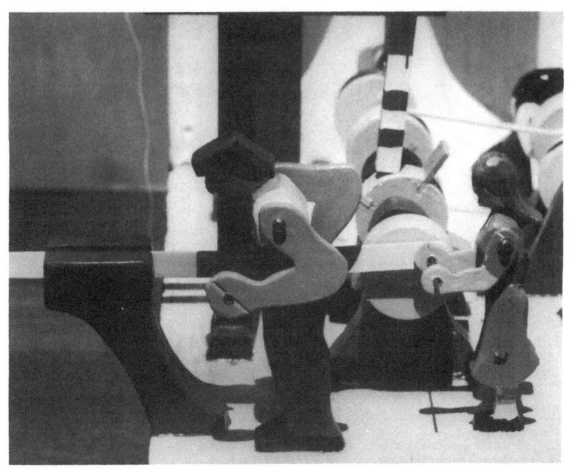

FACTORY FIGURES
FOR FOURTH WHEEL

1 SQUARE = 1/2 INCH

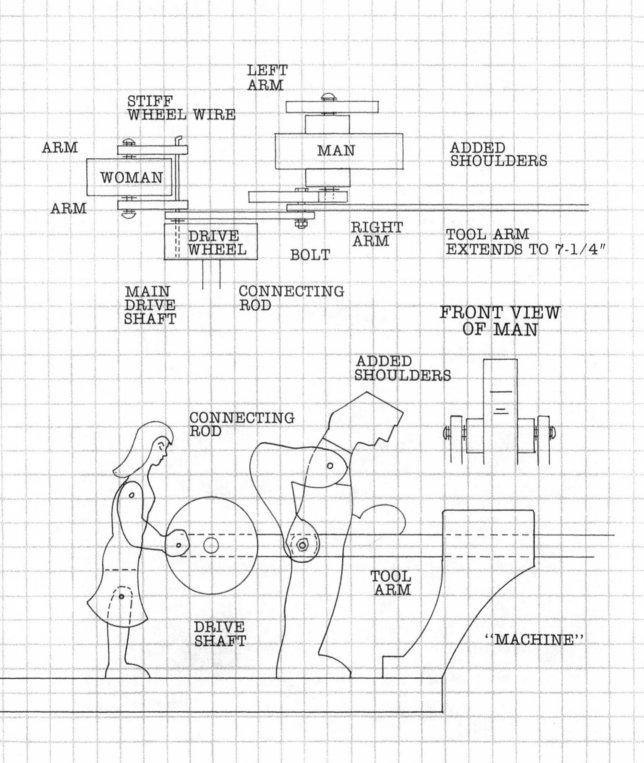

LEFT
ARM

STIFF
WHEEL WIRE

ARM

MAN

ADDED
SHOULDERS

WOMAN

ARM

RIGHT
ARM

TOOL ARM
EXTENDS TO 7-1/4"

DRIVE
WHEEL

BOLT

MAIN
DRIVE
SHAFT

CONNECTING
ROD

FRONT VIEW
OF MAN

ADDED
SHOULDERS

CONNECTING
ROD

TOOL
ARM

DRIVE
SHAFT

"MACHINE"

In the hole in the drive wheel (1/4″ in from the rim), force a stiff wire about 3″ long. Later it can be cut and glued in. This becomes the drive rod. One end of the connecting rod will be placed in it first. The woman's hands will come next.

Secure the machine; it is located so that the tool arm will rest in it horizontally and move back and forth when it is attached to the connecting rod and to the man's hand with a No. 4 or No. 6 machine bolt. The measurements in the illustration are correct, but test the movement of the man and machine, and mark their proper location. Drill holes through the platform and secure the man and machine to the platform with glue, screws, and nails.

Position the woman so her arms move easily when the drive rod moves as the wheel turns. Check and mark the position of her leg section. Test the entire movement. Then drill a hole in the platform and secure her legs.

Painting and Final Assembly: The tail can now be added in the tail slot. If metal, it is secured with nails and, if wood, with glue and nails.

The pivot base can be screwed in place and the entire whirligig mounted on a stand at least 12″ high and with a wide base.

All parts may be painted, at least with an undercoat, when they are first made, or the pieces may be disassembled and painted at this point. It is best to plan for a cohesive painting job. The whirligig may be made to look like a "factory" with steel gray machinery, or the pieces may be made more colorful. I made the front red, the floor yellow, the wall white, the machine supports dark blue-gray, and the drive shaft and wheels light gray-blue.

In final assembly, start with wheel No. 1 and make all the connections permanent. To keep the nut of the rider wheel bolt in place, turn it in with a spot of glue. Bend the ends of the axles so they won't become loose. Permanently fix the man and woman in position off wheel No. 2. Make sure the rods are tight and that the belt is fitted correctly. Check all the connections for the other wheels. Then test the entire movement and make any necessary alterations.

The Propeller: A large propeller at least 24″ in diameter with eight blades is recommended for this whirligig. It may be entirely of wood or have metal blades. The general dimensions of such a propeller are as follows:

Hub:	3/4″ X 3″ diameter, with hub center drilled for 3/8″ drive shaft; rim drilled for eight arms, 3/4″ deep with 3/8″ bit
Arms:	1/2″ X 1/2″ X 10″, whittled down at one end to fit in hub
Blades:	8″ lengths, tapered down from 5″ on the outside to 2″ on the inside. They are center-fastened to the arms with 1/2″ wire nails, and extend 2″ beyond the ends of the arms.

Final Features: Construction of a whirligig like this will indicate to any craftsperson why the old whirligigs were indeed one-of-a-kind. Even if you copied one, you would come up with something different; you would see new ways of doing things, additional activities to try, and new movements to experiment with. On The Nothing Factory, I changed my plan at least five times after I first laid it out, and I invented four new movements that were not in the script. That's how the more complicated whirligigs were made years ago, by trial and error.

Much can be added to a whirligig of this type to make it more exciting. For example, a human figure can stand at the edge of the platform under the end of the lever arm. Attach a wire or fishing line to the arm so that it moves as the lever moves. There are other possibilities. I will try these, too, and perhaps add a larger propeller. However, for this book I decided to stop with the original purpose—to illustrate how to change circular motion to other movements—completed.

Nonmoving features also make a whirligig intriguing. This whirligig can have flags flying here and there, on the building, and on any loose end such as at the tops of swinging poles. The flags can be made of lightweight metal and pressed over thin wire poles.

CHAPTER 13

EXHIBITING AND MARKETING WHIRLIGIGS

There is a market for whirligigs, and there are a number of opportunities to show whirligigs in exhibitions. The actual sales of whirligigs and their acceptance by judges will, of course, depend largely on the quality of workmanship, but the opportunities for involvement in the marketplace are many. There are local, state, regional, and national arts and crafts exhibitions, and, similarly, there are local and other outlets for crafts products. Entering such shows and marketing one's products may seem bewildering, if not somewhat frightening, to a beginner. How does one get into a show? How can one gain acceptance by a gallery or a store? There are ways to break into the crafts world of exhibitions and markets, and they are the same for the whirligig maker as for other craftspersons.

THE CRAFT ASSOCIATIONS

The whirligig maker should consider joining a craft association. There are several woodcraft and woodcarving organizations that encourage the craftsperson and support his or her enterprise. They publish papers and journals which contain articles on what others are doing in the field, drawings and photographs of models and products, and times and places of exhibitions related to woodwork. An example of such an organization is The National Wood Carvers Association, 7424 Miami Avenue, Cincinnati, OH 45243, a nonprofit organization dedicated to the interests of amateur and professional carvers and whittlers. It publishes the bimonthly Chip Chats, a journal entirely devoted to the wood craftsperson. This contains articles on what is occurring in the world of woodcrafts, tells where exhibitions, shows, and jamborees are being held, and includes a number of notes on new ideas, materials, and books. Mention is occasionally made of whirligigs.

On another level is the prestigious American Craft Council, a national, nonprofit membership organization which promotes interest in contemporary crafts. It maintains the American Craft Museum and publishes the magazine, American Craft. Each issue contains a calendar of exhibitions, by state and city. While many of these are organized special showings such as "New England Pewter" and "Shaker Furniture," other items provide information on arts and crafts fairs and juried shows open to craftspersons. The American Craft Council presents craft markets in various parts of the country through its subsidiary, American Craft Enterprises. The Council is an affiliate member of the World Craft Council and is located at 72 Spring Street, New York, NY 10012-0419. Membership includes a subscription to the magazine, various discounts, and free admission to the crafts markets sponsored by American Craft Enterprises, Inc.

In addition to national organizations there are state and regional crafts societies. These are usually listed in crafts publications and directories found in local libraries. Occasionally there are community associations of small membership, open only to persons who reside in the area. Affiliation with these organizations can be of considerable support to craftspersons. They will stimulate interest in pursuing new avenues of design and manufacture. Contact with other woodworkers will result in the sharing of knowledge and experience.

EXHIBITIONS

The whirligig maker should enter as many shows and exhibitions as is feasible for his or her own purposes. Some, whose purpose it is to make an income or even a living from crafts manufacture, may intend to enter all kinds of shows, regional and national. Others, whose purposes are more moderate, may wish to enter only an occasional or a local show. It should be pointed out that exhibitions often require that many whirligigs be available. In addition, there can be a considerable cost involved in exhibiting. Beginners should think of entering a local show when exhibiting for the first time. Shows and exhibitions fall into several categories.

Shows to Honor Crafts: First of all, there is the exhibition that has the highest prestige, which is organized to honor the crafts and craftspersons. In 1983, the State of North Carolina, through the North Carolina Museum of History and the sponsorship of the governor, held the state's first juried crafts exhibition in Raleigh. The jurors included a curator of the Smithsonian, the president of the Rhode Island School of Design, and a noted designer/craftsperson from Georgia. The exhibition was open without charge to all craftspersons who were residents of the state. With some misgivings, I entered four whirligigs; to my surprise, not only were two accepted, but they won honorable mentions. While products are available for purchase at such exhibitions, the main purpose is not commercial but to encourage arts and crafts. Take the opportunity to enter exhibitions of this character if they occur in your area.

Organizational Shows: Second, there is the arts and crafts exhibition sponsored by an organization for its members only. To become a member and be admitted to exhibitions, one must submit an application and a selected number of 35mm slides of one's work. This process helps maintain standards of high quality in craftsmanship. It also provides the judges with a chance to discourage people who have not shown much originality or who appear to know only how to make things from complete kits, and then not too well. Selection panels do not operate to shut new people out; they are most anxious to admit those who take pride in their work, who have a creative interest in woodcrafts, and who do a fairly good job. Whirligig makers who want the prestige of having such an organization behind them are encouraged to make application, because, among other advantages, it will give them confidence in their work and abilities. If one is not accepted the first time, one should try again the next time applications are called for.

The exhibitions sponsored by such organizations usually involve renting a booth or space for the period of the exhibition. This may be indoors or outdoors, and pity the poor outdoor exhibitor when the winds blow and the rains fall. However, one takes one's chances when one considers exhibiting!

Gallery Exhibitions: Another type of exhibition is a show put on by a gallery, where one is invited to submit pieces for exhibition. Under such circumstances, the gallery managers or curators take considerable care to display the objects to their best advantage. Once a person's work becomes well-known, invitations from galleries will be common. In these shows, which normally last up to one, or possibly two, months, the gallery owner accepts items on a consignment basis and takes a percentage of the sales price, customarily 40 to 50 percent. The craftsperson is provided the opportunity to show his work to a discriminating public and at the same time possibly to sell his or her work.

MARKETING

This discussion of marketing is geared to the individual craftsperson who does not produce a large number of products for wholesale. As in the case of the associations of woodcrafters, and the crafts shows, there are a number of opportunities for the maker of whirligigs on a small scale. One can, of course, go as far as one likes in business, and a small business may become a large business. But the focus here is on the person who likes to make whirligigs but doesn't want to store them in the living room for the rest of his or her life, the person who would like to make enough money to pay for the wood and the tools and would like to supplement his or her income rather than to make an entire living from whirligigs.

Stores: To market products, the craftsperson should first become acquainted with the retail outlets in the community and in the city, town, or adjoining towns. There are stores that specialize in crafts and others that handle some crafts, among other products. An appropriate approach is to make inquiries and then make an appointment to see the store owner or manager. Set up a meeting with the owner/manager and bring examples of the work and photographs with a price list of the amounts you expect to get for your work. The manager, if interested, will take it from there and establish a retail price based on your wholesale price. Stores usually work on a consignment basis; that is, they accept an article for sale conditionally. If it sells within a certain period, they pay the sales taxes on it and will send you your wholesale price. If the article is not sold, they will ask you to pick it up. In some shops, the owner/manager may pay you directly for the articles, but this is not customary. If you are new to doing business, do not be afraid of approaching merchants. They are in business because of you, the supplier. You may have just what they are looking for. If they are not interested, that, too, is a part of doing business. If a manager seems unappreciative of your work, or even rude, forget it and go to the next store.

On the subject of consignment, about thirteen states have enacted laws to protect the artist or craftsperson who leaves items on consignment with a dealer. According to the laws, the dealer has no legal interest in the item or its proceeds after sale until the artist or craftsperson is fully paid. The item, for example, cannot be claimed by the creditors in a bankruptcy case. Possession of an item on consignment with a dealer, in effect, remains with the craftsperson who submitted it.

Nonprofit Outlets: In some areas there are nonprofit crafts stores operated by groups who use the income for community service projects. For example, many towns have shops where the crafts products of senior citizens are offered for sale.

The Arts and Crafts Fair: Another avenue for marketing whirligigs is through the shows and exhibitions where exhibited items carry your price tag. Among these is the arts and crafts fair. For the best of these, you must write for an application; this is usually submitted with several slides and a jury fee. The fee is deducted from the booth fee if you are accepted. If you are rejected, the sponsors keep the fee. The amount of the booth fee will depend upon the importance of the event; it can range from a few dollars to several hundred dollars for one or two days. While the quality of your work may be acceptable, you will seriously have to consider whether it is worthwhile for you to participate in some events. If you expect to sell whirligigs worth thousands of dollars, you may not be concerned about paying a booth fee of five hundred dollars.

Perhaps the largest crafts fairs in the United States are organized by the American Craft Council, which sponsors ACC Craft Fairs in selected places throughout the country through their marketing arm, American Craft Enterprises, Inc., 21 So. Elting Corner Road, Highland, NY 12528. The goals of the ACC-sponsored events are the advancement of the craft movement and the promotion of excellence in craft marketing. For information regarding the locations and dates of events, and for application forms, craftspersons should write to American Craft Enterprises.

Notices in crafts magazines and publications regarding arts and crafts shows are, fortunately, quite specific, and you will not be tempted beforehand beyond your means. These give dates and locations, cost of participation, booth sizes, juried or nonjuried selection, number of exhibitors, number of expected visitors, whether there will be a related wholesale show, the deadline for applications, and where to get a prospectus.

Jewelers have very little difficulty transporting their tiny wares, except for their display cases, but whirligig makers with large whirligigs and their stands to handle sometimes need plenty of room. If you expect to enter shows and exhibits, you must plan for your transporting requirements. To move 25 large whirligigs may take a truck or station wagon. You may be able to fit a number of whirligigs into a compact, but this will not leave room for the spouse or the family pet. When considering exhibiting, also consider how you will get your whirligigs to the show.

It should perhaps be mentioned that some people make a kind of nomadic life out of moving from one crafts show to another. Others seem to decide to take their annual vacation in a part of the country away from home and make arrangements to participate in a major crafts show that will be held there at that time, thereby combining business with pleasure. Most craftspersons who enter shows do so within their own regions; they look forward to meeting old acquaintances at these gatherings.

State Fairs: Most state fairs have at least one building devoted to arts and crafts. For a fee, artists and craftspeople can reserve an exhibition space. To insure that you have a place in a State Fair Exhibition Hall, an application to the state office must be made several months in advance.

The Open Market Fair: At the other extreme is the crafts fair that is open to all comers. You just show up early in the morning, pay a small fee, set up a table, and you are in business. Some of these are in connection with certain weekly activities.

The Wholesale Market: There are also wholesale markets, which are closed to the public and open only to wholesalers. These markets are listed in crafts publications. For the craftsperson to participate in most wholesalers' shows, his or her work must be selected by a jury of craft professionals and retailers. The problem for most craftspersons is that even if their work is acceptable, they will not be able to supply the quantity expected. Wholesalers are not interested in only one or two articles.

National Retail Outlets: Up-to-date information on all kinds of craft business activity is contained in The Crafts Report: The Newsmonthly of Marketing, Management, and Money for Crafts Professionals. The focus of this paper, which contains news of much interest to amateurs also, is on "how to sell, where to sell, how to manage the business side of your craft activities, how other craftspersons do it, how to earn a better living in crafts." It also touches on many matters affecting the craftsperson: insurance, taxes, social security, new legislation, etc. Each month shows and fairs are listed by state. The Crafts Report may be obtained by writing Subscription Department, P.O. Box 1992, 300 Water Street, Wilmington, DE 19801.

Craft Marketplace, a monthly publication listing shows, malls, and other locations for exhibiting and selling merchandise, is available at newsstands and by subscription. Published by Betterway Books, 1507 Dana Avenue, Cincinnati, OH 45207.

ENTERING THE MERCHANT CLASS

As soon as you sell a whirligig yourself, whether you make a profit or take a loss, you are a "merchant." Legally, at the state and county level, you are also bound to report such a sale to the proper authorities, along with any tax collected on that item. Each state has a sales tax office, and it is advisable if you are planning to sell whirligigs at crafts fairs and the like to write that office for information. Be specific as to your intentions, as this helps the office identify your situation. Some states will issue you a merchant's license (a permit to collect sales taxes) for a small fee and provide you with forms on which you report monthly or quarterly on the merchandise sold and the taxes collected. Of course this refers only to items which you yourself sell, and ordinarily you do not have to collect taxes on goods sold outside your state. If you leave goods in a gallery or store on consignment, that dealer collects the taxes and files the reports.

When you enter the marketplace as a whirligig maker, and especially if you sell your products yourself, you are, in state and federal law, a self-employed person, which means that you must include with your annual income tax form the profit-

or-loss-from-business-or-profession form (Schedule C). This is not a disadvantage because you can list deductions and costs related to your operations. Some of the deductions, with examples, are as follow:

- Advertising—printing and distributing a handbill describing your work or a news ad.
- Car & truck expense—mileage at 31.5 cents/ mile on taking your whirligigs to a show.
- Depreciation—on selected tools or shop equipment.
- Office expense—mailing & shipping expenses, etc.
- Tools—purchase of a band saw for cutting the wood you use for whirligigs, carving tools, etc.
- Insurance—the deductions for these items will vary.
- Utilities and Telephone—on proof that this is connected with your crafts work or work space. You may be able to deduct space in your home.

Cost of materials is also indicated on Schedule C, and this includes "Materials and Supplies," like lumber, hardware, and paint. Other costs related to your operation also may be listed. These costs can then be subtracted, along with deductions, from your gross receipts or sales, after the inventory at the end of the year is taken into account. For small operations, the inventory need not list the paint left over in the bottom of each can, or the extra nut that is kicking around. A reasonable estimate of the total amount of paint left over, in quarts, by cost, is sufficient, as is a rational estimate of feet of lumber, and hardware items in group categories.

All this means that even if you operate in a very small way, it is essential that you keep good accounts. These need not be extensive or complicated. If you keep nothing else, at least keep a journal. This is a simple account book in which you list everything, all sales and all expenditures and purchases, item by item, line by line, by consecutive date. You can always go over a journal, line by line, and select those items that belong in one category or another. So can an auditor. You may also keep a ledger, in which separate pages identify receipts or expenditures by categories. Such ledger pages could be headed, for example, "Receipts from Consignment Sales," "Receipts from Sales at Shows," "Costs of Manufacture: Lumber," "Other Costs: Mailing, etc.," and so on.

In any events, keep records and be able to sort out income by source and expenditures by appropriate category. It is important to make out a sales slip for every sale or an invoice for every item ordered and sold through the mail. Also, keep receipts and checks for every expenditure; these should match the items in your journal or ledger. For example, every time I go to the post office or the United Parcel Service to ship a package, I get a receipt, and as soon as I get home, I make a line entry under "Costs: Mailing and Shipping Expenses," on a ledger page. Then I place the receipt in an envelope marked the same way. When I purchase wood in a lumberyard, I go through the same procedure. Sometimes you may lose a receipt; enter the item with an explanation.

The independent craftsperson can receive considerable assistance in these matters by making a personal visit to the local Internal Revenue Service office and requesting advice on how best to report on his or her business. For further reference or clarification, I have found it advisable to keep notes on the advice given me at IRS and to record the name of the person I consulted. IRS publication No. 334, Tax Guide for Small Business, available free of charge, will provide just about all the basic tax information an individual craftsperson requires.

SUMMARY OF MARKETING PRINCIPLES

Make sure you have a stock of marketable crafts products. They should be skillfully mounted. Take the best possible photographs of them, and make 35mm slides for distribution to judges and retailers. Make up a price list showing the money you would expect to get for each item.

Check on all the crafts shows in your vicinity, or on other arts and crafts shows you may be eligible for. Call or write for application blanks, and submit them with the jury fee, if required. You are not limited, of course, to your area; there are shows all over the United States, and in Canada, for which you may be eligible.

Check on the retailers of crafts products in your vicinity. Call on them or make an appointment with the manager or owner. Take an example of your work with you, photographs or slides of other work, and a price list.

Look up retailers in your state or in your region. Write to them, submitting photographs and slides of your work and your price list. Dealers all over the country are listed in some directories and crafts publications; you should write those that interest you.

Use the facilities offered by the crafts organizations. They list exhibitions and special opportunities for craftspersons.

Keep up-to-date on the crafts publications that provide current directory information on shows, retailers, special exhibitions, and other information related to marketing.

Keep accurate records on all expenditures and receipts for your own evaluation of your business and for reporting to state and federal tax authorities.

Check with your state tax office to find out how to handle sales and sales taxes, as well as how to report on gains and losses in your business.

Visit your local Internal Revenue Service office for advice on how to report your income and expenditures from your business.

An additional item that is impressive and useful is an attractive business card with your business name, address, phone number, and other pertinent information. Such a card may be given to exhibition directors and store managers for reference. Also, have letterhead stationery especially designed for your business; this can serve as general stationery for invoices as well as correspondence.

A FINAL WORD

In exhibiting or displaying whirligigs, serious attention should be given to the manner in which they are mounted. The stands for exhibition whirligigs should be well-designed and well-crafted, but they should be kept simple. An elaborate mount takes attention away from the whirligig itself. Throughout the book, a few stands were detailed; for the most part, the ones that I described gave practical suggestions related to the base needed to support the whirligig and the height needed to clear the propeller. There are many other, and more artistic, possibilities. At a recent exhibition, a whirligig was mounted on a long, slender iron spindle emerging from a low, solid base; it looked as if the whirligig were suspended in the air.

Whirligigs destined for the marketplace usually need stands that are even more simple. A standard pattern should be made for each type of whirligig that can then be mass-produced. In some shops, the whirligigs will be sold separately, and temporary display stands are needed, while other store owners prefer a simple stand that will be sold with the whirligig and will be included in the price. It is advisable to discuss stands or mountings with managers from the first. Most stands provided with whirligigs in the marketplace are functional only and are often unfinished, although most are stained or painted with an unobtrusive color such as flat black. If a customer wishes something more decorative for indoor display, the craftsperson should be ready to supply it.

We may conclude by repeating that there is a market for whirligigs in all kinds of shows and shops. Once you start to make inquiries, you may be surprised at the requests you will get to exhibit. Your enterprise will prosper if you continue to make products of quality and excellent design.

FOLDOUTS

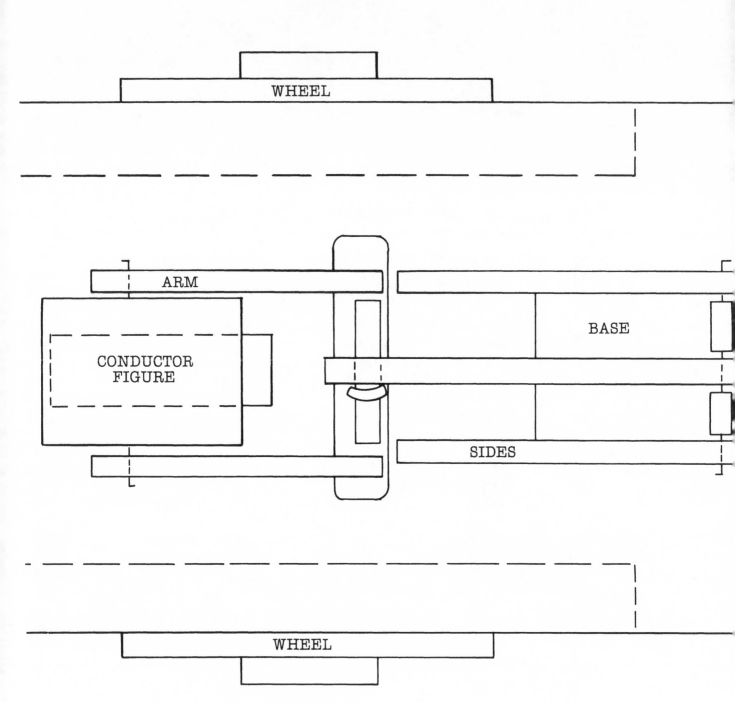

WHEEL

ARM

CONDUCTOR
FIGURE

BASE

SIDES

WHEEL

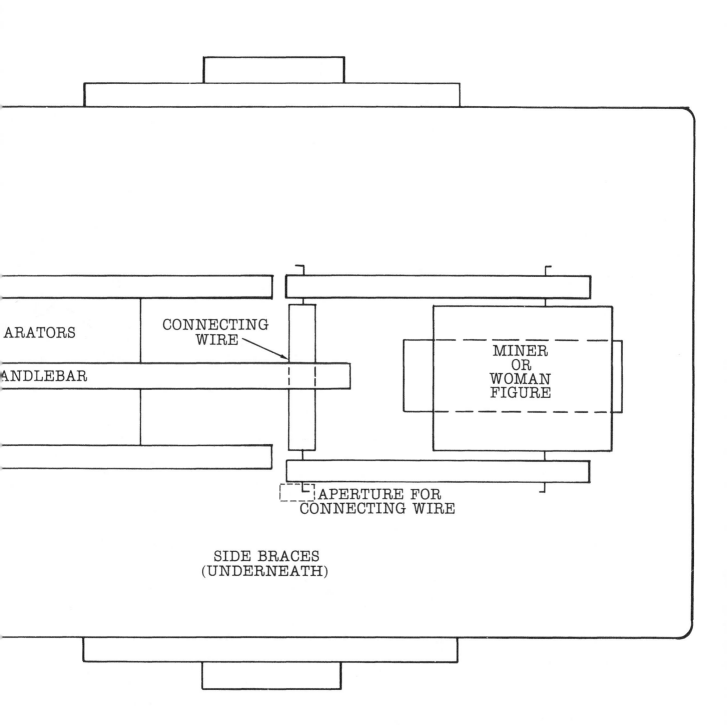

ARATORS

CONNECTING
WIRE

ANDLEBAR

MINER
OR
WOMAN
FIGURE

APERTURE FOR
CONNECTING WIRE

SIDE BRACES
(UNDERNEATH)

ANNE AT THE PUMP

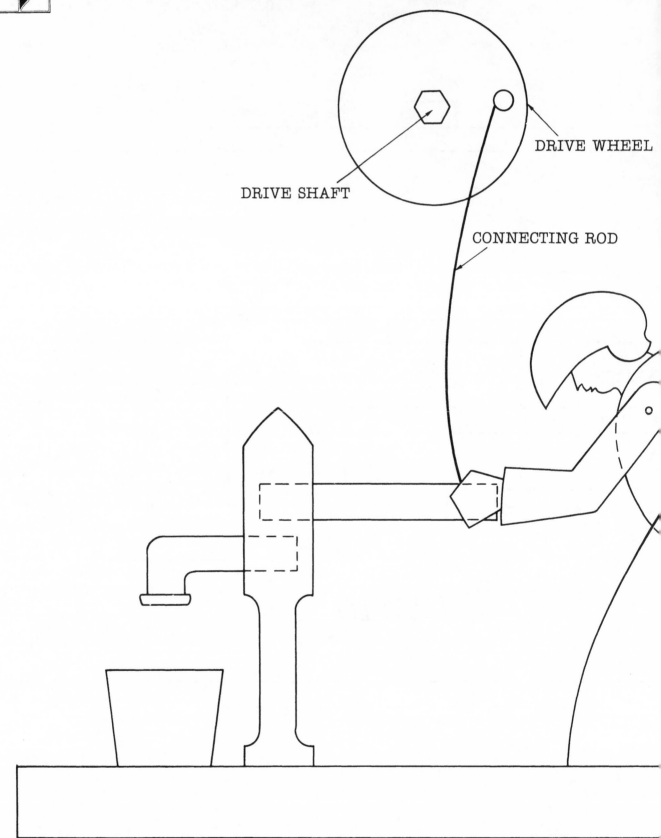

DRIVE WHEEL

DRIVE SHAFT

CONNECTING ROD

**SIDE VIEW OF CROSSPIECE
WITH PUMP AND FIGURE**

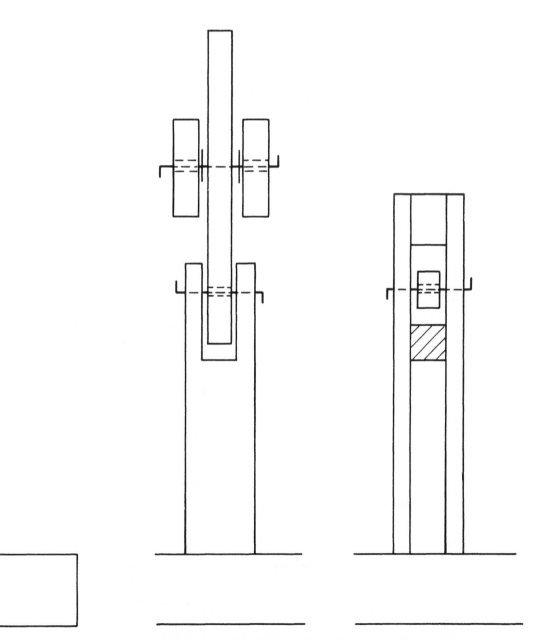

END VIEW OF FIGURE AND PUMP

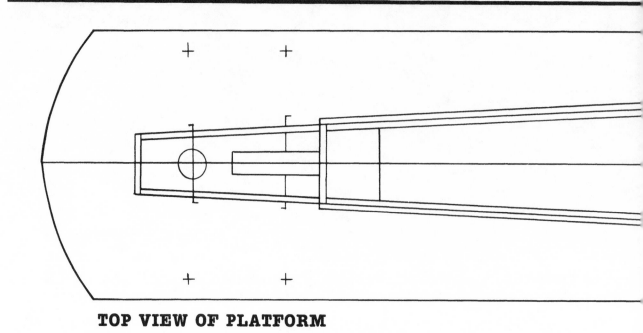

TOP VIEW OF PLATFORM

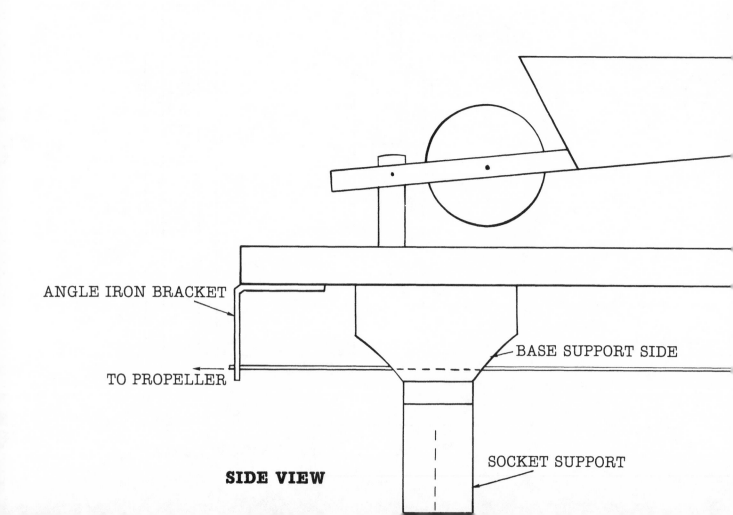

ANGLE IRON BRACKET

BASE SUPPORT SIDE

TO PROPELLER

SOCKET SUPPORT

SIDE VIEW

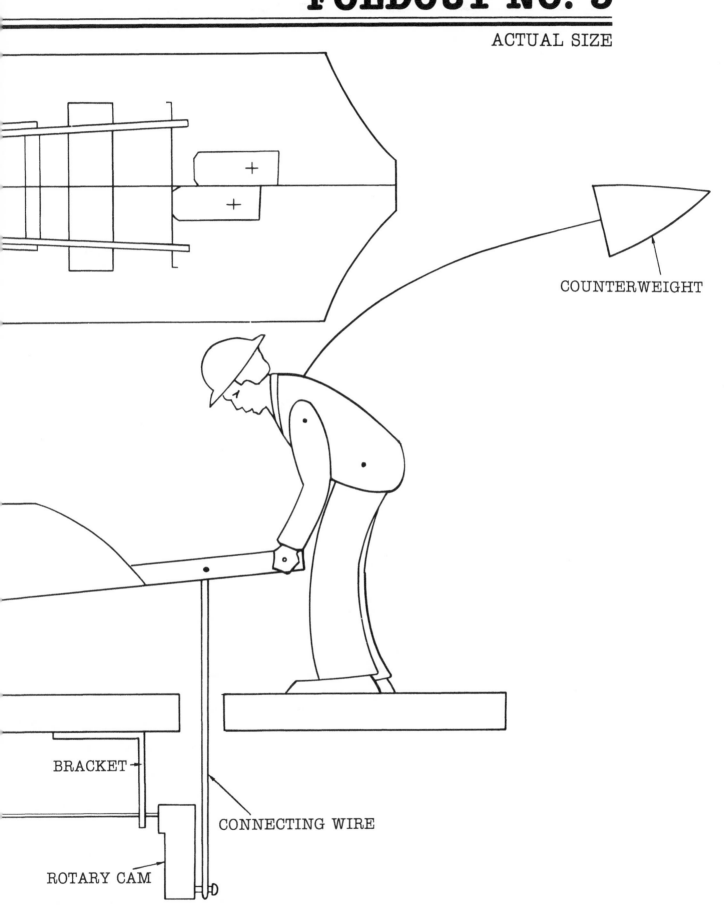

COUNTERWEIGHT

BRACKET

CONNECTING WIRE

ROTARY CAM

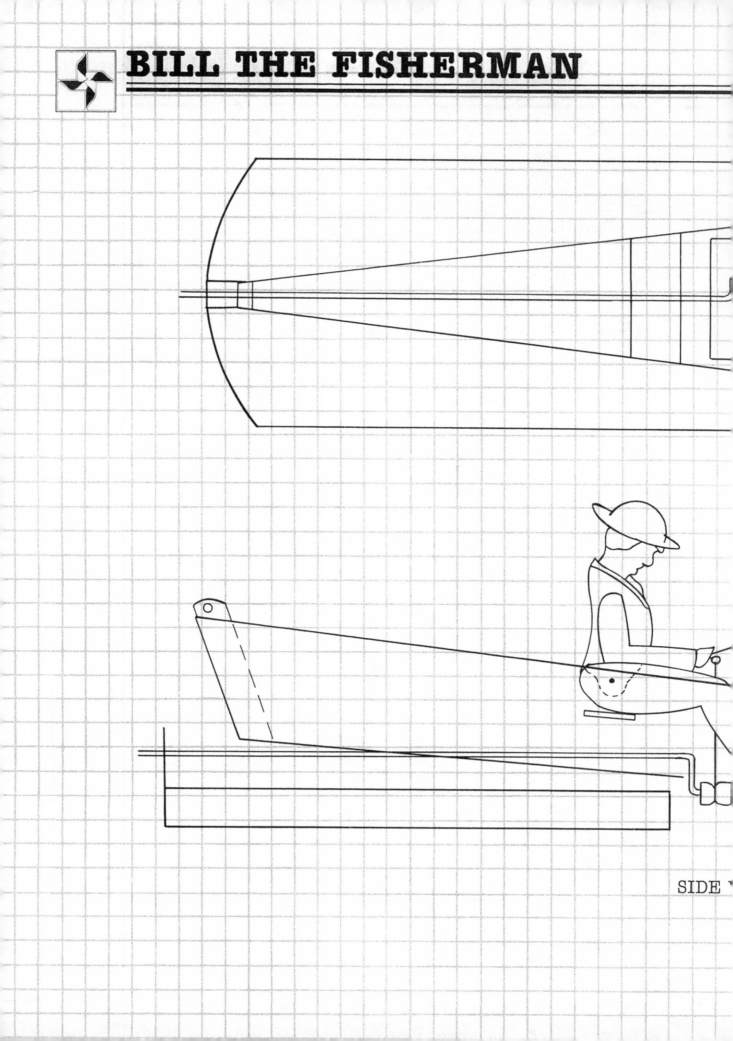

SIDE

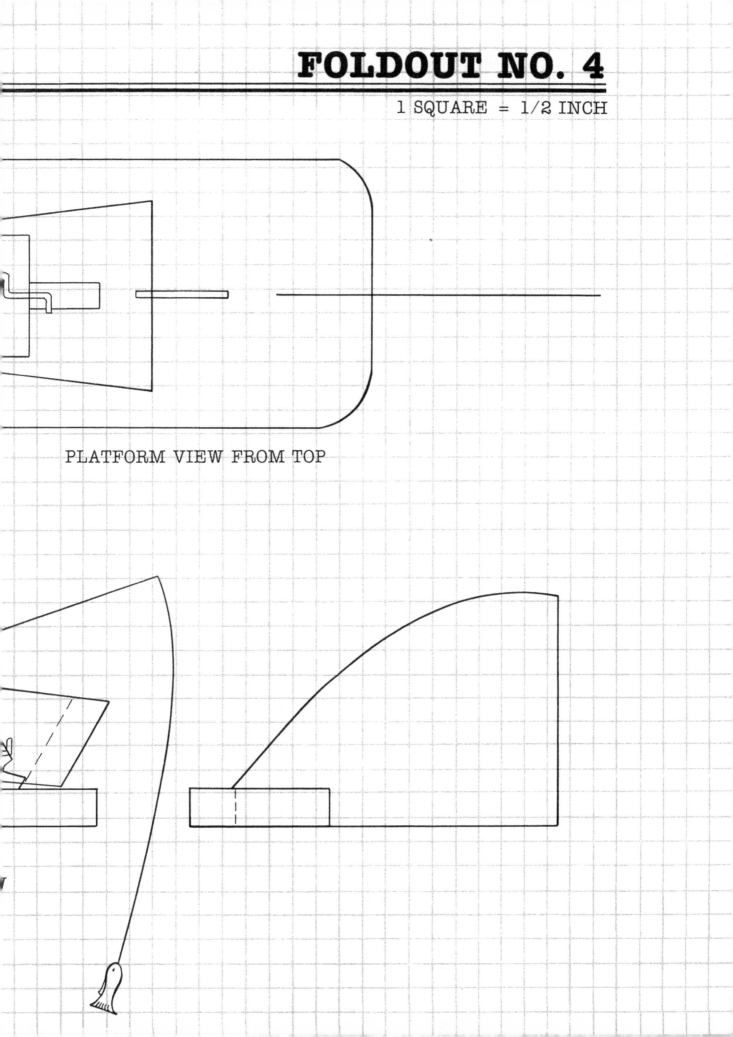

PLATFORM VIEW FROM TOP

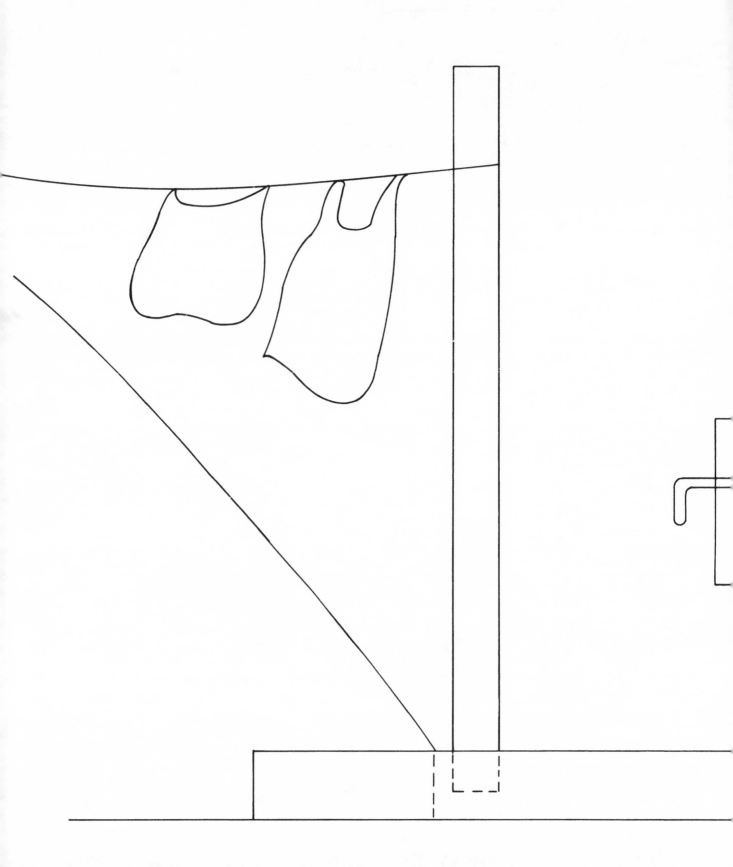

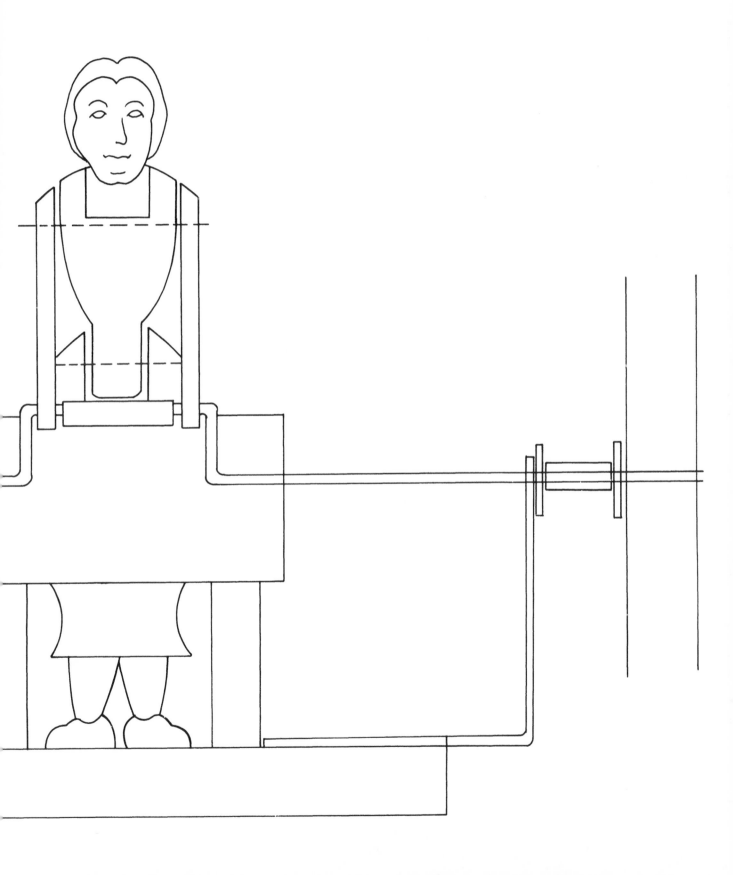

ELEANOR AT THE TUB

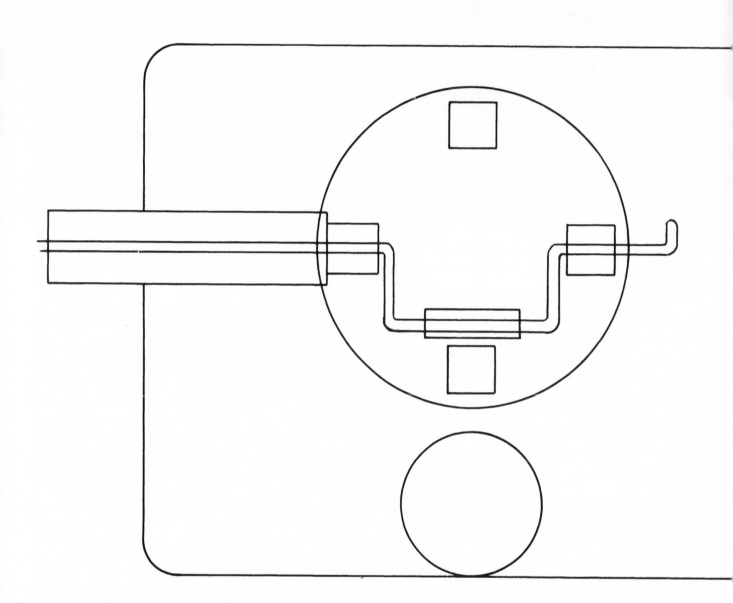

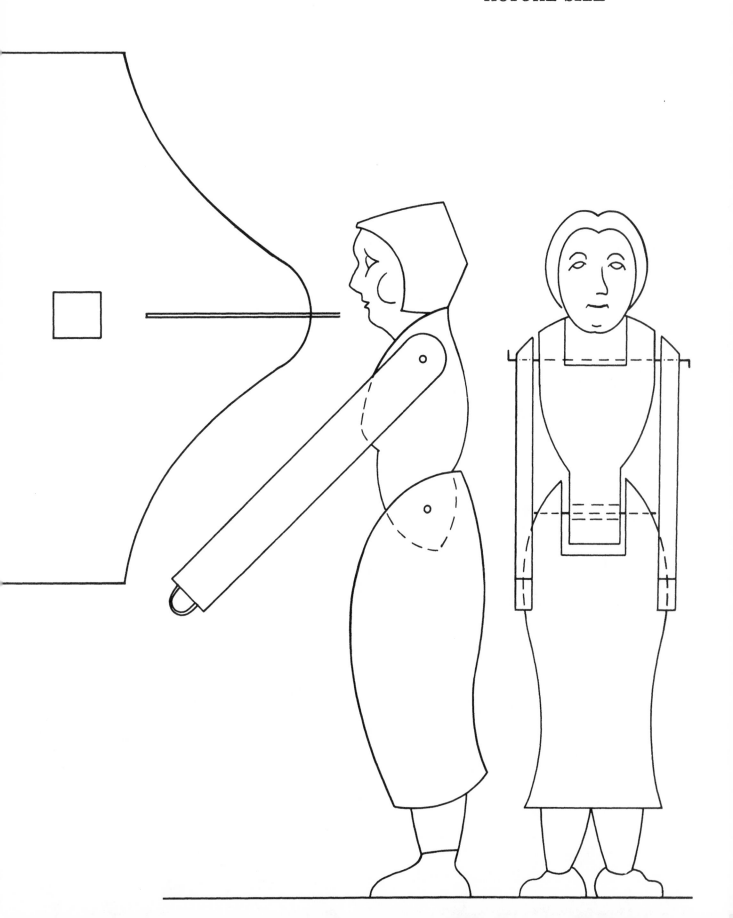

1 SQUARE = 1 INCH

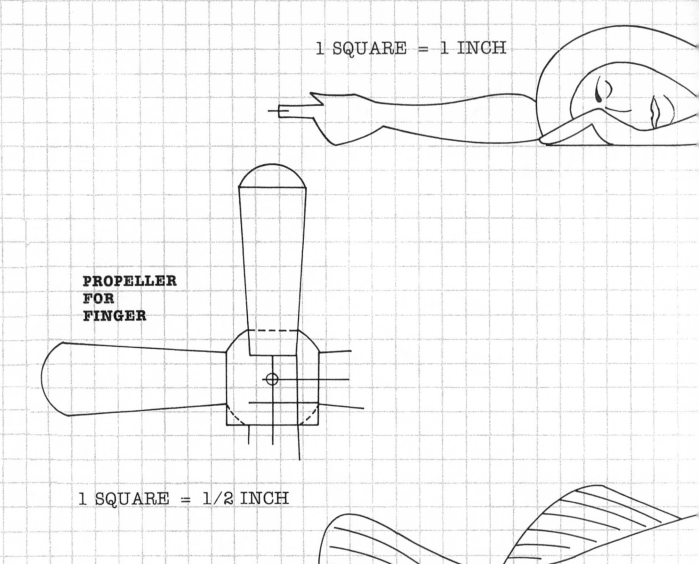

**PROPELLER
FOR
FINGER**

1 SQUARE = 1/2 INCH

NOTE: One dorsal fin (middle)
shows how fins may be made
1/4" longer in that dimen-
sion and inserted and glued
into a slot.

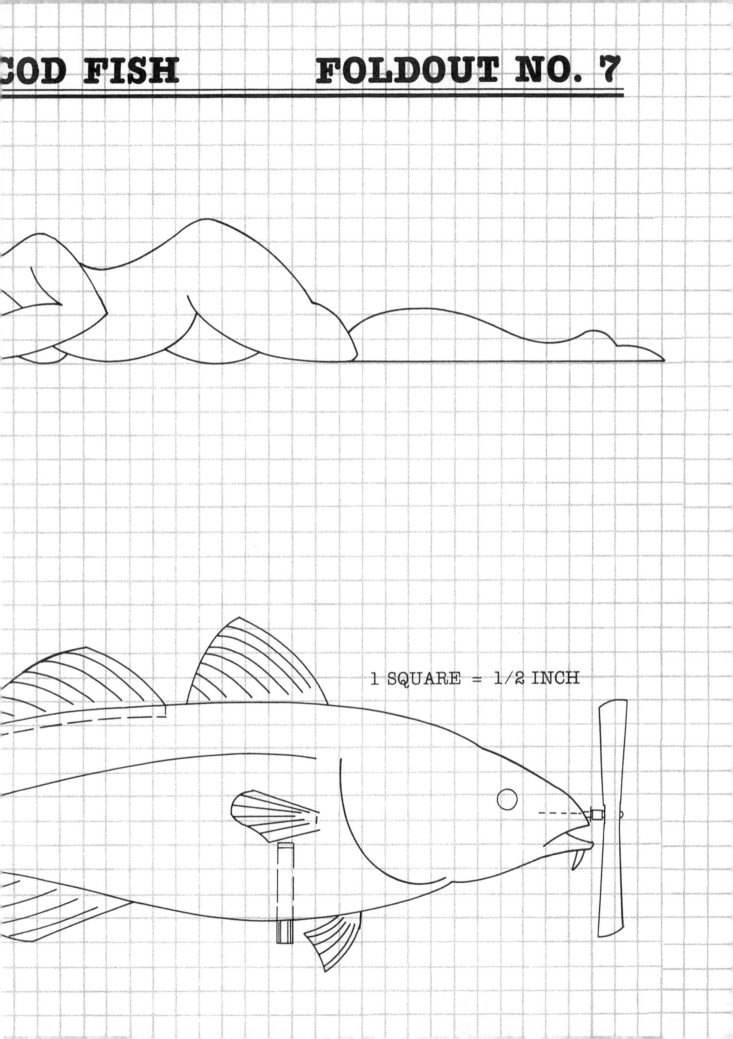

1 SQUARE = 1/2 INCH

THE WHALE

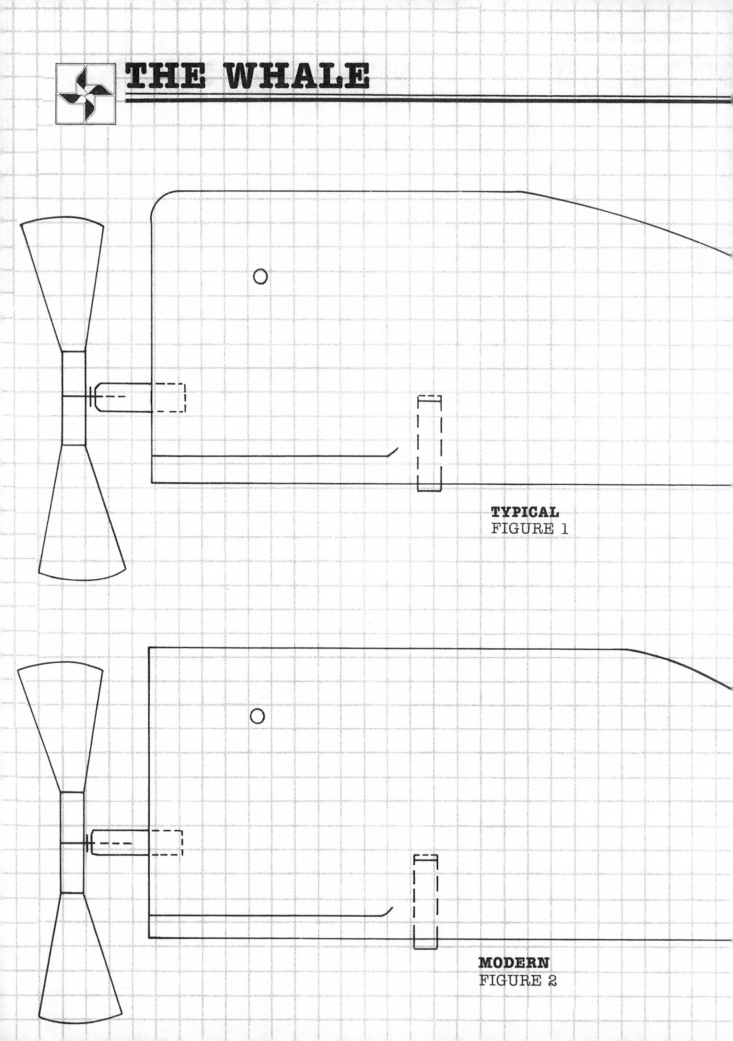

TYPICAL
FIGURE 1

MODERN
FIGURE 2

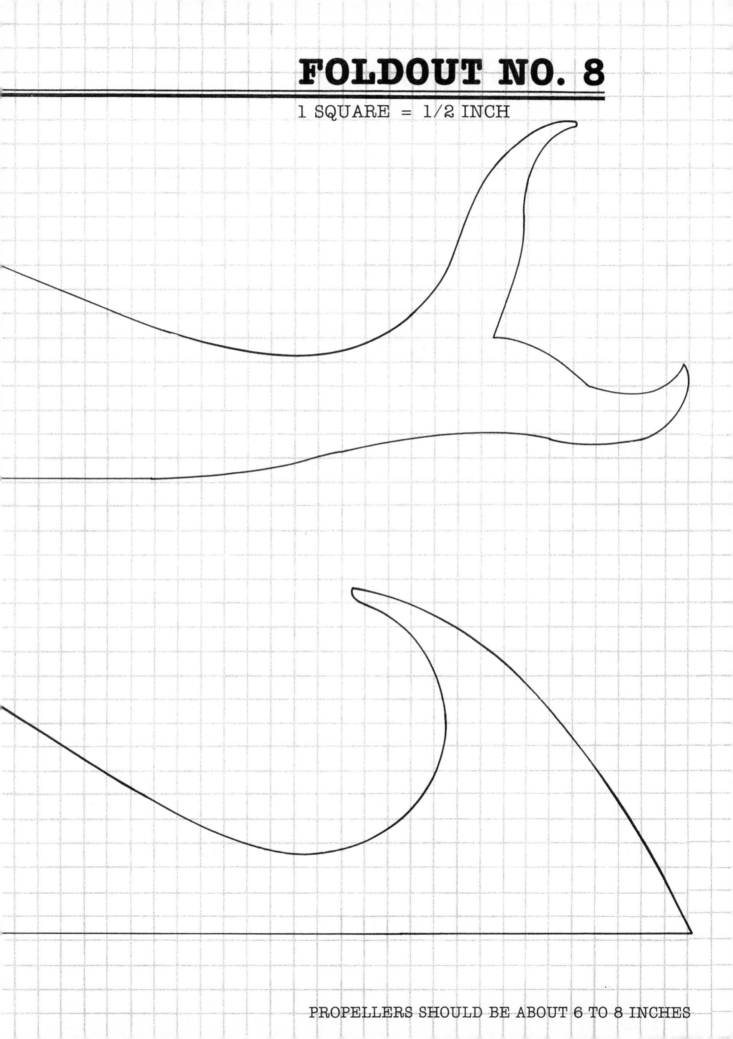

PROPELLERS SHOULD BE ABOUT 6 TO 8 INCHES

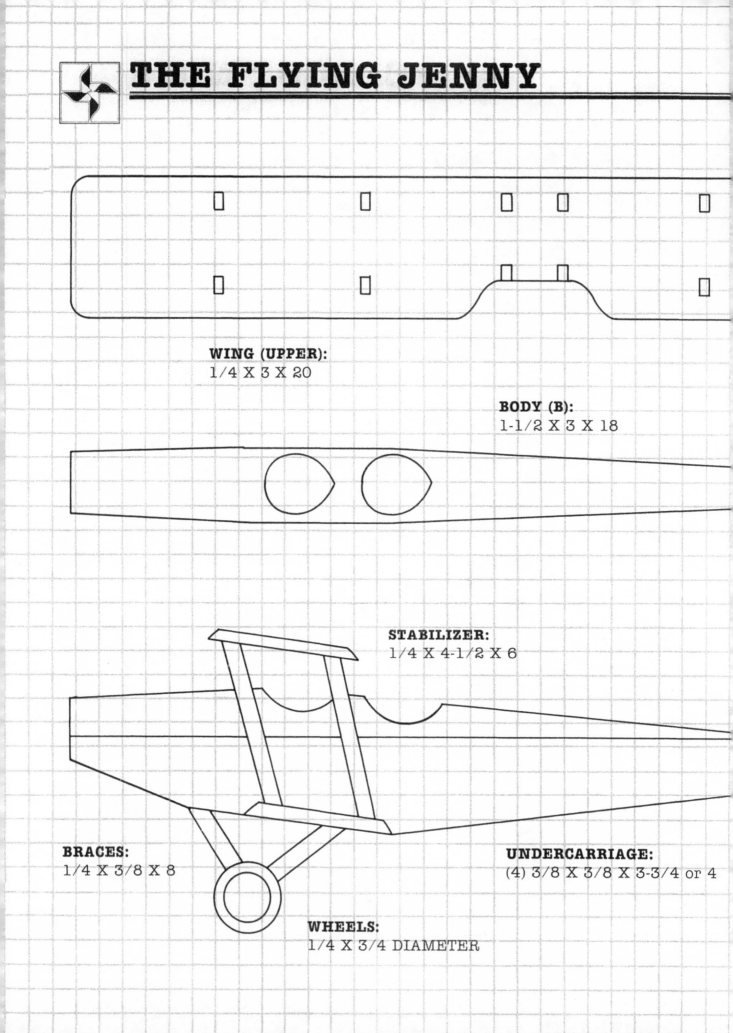

THE FLYING JENNY

WING (UPPER):
1/4 X 3 X 20

BODY (B):
1-1/2 X 3 X 18

STABILIZER:
1/4 X 4-1/2 X 6

BRACES:
1/4 X 3/8 X 8

UNDERCARRIAGE:
(4) 3/8 X 3/8 X 3-3/4 or 4

WHEELS:
1/4 X 3/4 DIAMETER

FOLDOUT NO. 9

1 SQUARE = 1/2 INCH

PROPELLER:
3/4 X 3/4 X 6 or 8

STRUTS:
1/4 X 3/8 X 3-3/4 or 4

RUDDER:
1/4 X 4 X 4-1/2

AXLE:
1/8 INCH ROD

WING (LOWER):
1/4 X 3 X 16

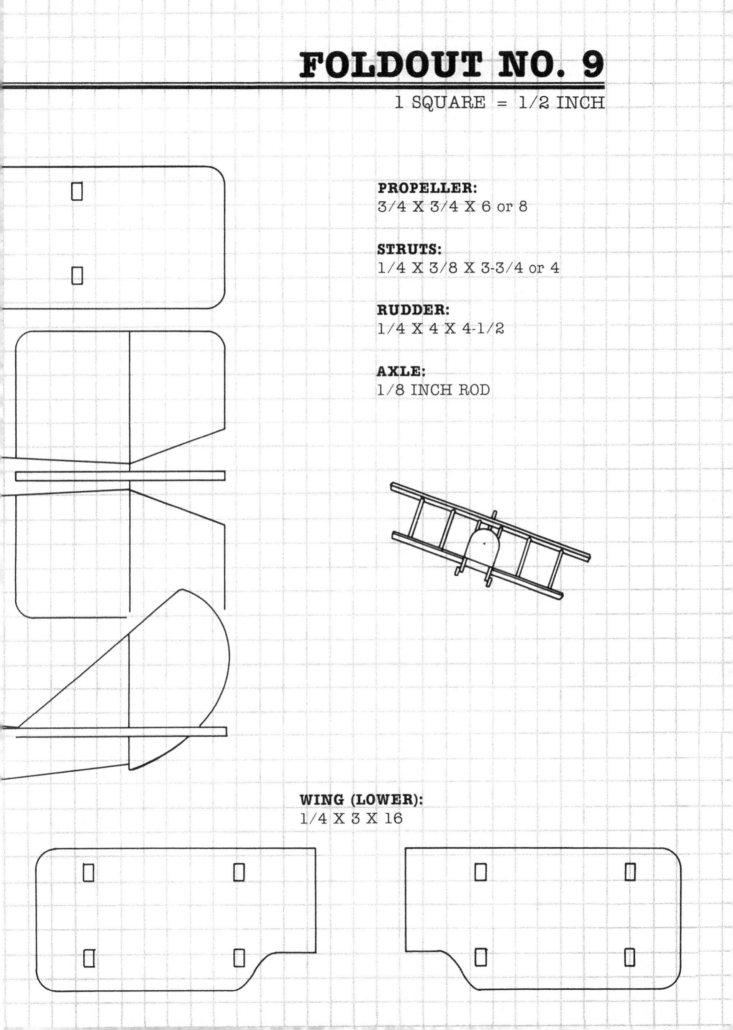

THE TIN GOOSE

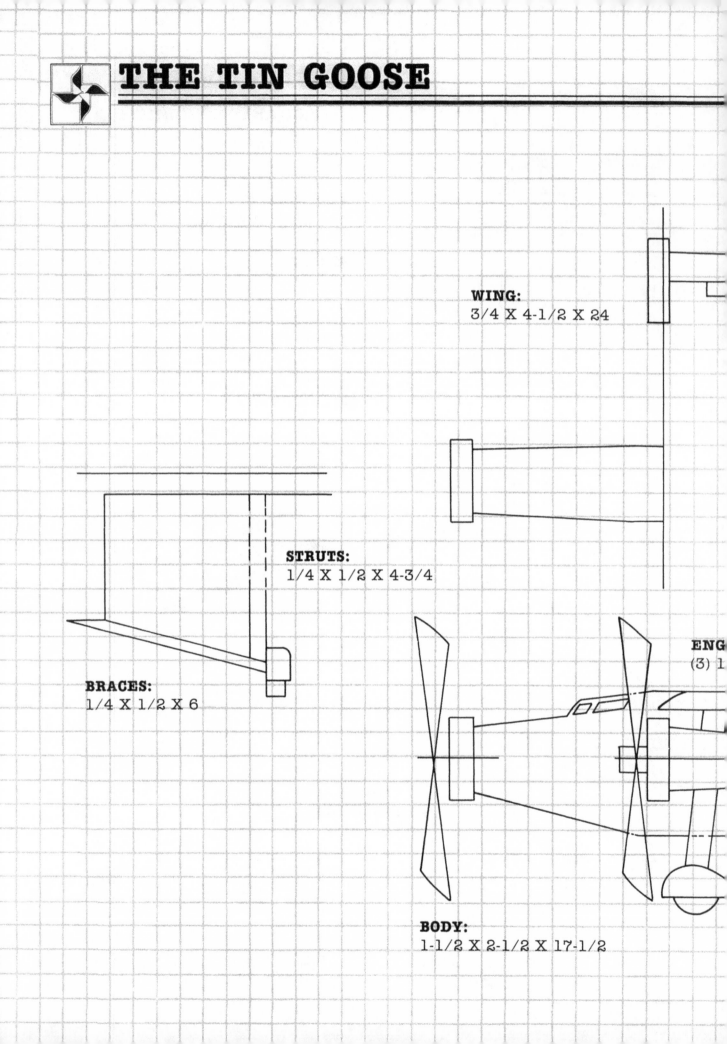

WING:
3/4 X 4-1/2 X 24

STRUTS:
1/4 X 1/2 X 4-3/4

BRACES:
1/4 X 1/2 X 6

ENG
(3) 1

BODY:
1-1/2 X 2-1/2 X 17-1/2

FOLDOUT NO. 10

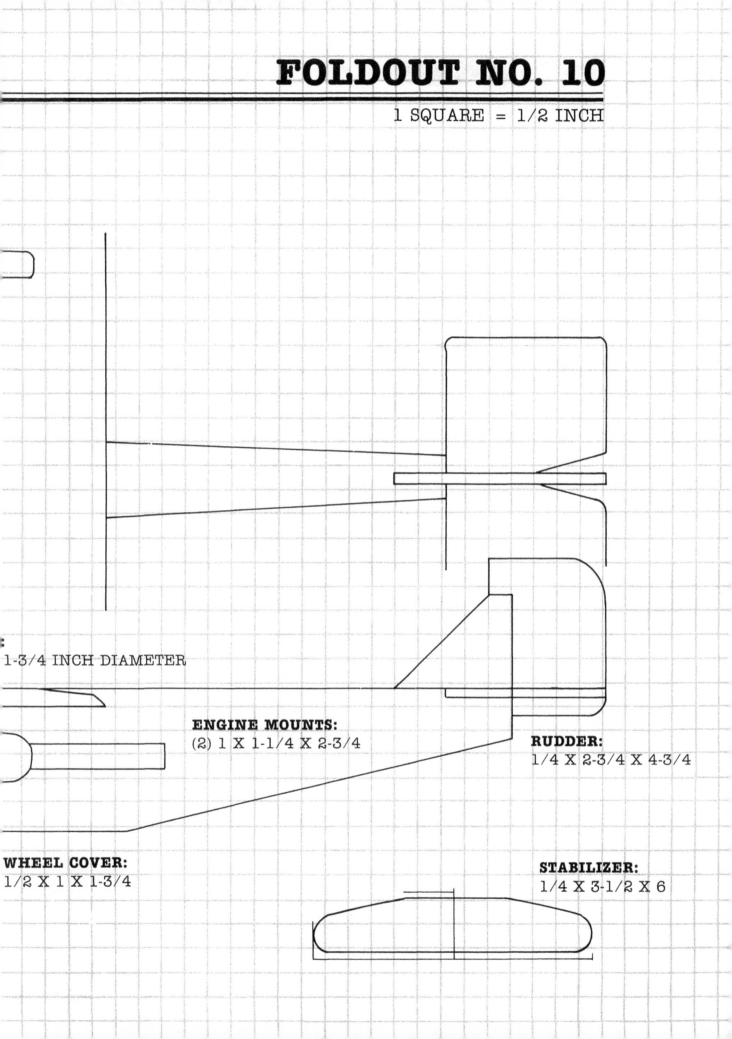

1-3/4 INCH DIAMETER

ENGINE MOUNTS:
(2) 1 X 1-1/4 X 2-3/4

RUDDER:
1/4 X 2-3/4 X 4-3/4

WHEEL COVER:
1/2 X 1 X 1-3/4

STABILIZER:
1/4 X 3-1/2 X 6

TOO MANY CHICKENS

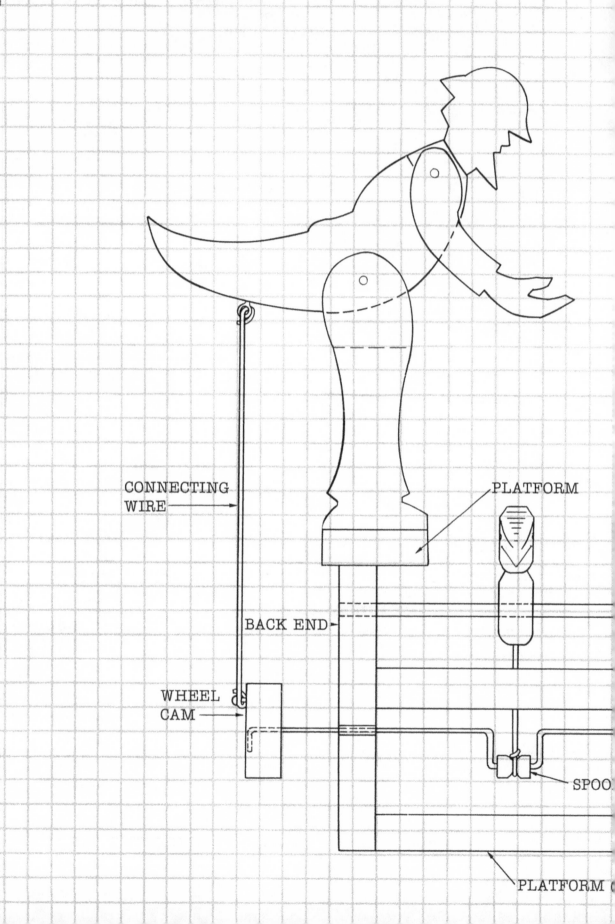

CONNECTING
WIRE

PLATFORM

BACK END

WHEEL

CAM

SPOO

PLATFORM

1 SQUARE = 1/2 INCH

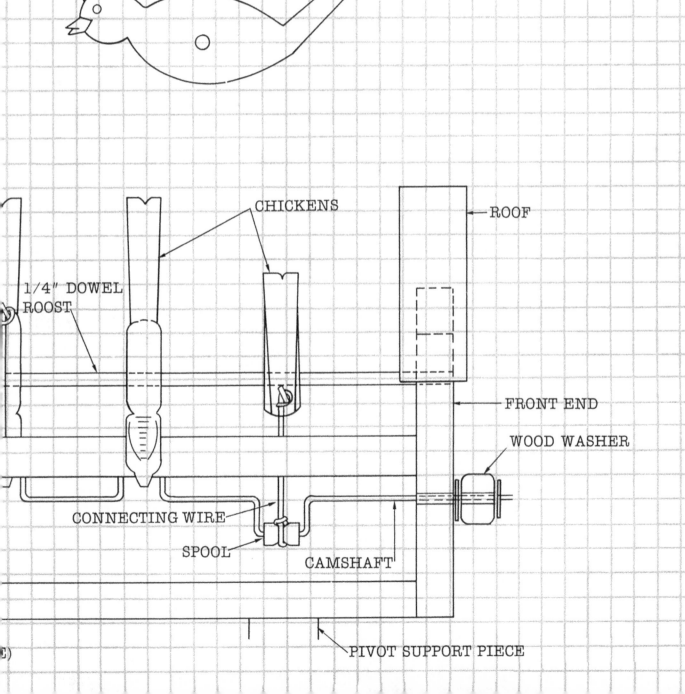

CHICKENS

ROOF

1/4" DOWEL
ROOST

FRONT END

WOOD WASHER

CONNECTING WIRE

SPOOL

CAMSHAFT

PIVOT SUPPORT PIECE

THE NOTHING FACTORY

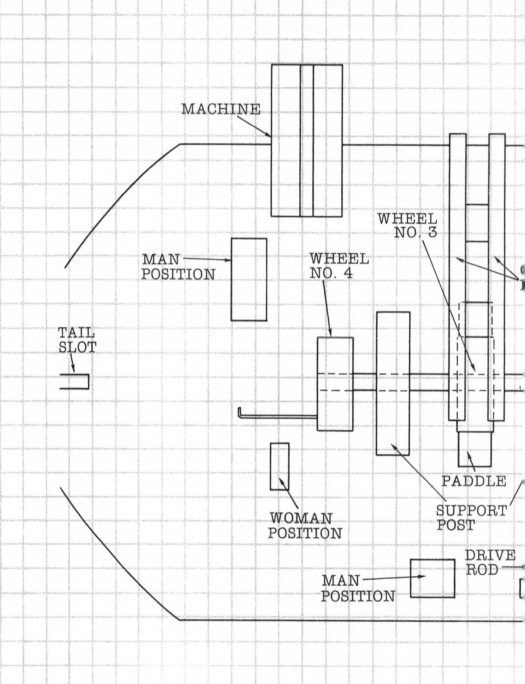

MACHINE

MAN POSITION

TAIL SLOT

WHEEL NO. 4

WHEEL NO. 3

WOMAN POSITION

SUPPORT POST

PADDLE

MAN POSITION

DRIVE ROD

1 SQUARE = 1/2 INCH

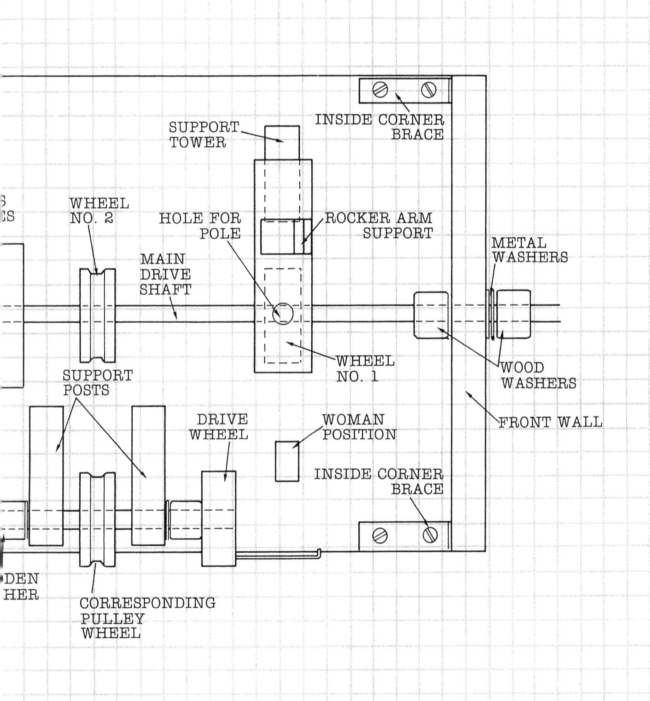

SUPPORT
TOWER

INSIDE CORNER
BRACE

WHEEL
NO. 2

HOLE FOR
POLE

ROCKER ARM
SUPPORT

METAL
WASHERS

MAIN
DRIVE
SHAFT

SUPPORT
POSTS

WHEEL
NO. 1

WOOD
WASHERS

DRIVE
WHEEL

WOMAN
POSITION

FRONT WALL

INSIDE CORNER
BRACE

DEN
HER

CORRESPONDING
PULLEY
WHEEL